ON THE RIVER

OTHER BOOKS BY WALTER TELLER

The Farm Primer, 1941
Roots in the Earth (with P. Alston Waring), 1943
Starting Right With Sheep, 1945
An Island Summer, 1951
The Search for Captain Slocum: A Biography, 1956
The Voyages of Joshua Slocum: 1958
Five Sea Captains, 1960
Area Code 215: A Private Line in Bucks County, 1963
Cape Cod and the Offshore Islands, 1970
Joshua Slocum, 1971
Twelve Works of Naïve Genius, 1972
Walt Whitman's Camden Conversations, 1973

ON THE RIVER

A Variety of
Canoe & Small Boat Voyages

SELECTED, EDITED,
AND WITH AN INTRODUCTION BY
WALTER MAGNES TELLER

SHERIDAN HOUSE

Published 1988 by
Sheridan House Inc.
Dobbs Ferry, NY 10522

First published 1976 by
Rutgers University Press

Copyright © 1976 by Walter Magnes Teller
Copyright © 1988 by Walter Magnes Teller

Library of Congress Cataloging in Publication Data
Main entry under title:

On the river.

    Includes index.
    CONTENTS: Teller, W. Theme and variations.—Thoreau, H. D. Journal.—Bishop, N. H. Voyage of the paper canoe. Four months in a sneak-box. [etc.]
    1. United States—Description and travel—Addresses, essays, lectures. 2. Canoes and canoeing—United States—Addresses, essays, lectures.
I. Teller, Walter Magnes.
E161.05   917.3'04   76-12467
ISBN 0-911378-77-4

Manufactured in the United States of America

PREFACE

In the twelve years since this book first appeared, new men and women have been turning to the paddling arts—to canoeing, kayaking, and all manner of boating. Not long ago I received a letter from a psychiatrist, Dr. Grover Wald. "To handle one's self and one's boat well—even at a very modest level—is sufficient to provide me with great pleasure and much inspiration for other areas of my life," he wrote. "On a recent outing with my wife on the Oakland [California] estuary in an open cockpit kayak for two, I was somewhat heedless of the strong gusty winds, not taking their full measure till we turned about, straight into them for the homeward leg. With a ways to go, both of us became quite soaked by the spray and occasional swamping wave. Although we were tired from the effort of paddling into the wind, I calmly encouraged her to keep it up. I had to adjust my strokes to hers so that we paddled in unison. It was a wonderful sense of intimacy as we both shared the strain and the need to manage a common plight. Can you imagine how many domestic tensions could be successfully dealt with with that sort of model!"

As for canoe and small boat voyages in the 19th and early 20th centuries (the subject matter of this book), just the other day I learned of an extraordinary piece of canoeing performed in 1863. In *Personal Memoirs of U. S. Grant* the general wrote, "Knowing the difficulty Sherman would have to supply himself from Memphis, I had previously ordered supplies sent from St. Louis on small steamers, to be convoyed by the navy.... I now ordered him to... move on with his whole force to Stevenson, Alabama, without delay. This order was borne to Sherman by a messenger, who paddled down the Tennessee in a canoe and floated over Muscle Shoals..."

Think of it—the unknown canoeist (what kind of canoe?) gliding downstream through murderous enemy territory in Mississippi and Alabama, sliding over the Shoals, the most important waterpower site on the river, and delivering Grant's orders.

Quite another variety of canoeing adventure began in the summer of 1930 when Eric Sevareid, seventeen, and Walter Port, nineteen, launched an 18-footer at Minneapolis and canoed to the North Atlantic Ocean. Going via the Minnesota River, the Red River of the North, Lake Winnipeg, God's Lake, God's River, the Shamattawa and Hayes Rivers, they paddled through Indian country changed hardly at all since the 17th century, to York Factory on Hudson Bay. But then change accelerating all down the line, their long trip soon became historic, and Sevareid's narration, *Canoeing With the Cree* (reissued by the Minnesota Historical Society), took its place in the literature of canoeing. Were the two young men the first to make the 2250 mile voyage? Or had the trip been made in reverse, centuries earlier, by Vikings penetrating deep into North America?

September 1987   W. T.

NOTE

Except for conforming spelling, capitalization, punctuation, and hyphenization to current usage—and cutting where indicated—I made no changes in these narratives.

Betty Vas Nunes Burroughs, whose assistance I have had previous occasions to be grateful for, helped with this book from beginning to end.

William L. Howarth read the manuscript and gave counsel.

W. T.

. . . the pursuits of the simpler nations are still the sports of the more artificial.

Thoreau, *Walden*, I

CONTENTS

WALTER TELLER: Theme and Variations	ix
HENRY DAVID THOREAU: *Journal*	5
NATHANIEL HOLMES BISHOP: *Voyage of the Paper Canoe*	29
Four Months in a Sneak-Box	57
RALPH K. WING: Canoeing on the Genesee	105
REUBEN GOLD THWAITES: Historic Waterways	121
JOHN BOYLE O'REILLY: *Athletics and Manly Sport*	149
Canoeing on the Connecticut	149
Down the Susquehanna in a Canoe	158
Down the Delaware River in a Canoe	171
Canoeing in the Dismal Swamp	187
EDWARD L. CHICHESTER: The Cruise of the *Sybaris* and *Shaw Shaw*	215
FREDERIC REMINGTON: Black Water and Shallows	233
GEORGE ELMER BROWNE: Canoeing Down the Androscoggin	243
GERRIT SMITH STANTON: "Where the Sportsman Loves to Linger"	257
ISOBEL KNOWLES: Two Girls in a Canoe	279
ANTHONY WESTON DIMOCK: Yachting in a Canoe	285
CHARLES PHELPS CUSHING: Floating Through the Ozarks	299
ANNA KALLAND: It Can't Be Done	311
Sources	321
Index	323

THEME AND VARIATIONS

On a sparkling fresh day (wind from the north, light to gentle), the cloudless sky summer blue, I set out with Charlie, a long-standing friend, and his thirteen-year-old grandson. We were bound for the shore of Tashmoo Lake on Martha's Vineyard where Charlie keeps a canoe.

My first glimpse of a fabric-skinned hull of unconventional hue, bottom up on the grassy bank, told me whose canoe it was. Charlie is a painter very much at home with earthy shades and tones. "What do you call the color," I asked. "Indian mud," he replied. He had begun, he said, with run-of-the-mill marine buff, added chrome yellow, burnt umber, a touch of black, and stirred until the blend pleased him. A soft, warm, handcrafted color, it suited perfectly his vintage handmade wood and canvas Old Town, sixteen feet long, its high ends curving down to a wide flat floor. The canoe had been bought from the local Girl Scouts who had been phasing out these venerable craft and replacing them with the aluminum kind, for who has the love and labor to spare to keep an old canoe alive? Charlie had spent many hours slapping on the "Indian mud," varnishing the interior, the outside gunwales, and refastening the keel.

We carried it to the water's edge, put our cushions and paddles aboard and in the spirit of treasure-hunting, a pail—in case we encountered a clam or other largesse of the lake. Three narrow thwarts extended across the canoe Algonkin fashion; there were no ash-framed and cane-filled seats as there had been in the Kennebec models I had once known. Charlie took the stern, his grandson Thorp the bow, and I the space amidships. Stepping in, arranging my cushion on the floor, and settling against the center thwart, I heeded inwardly the words the Jesuit priest Jean Brébeuf had addressed to his brethren more than three hundred years ago.

"Take from the start the place in the canoe that you wish to keep. . . ." Barefoot, Thorp shoved off.

The canoe wafted out stern foremost and as it bobbed to the rhythm of the water I felt (not for the first time) the strangeness of the familiar—the expansiveness of the water on the one hand, the narrowness of the cockleshell on the other. How glorious the water—the wonder of it—the fact that it exists at all.

From a point near the northern end of Tashmoo we started south toward the head of the lake, Charlie the veteran paddler setting the course and the boy kneeling in the Indian way, a splendid bowsman. Listening to the water rippling, enjoying the body feeling of the canoe in motion, I recalled another of Father Brébeuf's recommendations to his fellow explorers and missionaries when they were young and zealous. "Do not undertake anything unless you desire to continue it; for example, do not begin to paddle unless you are inclined to continue paddling." Finest kind of advice for one with an unreliable back. I laid my paddle beside me but later when homeward bound and the day began breezing up, I held it aloft for a sail.

Canoeing invites exploring. Poking along an unfamiliar shore, each of us is a discoverer in the sense that matters most. I had spent many moons on Martha's Vineyard but had not been on the lake before, really a lake in name only. Tashmoo has long been a deep sheltered arm of the sea; a dredged inlet connects it with Vineyard Sound. So while it looks like the freshwater lake it once was, and calls to mind many a pleasant lakeside resort, there is this singular difference; Tashmoo smells of saltwater life and the sea.

We glided through a panorama of closely colonized waterfront. This section of the onetime lake—a consequence of the sea change it underwent—has become a harbor for private seagoing craft, a parking lot one might call it, for power boats. Slipping by in our silent conveyance we resembled walkers beside a highway, anachronistic and out of phase with the traffic, yet pleased with and proud of our progress, no way wanting it otherwise, and like the aquatic birds that frequent this coast, adapting—accepting the changing conditions.

The scene altered as we advanced. Low-sweeping houses came into view, modest buildings tucked away among Japanese black pine and scrub pine, in scale with the land and the lakefront. Spotted in here and there was an old summer cottage, a turn-of-the-century bungalow; we seemed to be going back in time but in landscape the past is always vividly present enhancing the now, the hour arrived at, and surely this very moment, fair as any since God called the light day. Early morning of summer. Great splashes and globs of blooming viburnum brightened the uplands with yellows and whites. Pink-faced wild roses bordered the fields and the shores. Coming to the head of the lake we found a weathered ramshackle dock in the lee of a clump of windblown beetlebung trees where we tied up and disembarked. From the dock I looked down on our unloaded craft with its white cedar ribs and red cedar planking, riding so lightly the water's elastic tension. I thought it looked exactly right —the epitome of canoe.

Just ahead lay an English lake country vista; an informal park—umbrageous trees and well mowed grass, and a pond framed by native wild shrubs with a pair of mallards cruising, now and again upending themselves to fish. Herring gulls standing around on rotted-down spiling, coming and going were, however, a reminder that I was after all off the southern coast of Massachusetts. Deep in the apex of an imperfect triangle, the land shelving upward on either side, and backed to a wooded hill, stood a noble large red brick building, sturdy, old, and elegant. Though it resembled somewhat a carriage house on an estate, the tall, square-cornered, tapering stack suggested it had been designed for a different purpose. The structure, built for a pumping station, was now in disuse. Overall was a stillness I liked.

I knew from reading that I was standing in a noteworthy vertex —where the northwest leg of the triangle, the Buzzards Bay Lobe, met the northeast leg, the Cape Cod Bay Lobe—a spot a geologist might journey far to see, a meeting place of moraines. I looked but saw a trained eye was needed; I could not fix the precise location. I love these green-mantled spines and boulder-strewn ridges rising above the surrounding level, pushed up by the mighty bulldozing power of glaciers, their features plowed and furrowed by ice. I affiliate with moraines, feel more attuned to them than to the outwash plains. I like hilly land and flat water, prefer them that way to the other way around.

Tashmoo, it is said, derives from an Indian word meaning where there is a great spring and the great spring is here—gushing forth from a twelve-inch-diameter pipe and into the pond which in turn spills into the lake. I lay face down on the grassy bank and drank the sweet cold water. In former times the water was bottled and sold for alleged mineral virtues; today one can come and take it away for free.

Leaving the copious flowing spring, the well-tended grass, the leafy trees and the pond, we returned to the dock, its bleached boards (a few missing) pearly gray in bright sunshine. Smallest of small fry darted and scooted beneath it as though enjoying the shoal brackish water but more likely swimming for dear life. An attractively speckled crab came sidling along, a calico crab I thought, snatched up a mussel, cracked it open and using an arm and a hand (anterior limb modified as pincer) drew out the saffron-colored meat, fed on it hand to mouth, morsel by morsel—amusingly human in its behavior. We got under way again, pointing down the farther and less busy side of the lake. I saw sedges, reeds and the sapphire gleam of the last blue flag left over from spring. Waterfowl seemed to favor this shore but then for the inhabitants, bird or human, a lake is a very shared thing. Those on the relatively lightly settled west side enjoyed the advantage of more elbow room but their view of the opposite strand was cluttered; on the east side, vice versa.

The shape of Tashmoo appeared like a cutout, a jigsawed piece of the grand cosmic puzzle. While a scalloped shoreline went sliding by I looked down into the water scanning the sands. Would I find something to gladden the pail we had brought? I did not. The water looking clean and inviting was doubtless teeming with all manner of life—lives that I could not know and living conditions I never would fathom but in these moments and circumstances, not-knowing let me see the thing in my own way, adding to my enjoyment; I too was among the uncounted myriads playing my role in the incidents of the spheres. The random talk died away; water dripping from the paddles became the most conspicuous sound. As we passed a seemingly houseless expanse, wooded with pine to the watery margin, one could imagine that this was a lake in the mountains, or somewhere deep in the woods in Maine.

Hauling down to the northwest corner, Charlie steered into a cove known as Aunt Rhody's Pond where, says tradition, Aunt Rhody throve and lived to an age that rivaled Methuselah's. Oh, the Rhody aunts of fable and song. "Go tell Aunt Rhody/The old gray goose is dead." Salt marshes, meadows by the sea, graced the pond shores. Some of these marshlands—among the most unspoiled in the nation—are now protected; they cannot be drained or filled or built on. Long may their grasses wave. We approached the tidal flats where summertime clammers bent to their task, for the tide was low and ebbing rapidly. We ran aground. Quickly our bowsman Thorp jumped out and seizing the painter (the line at the bow, not his grandfather), dragged the canoe through the shoals to the inlet channel. Suddenly, the wind picked up. I raised my paddle blade broadside to it, and now with three paddles working we crossed the channel. Before long we were home again, back where we started.

The canoe-idea is so old that one might say the canoe has always been with us. The first Europeans to land in the western hemisphere saw canoes. Viking legends told of boats made of skins stretched over wooden frames; Columbus arriving in the Caribbean saw the hollowed out tree trunk called canoa. (Canoe is a Carib word.) John Smith's Indians had dugouts, Champlain's birchbarks. Faster and lighter than the white man's longboat, the bark canoe won immediate adoption. Starting from the Indian village of Quebec a long line of French explorers, soldiers, and Jesuit missionaries carried the French flag up the St. Lawrence and Ottawa Rivers, through the Great Lakes region and into Wisconsin. They went by canoe and one of their number, the Father Brébeuf spoken of earlier, formulated a set of instructions concerning the etiquette and logistics of traveling with native Americans.

To conciliate the Savages, you must be careful never to make them wait for you in embarking. . . .
You must be prompt . . . and tuck up your gowns so that they will not get wet, and so that you will not carry either water or sand into the canoe. To be properly dressed, you must have your feet and legs bare; while crossing the rapids you can wear your shoes, and, in the long portages, even your leggings. . . .

It is well not to ask many questions. . . . You must relieve those in your canoe of this annoyance. . . .

Each one will try at the portages, to carry some little thing, according to his strength; however little one carries, it greatly pleases the Savages, even if it be only a kettle. . . .

Be careful not to annoy anyone in the canoe with your hat. . . .*

Jacques Marquette, Jesuit priest, and Louis Jolliet, Canadian explorer, traveling the Wisconsin River in two big canoes with a party of twenty-five Indians and three Frenchmen, entered the Mississippi in 1673. Nine years later LaSalle pushed down the Illinois River, reached the Mississippi and journeyed to its mouth.

North America, blessed with an abundance of rivers, seems to have been the only continent opened up and explored by canoe. For more than two hundred years canoes made the inland thrust. Proselyting went hand in hand with trading. The fur trade depended on the canoe, especially on a high-ended model designed to meet the demands of the business, the freight-and-passenger *maître canot*.† The canoe served the licensed and the unlicensed—company men called voyageurs, and also roving free lances who bootlegged furs, known as *coureurs de bois*. Canoes carried cargo and goods for exchange, brought letters, orders, and information. Crown officials, soldiers, churchmen, judges on circuit, doctors and quacks—all employed the canoe. Canoeing put place names on newly drawn maps—many a Portage and Portageville, names strong and blunt as directives.

From the St. Lawrence to the Gulf of Mexico, rivers and lakes became imperial highways threading the vast untouched American forest. The Brule–St. Croix corridor, well known to red men of the region, furnished the shortest north-south passage between Lake Superior and the lower Mississippi. The first written record of the

---

* *The Jesuit Relations and Allied Documents* . . . , 73 vols., edited by Reuben Gold Thwaites (Cleveland: The Burrows Brothers Co., 1896–1901). *The Jesuit Relations,* one-volume selection edited by Edna Kenton (New York: Albert & Charles Boni, 1925). Relation of what occurred in New France in the year 1637 . . . By Father Paul le Jeune . . . Superior of the Residence of Kebec.

† The preeminent study of the workhorse canoe is Edwin Tappan Adney and Howard I. Chapelle, *The Bark Canoes and Skin Boats of North America* (Washington: The Smithsonian Institution, 1964), 242 pp., 224 illustrations, and a fine bibliography.

route was penned by Daniel Graysolon, sieur Duluth, who went that way in 1680. Further evidence of voyageurs passing through is given by the fleur-de-lis (yellow iris) that grows on the banks of the St. Croix River; the plant is not indigenous but came from European gardens.

Meriwether Lewis and William Clark led an official party including Sacajawea, squaw-wife and guide, that began the ascent of the Missouri River in the spring of 1804. Seeking a still undiscovered northwest passage they traveled as far upstream as they could in canoes and small boats, crossed the mountains to the Snake River, then descended the Snake and Columbia Rivers to reach the Pacific Ocean two years later. The Lewis and Clark Expedition crossed the greater part of an immense uncharted continent by water, a pioneer pathbreaking journey. Meriwether Lewis's diary account is a fascinating American document.

Presently western waters churned with all manner of exploration. In 1820, Henry Rowe Schoolcraft, known for his later Indian studies, joined the Cass expedition, three canoe loads of soldiers, voyageurs, and Indians led by the governor of Michigan Territory. Schoolcraft's *Narrative Journal of Travels . . . through the Great Chain of American Lakes to the Sources of the Mississippi . . .* is typical of the geographical-geological discovery genre—daily, descriptive, factual—useful notes but not inspired.

Shortly after the Civil War, John Wesley Powell, a one-armed Union veteran officer, undertook a remarkable piece of river investigation. He and ten companions—athletes, scouts, and geographers—risked their lives on the nine-hundred-mile descent of an unexplored and legendary stream that coursed through wild and impassable badlands. Powell kept a log of the trip and later produced a superb book—one of the great contributions—*Canyons of the Colorado*.

By that time however, and even earlier, canoeing had come full circle. It had carried civilization into the wilds; now people were seeking the wilderness. The literature of canoeing and voyages in canoe-like craft seems to me to fall into two broad and general categories; one, the records of professional subsidized explorations and commercial travels; the other, the narratives of men and women—amateurs in the good sense of the word—who canoed independently for pleasure or other individual reason. Since my kinship feeling is with the latter, I confined my selections to writings by persons in the second group.

Henry Thoreau discovered that in a few days in a rowboat he could make a significant odyssey, and I would have begun this collection with *A Week on the Concord and Merrimack Rivers,* his account of a trip made in 1839, were it not so well known and available. In the 1850s he traveled to Maine where he canoed with Joe Polis, an Old Town Indian. Thoreau's trip on the Allagash and East Branch, told in *The Maine Woods,* lies at the heart of canoeing but since three editions of that work are now (1975) in print, I passed it up in order to give the space to reports not readily obtainable.

Modern canoeing came into its own as the nation became more urbanized. I believe the reason personal and recreational uses of the canoe increased was because the canoe remained very much the same as it was. Few of man's early inventions have absorbed and survived technological progress so brilliantly; few primitive concepts have come through so clearly. The clean line and simple functional forms of the Indian birchbark have not been improved, nor has the cost greatly increased—it is still comparatively inexpensive.*
The silent action drawing it forward remains the same—the hand-driven paddle with no fixed fulcrum, and no fuel and no crew required. Furthermore it continues to be lightweight and transportable. Indefinitely ancient, eternally youthful, a tangible reminder of freedom and unclouded rivers, the canoe lasts into our time from days when man lived closer to nature and it retains the aura.

Rivers have long represented the flow of time, continuity of cause and effect, antecedents and successors. Many American settlers, however, ignored or turned their backs on them. In New Hope, Pennsylvania, a Delaware River village where my friend Charlie and I published a local paper some years ago, all the older houses built on the river's bank faced away from the water. Regarded as a convenience, a way of disposing of human waste, garbage, trash, and industrial effluents, the river was honored accordingly; and this

---

* Today the most expensive canoe is the paper birch. See *The Survival of the Bark Canoe,* by John McPhee (New York: Farrar, Straus & Giroux, 1975). The standard wood and canvas model commands a higher price than the canoe manufactured of fiberglass or acrylonitrile-butadiene-styrene, ABS. The aluminum canoe costs least.

has long been the common everyday usage in many villages, towns, and cities. There are, however, signs that these reckless don't-give-a-damn practices are being checked, that rivers are being cleaned up and riparian beauties, rights, and respects restored.

The theme—voyages by canoe and canoe-like boat—is inherent to the growth of the nation and continent. The variations in time and place give close-up views of environment, history, and culture. They celebrate journeys long and short, this way and that, in search of values. Some were written by recognized names, some by persons known in the annals of their occupations and professions, and others by persons whose backgrounds remain obscure. A number lay buried in fading files of old magazines, or in little known and seldom read books. Though their qualities vary consonant with the talents and gifts of the authors, arranged chronologically they effect new and interesting juxtapositions. Most of the narratives come from the years when the population was shifting from open country to city, when immigration was swelling the urban centers and the frontier was closing down; most of the authors in so far as I know them, came from cities and towns. I have not included anyone contemporary; everyone here has received the benefit of the perspective of time.

W. T.

October 1975

ON THE RIVER

Henry David Thoreau
1817 - 1862

Thoreau gave the world a noble example of civilized man in tune with the natural environment. A native son and lifelong resident of Concord, Massachusetts, he was an enthusiastic canoeist, boater, and sailor, and a joyful walker in rivers—fluvial walks he called them. Waters were as necessary as woods to his pleasure, well-being, and inspiration. River trips were an integral element in his quest for a way of life.

The record of that quest, the six thousand pages of his Journal, includes impressions, observations, and accounts of simple soul-delighting adventures met with on little journeys by water. Excursions in springtime, summer, and fall on hometown rivers he loved and studied until he knew them by heart—they were voyages inward as well as outward; many times in a few miles he traveled far.

THE *JOURNAL* OF
HENRY D. THOREAU

1850

Sept. 19. . . . Water is so much more fine and sensitive an element than earth. A single boatman passing up or down unavoidably shakes the whole of a wide river, and disturbs its every reflection. The air is an element which our voices shake still further than our oars the water. . . .

The forms of trees and groves change with every stroke of the oar. . . .

* * *

1851

Oct. 6. Monday. . . . 7.30 P.M.—To Fair Haven Pond by boat, the moon four-fifths full, not a cloud in the sky; paddling all the way.

The water perfectly still, and the air almost, the former gleaming like oil in the moonlight, with the moon's disk reflected in it.

When we started, saw some fishermen kindling their fire for spearing by the riverside. It was a lurid, reddish blaze, contrasting with the white light of the moon, with dense volumes of black smoke from the burning pitch-pine roots rolling upward in the form of an inverted pyramid. The blaze reflected in the water, almost as distinct as the substance. It looked like tarring a ship on the shore of the Styx or Cocytus. For it is still and dark, notwithstanding the moon, and no sound but the crackling of the fire. The fishermen can be seen only near at hand, though their fire is visible far away; and

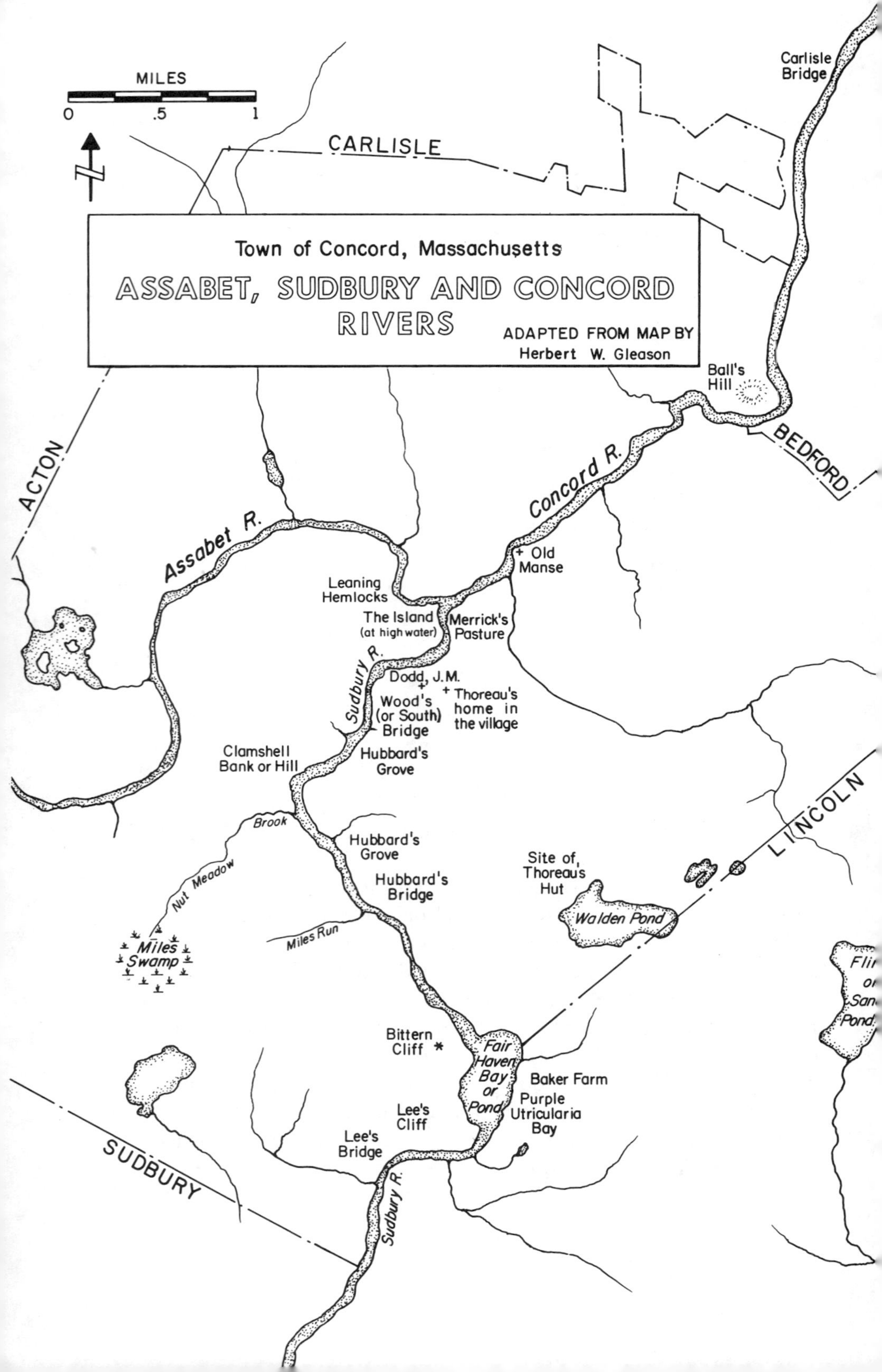

MILES
0
.5
1
CARLISLE
Town of Concord, Massachusetts
ASSABET, SUDBURY AND CONCORD RIVERS
ADAPTED FROM MAP BY
Herbert W. Gleason
Carlisle Bridge
Ball's Hill
BEDFORD
ACTON
Concord R.
Assabet R.
Old Manse
Leaning Hemlocks
The Island (at high water)
Merrick's Pasture
Sudbury R.
Dodd, J.M.
Thoreau's home in the village
Wood's (or South) Bridge
Clamshell Bank or Hill
Hubbard's Grove
LINCOLN
Brook
Hubbard's Grove
Nut Meadow
Hubbard's Bridge
Site of, Thoreau's Hut
Walden Pond
Miles Run
Miles Swamp
Bittern Cliff
Fair Haven Bay or Pond
Baker Farm
Purple Utricularia Bay
Lee's Cliff
Lee's Bridge
SUDBURY
Sudbury R.

then they appear as dusky, fuliginous figures, half enveloped in smoke, seen only by their enlightened sides. Like devils they look, clad in old coats to defend themselves from the fogs, one standing up forward holding the spear ready to dart, while the smoke and flames are blown in his face, the other paddling the boat slowly and silently along close to the shore with almost imperceptible motion.

The river appears indefinitely wide; there is a mist rising from the water, which increases the indefiniteness. A high bank or moonlit hill rises at a distance over the meadow on the bank, with its sandy gullies and clamshells exposed where the Indians feasted. The shore line, though close, is removed by the eye to the side of the hill. It is at high-water mark. It is continued till it meets the hill. Now the fisherman's fire, left behind, acquires some thick rays in the distance and becomes a star. As surely as sunlight falling through an irregular chink makes a round figure on the opposite wall, so the blaze at a distance appears a star. Such is the effect of the atmosphere. The bright sheen of the moon is constantly traveling with us, and is seen at the same angle in front on the surface of the pads; and the reflection of its disk in the rippled water by our boatside appears like bright gold pieces falling on the river's counter. This coin is incessantly poured forth as from some unseen horn of plenty at our side. . . .

Oct. 7. This morning the fog over the river and the brooks and meadows running into it has risen to the height of forty or fifty feet.

1 P.M—To river; by boat to Corner Bridge.

A very still, warm, bright, clear afternoon. Our boat so small and low that we are close to the water.

The muskrats all the way are now building their houses, about two thirds done. . . . Their unfinished, rapidly rising nests look now like truncated cones. They seem to be all building at once in different parts of the river, and to have advanced equally far.

The weeds being dead and the weather cooler, the water is more transparent. Now is the time to observe such weeds as have not been destroyed. The fishes are plainly seen. Saw a pickerel which had swallowed a smaller fish, with the tail projecting from his mouth. There is a dirty-looking weed quite submerged, with short, densely crowded, finely divided leaves, in dense masses atop, like the tops of spruce trees, more slender below. The shores for a great width are occupied by the dead leaves and stems of the pontederia, which give the river a very wild look. There is a strong-scented, green plant which looks like a fresh-water sponge or coral, clumsy-limbed like a dead tree, or a cactus. A long narrow grass like a fresh-water eel grass. . . .

There is a great difference between this season and a month ago —warm as this happens to be—as between one period of your life and another. A little frost is at the bottom of it.

It is a remarkable difference between night and day on the river, that there is no fog by day.

Nov. 9. The boat which we paddled that elysian day, Oct. 7th, was made of three distinct boxes shaped like bread-troughs, excepting the bow piece, which was rounded, . . . fastened together by screws and nuts, with stout round leather handles by which to carry the separate parts. It was made of the thinnest and lightest material, without seats or tholepins, for portability. So that the three passengers could sit in three different boats which, by turning the hand-nuts(?), they might separate and steer different ways. . . .

* * *

1852

June 16. Wednesday. 4.30 A.M. . . . A new season. The earth looks like a debauchee after the sultry night. Birds sing at this hour as in the spring. You hear that spitting, *dumping* frog and the bullfrogs occasionally still, for the heat is scarcely less than the last night. *No toads now.* The white lily is budded.

Paddle from the ash tree to the swimming place. The further shore is crowded with polygonums (leaves) and pontederia leaves. There seems to have intervened no night. The heat of the day is unabated. You perspire before sunrise. The bullfrogs boom still. The river appears covered with an almost imperceptible blue film. The sun is not yet over the bank. What wealth in a stagnant river! There is music in every sound in the morning atmosphere. As I look up over the bay, I see the reflections of the meadow woods and the Hosmer hill at a distance, the tops of the trees cut off by a slight ripple. Even the fine grasses on the near bank are distinctly reflected. Owing to the reflections of the distant woods and hills, you seem to be paddling into a vast hollow country, doubly novel and interesting. Thus the voyageur is lured onward to fresh pastures. . . .

July 10. *Saturday.* Another day, if possible still hotter than the last. We have already had three or four such, and still no rain. The soil under the sward in the yard is dusty as an ash heap for a foot in depth, and young trees are suffering and dying. . . .

The long, narrow open intervals in the woods near the Assabet are quite dry now, in some parts yellow with the upright loosestrife. One of these meadows, a quarter of a mile long by a few rods wide, narrow and winding and bounded on all sides by maples, showing the under sides of their leaves, swamp white oaks with their glossy dark-green leaves, and birches, etc., and full of meadowsweet just coming into bloom and cranberry vines and a dry kind of grass, is a very attractive place to walk in. We undressed on this side, carried our clothes down in the stream a considerable distance, and finally bathed in earnest from the opposite side. The heat tempted us to prolong this luxury. I think that I never felt the water so warm, yet it was not disagreeably so, though probably bathing in [it] was the less bracing and exhilarating, not so good as when you have to make haste, shivering, to get your clothes on in the wind, when ice has formed in the morning. But this is certainly the most luxurious. The river has here a sandy bottom and is for the most part quite shallow. I made quite an excursion up and down it in the water, a fluvial, a water, walk. It seemed the properest highway for this weather. Now in water a foot or two deep, now suddenly descending through valleys up to my neck, but all alike agreeable. Sometimes the bottom looked as if covered with long, flat, sharp-edged rocks. I could break off cakes three or four inches thick and a foot or two square. It was a conglomeration and consolidation of sand and pebbles, as it were cemented with oxide of iron, quite red with it, iron-colored, to the depth of an inch on the upper side—a hard kind of pan covering or forming the bottom in many places. When I had left the river and walked in the woods for some time, and jumped into the river again, I was surprised to find for the first time how warm it was—as it seemed to me, almost warm enough to boil eggs—like water that has stood a considerable while in a kettle over a fire. There are many interesting objects of study as you walk up and down a clear river like this in the water, where you can see every inequality in the bottom and every object on it. The breams' nests are interesting and even handsome, and the shallow water in them over the sand is so warm to my hand that I think their ova will soon be hatched. Also the numerous heaps of stones, made I know not certainly by what fish, many of them rising above the surface. There are weeds on the bottom which remind you of the sea. The radical leaves of the floating heart, which I have never seen mentioned, very large, five inches long and four wide, dull claret (and green where freshest), pellucid, with waved edges, in large tufts or dimples on the bottom, oftenest without the floating leaves, like lettuce or some kelps or carrageen moss (?). The bottom is also scored with furrows made by the clams moving about, sometimes a rod long; and always the clam lies at one end, so this fish can change its position and get into deeper and cooler water. I was in doubt before whether the clam made these furrows, for one apparently fresh that I examined had a "mud clam" at the end; but these, which were very numerous, had living clams.

There are but few fishes to be seen. They have, no doubt, retreated to the deepest water. In one somewhat muddier place, close to the shore, I came upon an old pout cruising with her young. She dashed away at my approach, but the fry remained. They were of various sizes from a third of an inch to an inch and a half long, quite black and pout-shaped, except that the head was most developed in the smallest. They were constantly moving about in a somewhat circular, or rather lenticular, school, about fifteen or eighteen inches in diameter, and I estimated that there were at least a thousand of them. Presently the old pout came back and took the lead of her brood, which followed her, or rather gathered about her, like chickens about a hen; but this mother had so many children she didn't know what to do. Her maternal yearnings must be on a great scale. When one half of the divided school found her out, they came down upon her and completely invested her like a small cloud. She was soon joined by another smaller pout, apparently her mate, and all, both old and young, began to be very familiar with me; they came round my legs and felt them with their feelers, and the old pouts nibbled my toes, while the fry half concealed my feet. Probably if I had been standing on the bank with my clothes on they would have been more shy. Ever and anon the old pouts dashed aside to drive away a passing bream or perch. The larger one kept circling about her charge, as if to keep them together within a certain compass. If any of her flock were lost or devoured she could hardly have missed them. I wondered if there was any calling of the roll at night. . . .

I wonder if any Roman emperor ever indulged in such luxury as this—of walking up and down a river in torrid weather with only a hat to shade the head. . . .

July 12. . . . 2 P.M.—To the Assabet. . . . Now for another fluvial walk. There is always a current of air above the water, blowing up or down the course of the river, so that this is the coolest highway. Divesting yourself of all clothing but your shirt and hat, which are to protect your exposed parts from the sun, you are prepared for the fluvial excursion. You choose what depths you like, tucking your toga higher or lower, as you take the deep middle of the road or the shallow sidewalks. Here is a road where no dust was ever known, no intolerable drouth. Now your feet expand on a smooth sandy bottom, now contract timidly on pebbles, now slump in genial fatty mud—greasy, saponaceous—amid the pads. You scare out whole schools of small breams and perch, and sometimes a pickerel, which have taken shelter from the sun under the pads. This river is so clear compared with the South Branch * or main stream, that all their secrets are betrayed to you. Or you meet with and interrupt a turtle taking a more leisurely walk up the stream. Ever and anon you cross some furrow in the sand, made by a muskrat, leading off to right or left to their galleries in the bank, and you thrust your foot into the entrance, which is just below the surface of the water and is strewn with grass and rushes, of which they make their nests. In shallow water near the shore, your feet at once detect the presence of springs in the bank emptying in, by the sudden coldness of the water, and there, if you are thirsty, you dig a little well in the sand with your hands, and when you return, after it has settled and clarified itself, get a draught of pure cold water there. The fishes are very forward to find out such

* The South Branch of the Concord River, namely the Sudbury. W. T.

places, and I have observed that a frog will occupy a cool spring, however small.

The most striking phenomenon in this stream is the heaps of small stones about the size of a walnut, more or less, which line the shore in shallow water, one every rod or two, the recent ones frequently rising by more than half their height above the water, at present, *i.e.* a foot or a foot and a half, and sharply conical, the older flattened by the elements and greened over with the thread-like stem of *Ranunculus filiformis,* with its minute bright yellow flower. Some of these heaps contain two cartloads of stones, and as probably the creature that raised them took up one at a time, it must have been a stupendous task. They are from the size of a hen's egg down to the smallest gravel, and some are so perfect that I cannot believe they were made before the river fell.

Now you walk through fields of the small potamogeton (*heterophyllus* or *hybridus*), now in flower; now through the glossy pads of the white or the yellow waterlily, stepping over the now closed buds of the latter; now pause in the shade of a swamp white oak (up to your middle in the cool element), to which the very skaters and water bugs confine themselves for the most part. It is an objection to walking in the mud that from time to time you have to pick the leeches off you. The stinkpot's shell, covered with mud and fine green weeds, gives him exactly the appearance of a stone on the bottom, and I noticed a large snapping turtle on one of the dark-brown rocks in the middle of the river (apparently for coolness, in company with a painted tortoise), so completely the color of the rock that, if it had not been for his head curved upwardss to a point from anxiety, I should not have detected him. Thus nature subjects them to the same circumstances with the stones, and paints them alike, as with one brush, for their safety.

What art can surpass the rows of maples and elms and swamp white oaks which the water plants along the river—I mean in variety and gracefulness—conforming to the curves of the river.

Aug. 31. *Tuesday.* 9 A.M.—Up river in boat to the bend above the Pantry.*

It is pleasant to embark on a voyage, if only for a short river

---

*Pantry Brook, coming from the west, enters the Sudbury south of Concord about 4.5 miles upriver from the village. W. T.

excursion, the boat to be your home for the day, especially if it is
neat and dry. A sort of moving studio it becomes, you can carry
so many things with you. It is almost as if you put oars out at your
windows and moved your house along. A sailor, I see, easily becomes attached to his vessel. How continually we [are] thankful
to the boat if it does not leak! . . .

I rigged my mast by putting a post across the boat, and putting
the mast through it and into a piece of a post at the bottom, and
lashing and bracing it, and so sailed most of the way. The water,
methinks, has a little of the fall sparkle on it after the rain. It has
run over the meadows considerably and drowned the flowers. I feel
as if it was a month later than it was a week ago. . . .

How much he knows of the wind, its strength and direction,
whose steed it is—the sailor. With a good gale he advances rapidly;
when it dies away he is at a standstill. The very sounds made by
moving the furniture of my boat are agreeable, echoing so distinctly
and sweetly over the water; they give the sense of being abroad.
I find myself *at home* in new scenery. I carry more of myself with
me; I am more entirely abroad, as when a man takes his children
into the fields with him. I carry so many me's with [me]. This large
basket of melons, umbrella, flowers, hammer, etc., etc., all go with
me to the end of the voyage without being the least incumbrance,
and preserve their relative distances. Our capacity to carry our
furniture with us is so much increased. There is little danger of
overloading the steed. We can go completely equipped to fields a
dozen miles off. The tent and the chest can be taken as easily as not.
We embark; we go aboard a boat; we sit or we stand. If we sail,
there is no exertion necessary. If we move in the opposite direction,
we nevertheless progress. And if we row, we sit to an agreeable
exercise, akin to flying. A student, of course, if it were perfectly
convenient, would always move with his escritoire and his library
about him. If you have a cabin and can descend into that, the charm
is double. . . .

It is worth the while to have had a cloudy, even a stormy, day
for an excursion, if only that you are out at the clearing up. The
beauty of the landscape is the greater, not only by reason of the
contrast with its recent lowering aspect, but because of the greater

freshness and purity of the air and of vegetation, and of the repressed and so recruited spirits of the beholder. . . .

I float slowly down from Fair Haven till I have passed the bridge. The sun, half an hour high, has come out again just before setting, with a brilliant, warm light, and there is the slightest undulation discernible on the water, from the boat or other cause, as it were its imitation in glass. The reflections are perfect. A bright, fresh green on fields and trees now after the rain, springlike with the sense of summer past. The reflections are the more perfect for the blackness of the water. I see the down of a thistle, probably, in the air, descending to the water two or three rods off, which I mistake for a man in his shirt sleeves descending a distant hill, by an ocular delusion. How fair the smooth green swells of those low grassy hills on which the sunlight falls! Indian hills.

This is the most glorious part of this day, the serenest, warmest, brightest part, and the most suggestive. Evening is fairer than morning. It is chaste eve, for it has sustained the trials of the day, but to the morning such praise was inapplicable. It is incense-breathing. Morning is full of promise and vigor. Evening is pensive. The serenity is far more remarkable to those who are on the water. That part of the sky just above the horizon seen reflected, apparently, some rods off from the boat is as light a blue as the actual, but it goes on deepening as your eye draws nearer to the boat, until, when you look directly down at the reflection of the zenith, it is lost in the blackness of the water. . . .

* * *

1853

March 22. . . . P.M.—To Martial Miles Meadow, by boat to Nut Meadow Brook.

Launched my new boat. It is very steady, too steady for me; does not toss enough and communicate the motion of the waves. Beside, the seats are not well arranged; when there are two in it, it requires a heavy stone in the stern to trim. But it holds its course very well with a side wind from being so flat from stem to stern.

The cranberries now make a show under water, and I always make it a point to taste a few. . . .

March 23. 5 A.M.—I hear the robin sing before I rise.

6 A.M.—Up the North River.*

A fresh, cool spring morning. . . .

My boat is very good to float and go before the wind, but it has not *run* enough to it—if that is the phrase—but lugs too much dead water astern. However, it is all the steadier for it. Methinks it will not be a bad sailer. . . .

Without being the owner of any land, I find that I have a civil right in the river—that, if I am not a landowner I am a water-owner. It is fitting, therefore, that I should have a boat, a cart, for this my farm. Since it is almost wholly given up to a few of us, while the other highways are much traveled, no wonder that I improve it. Such a one as I will choose to dwell in a township where there are most ponds and rivers and our range is widest. In relation to the river, I find my natural rights least infringed on. It is an extensive "common" still left. . . .

May 30. The morning wind forever blows; the poem of the world is uninterrupted, but few are the ears that hear it. . . .

P.M.—To Carlisle Bridge by boat.

A strong but somewhat gusty southerly wind, before which C.† and I sailed all the way from home to Carlisle Bridge in not far from an hour; the river unusually high for the season. Very pleasant to feel the strong, fresh southerly wind from over the water. There are no clouds in the sky, but a high haziness, as if the moisture drawn up by yesterday's heat was condensed by to-day's comparative coolness. The water a dull slate-color and waves running high —a dirty yellow where they break—and long streaks of white foam, six or eight feet apart, stretching north and south between Concord and Bedford—without end. The common blue flag just out at Ball's Hill. The white maples, especially those shaped like large bushes, on the banks are now full of foliage, showing the

---

* The Assabet River. W. T.

† William Ellery Channing (1818-1901), poet, journalist, and author of *Thoreau, the Poet-Naturalist,* 1873. He moved to Concord in 1842 and for twenty years roamed the fields, woods, and rivers with Thoreau. W. T.

white under sides of the leaves in the wind, and the swamp white oak, having similar silvery under sides to its leaves, and both growing abundantly and prevailing here along the river, make or impart a peculiar flashing light to the scenery in windy weather, all bright, flashing, and cheerful. On the meadows are large yellow-green patches of ferns beginning to prevail. Passed a large boat anchored off in the meadows not far from the boundary of Concord. It was quite a piece of ocean scenery, we saw it so long before reaching it and so long after; and it looked larger than reality, what with the roaring of the wind in our shrouds and the dashing of the waves. The incessant drifting about of a boat so anchored by a long cable, playing with its halter, now showing more, now less, of its side, is a pleasing sight. . . . The pines now dotted with white shoots, the pitch pines a little reddish, are an interesting sight now. Whence came all those dead suckers, a dozen at least, which we saw floating today, some on their sides, transversely barred, some on their backs with their white bellies up and dark fins on each side? Why are they suckers only that we see? Can it be because the spearers have thrown them away? Or has some bird of prey dropped them? I rarely see other fish floating . . . .

Nov. 11. . . . 9 A.M.—To Fair Haven Pond by boat.

The morning is so calm and pleasant, winterlike, that I must spend the forenoon abroad. The river is smooth as polished silver. A little ice has formed along the shore in shallow bays five or six rods wide. It is for the most part of crystals imperfectly united, shaped like birds' tracks, and breaks with a pleasant crisp sound when it feels the undulations produced by my boat. I hear a linaria-like mew from some birds that fly over. Some muskrat houses have received a slight addition in the night. The one I opened day before yesterday has been covered again, though not yet raised so high as before. The hips of the late rose still show abundantly along the shore, and in one place nightshade berries. I hear a faint cricket (or locust?) still, even after the slight snow. I hear the cawing of crows toward the distant wood through the clear, echoing, resonant air, and the lowing of cattle. It is rare that the water is smooth in the forenoon. It is now as smooth as in a summer evening or a September or October afternoon. There is frost on all the weeds that rise above the water or ice. The *Polygonum Hydropiper* is the most conspicuous, abundant, and enduring of those in the water. I see the spire of one white with frost crystals, a perfect imitation at a little distance of its loose and narrow spike of white flowers, that have withered. I have noticed no turtles since October 31st, and no frogs for a still longer time. At the bathing[place] I looked for clams, in summer almost as thick as paving stones there, and found none. They have probably removed into deeper water and into the mud (?). When did they move? . . .

I counted nineteen muskrat cabins between Hubbard Bathing Place and Hubbard's further wood, this side the Hollowell place, from two to four feet high. They thus help materially to raise and form the river bank. I opened one by the Hubbard Bridge. The floor of the chamber was two feet or more beneath the top and one foot above the water. It was quite warm from the recent presence of the inhabitants. I heard the peculiar plunge of one close by. The instant one has put his eyes noiselessly above water he plunges like a flash, showing tail, and with a very loud sound, the first notice you have of his proximity—that he has been there—as loud as if he had struck a solid substance. This had a sort of double bed, the whole about two feet long by one foot wide and seven or eight inches high, floored thinly with dry meadow grass. There were in the water green butts and roots of the pontederia, which I think they eat. I find the roots gnawed off. Do they eat flagroot? A good deal of a small green hypnum-like river weed forms the mouthfuls in their masonry. It makes a good sponge to mop the boat with.

The wind has risen and sky overcast. I stop at Lee's Cliff, and there is a *Veronica serpyllifolia* out. Sail back. Scared up two small ducks, perhaps teal. I had not seen any of late. They have probably almost all gone south.

Nov. 12. . . . I cannot but regard it as a kindness in those who have the steering of me that, by the want of pecuniary wealth, I have been nailed down to this my native region so long and steadily, and made to study and love this spot of earth more and more. . . .

8 P.M.—Up river to Hubbard Bathing Place.

Moon nearly full. A mild, almost summer evening after a very warm day, alternately clear and overcast. The meadows, with perhaps a little mist on them, look as if covered with frost in the moonlight. . . . There is now and of late months no smell of muskrats, which is probably confined to the spring or rutting season. While the sense of seeing is partly slumbering, that of hearing is more wide awake than by day, and, now that the wind is rising, I hear distinctly the chopping of every little wave under the bow of my boat. Hear no bird, only the loud plunge of a muskrat from time to time. The moon is wading slowly through broad squadrons of clouds, with a small coppery halo, and now she comes forth triumphant and burnishes the water far and wide, and makes the reflections more distinct. Trees stand bare against the sky again. This the first month in which they do. I hear one cricket singing still, faintly deep in the bank, now after one whitening of snow. His theme is life immortal. The last cricket, full of cheer and faith, piping to himself, as the last man might. The dark squadrons of hostile clouds have now swept over the face of the moon, and she appears unharmed and riding triumphant in her chariot. Suddenly they dwindle and melt away in her mild and all-pervading light, dissipated like the mists of the morning. They pass away and are forgotten like bad dreams.

Landed at the bathing place. There is no sound of a frog from all these waters and meadows which a few months ago resounded so with them; not even a cricket or the sound of a mosquito. I can fancy that I hear the sound of peeping hylodes ringing in my ear, but it is all fancy. How short their year! How early they sleep! Nature is desert and iron-bound; she has shut her door. How different from the muggy nights of summer, teeming with life! That resounding life is now buried in the mud, returned into Nature's womb, and most of the birds have retreated to the warm belt of the earth. . . .

1854

May 8. . . . P.M.—By boat to Fair Haven.

The water has fallen a foot or more, but I cannot get under the stone bridge, so haul over the road. There is a fair and strong wind with which to sail upstream, and then I can leave my boat, depending on the wind changing to southwest soon. It is long since I have sailed on so broad a tide. How dead would the globe seem, especially at this season, if it were not for these water surfaces! We are slow to realize water—the beauty and magic of it. It is interestingly strange to us forever. Immortal water, alive even in the superficies, restlessly heaving now and tossing me and my boat, and sparkling with life! I look round with a thrill on this bright fluctuating surface on which no man can walk, whereon is no trace of footstep, unstained as glass. When I got off this end of the Hollowell place I found myself in quite a sea with a smacking wind directly aft. I felt no little exhilaration, mingled with a slight awe, as I drove before this strong wind over the great black-backed waves I judged to be at least twenty inches or two feet high, cutting through them, and heard their surging and felt them toss me. I was even obliged to head across them and not get into their troughs, for then I could hardly keep my legs. They were crested with a dirty-white foam and were ten or twelve feet from crest to crest. They were so black—as no sea I have seen—large and powerful, and made such a roaring around me that I could not but regard them as gambolling monsters of the deep. They were *melainai*—what is the Greek for waves? This is our black sea. You see a *perfectly black* mass about two feet high and perhaps four or five feet thick and of indefinite length, round-backed, or perhaps forming a sharp ridge with a dirty-white crest, tumbling like a whale unceasingly before you. Only one of the epithets which the poets have applied to the color of the sea will apply to this water—*melaina,* μέλαινα θάλασσα. I was delighted to find that our usually peaceful river could toss me so. How much more exciting than to be planting potatoes with those men in the field! What a different world! The waves increased in height till [I] reached the bridge, the impulse of wind and waves increasing with the breadth of the sea. It is remarkable that it requires a very wide expanse to produce so great an undulation. The length of this meadow lake in the direction of the wind is about a mile, its breadth varying from a mile to a quarter of a mile, and the great commotion is toward the southerly end. Yet after passing the bridge I was surprised to find an almost smooth expanse as far as I could see, though the waves were about three inches high at fifty rods' distance. I lay awhile in that smooth water, and though I heard the waves lashing the other side of the causeway I could hardly realize what a sea I [had] just sailed through. It sounded like the breakers on the seashore heard from *terra firma*. . . .

As I returned I saw, in the Miles meadow, on the bottom, two painted tortoises fighting. Their sternums were not particularly depressed. The smaller had got firmly hold of the loose skin of the larger's neck with his jaws, and most of the time his head was held within the other's shell; but, though he thus had the "upper hand," he had the least command of himself and was on his edge. They were very moderate—for the most part quite still, as if weary—and were not to be scared by me. Then they struggled a little, their flippers merely paddling the water, and I could hear the edges of their shells strike together. I took them out into the boat, holding by the smaller, which did not let go of the larger, and so raising both together. Nor did he let go when they were laid in the boat. But when I put them into the water again they instantly separated and concealed themselves. . . .

July 17. Monday. Last night and this morning another thick dog-dayish fog. I find my chamber full this morning. It lasts till 9 A.M.

11 A.M.—By river to Fair Haven.

I go to observe the lilies. I see a rail lodged in the weeds with seven tortoises on it, another with ten, another with eleven, all in a row sunning now at midday, hot as it is. They are mostly the painted tortoise. Apparently no weather is too hot for them thus to bask in the sun. The pontederia is in its prime, alive with butterflies, yellow and others. I see its tall blue spikes reflected beneath the edge of the pads on each side, pointing down to a heaven beneath as well as above.

At Purple Utricularia Shore, there are, within a circle of four or five rods' diameter, ninety-two lilies fairly open and about half a dozen which appear to have already partly closed. I have seen them far more numerous. I watch them for an hour and a half.

        At 11.45 . . . . 92 fairly open
        At 12   88
        At 12.15 75
        At 12.30 46
        At 12.45 26
        At 1   . . . . 4 which are more or less stale

By about 1.30 they are all shut up, and no petal is to be seen up and down the river unless a lily is broken off. You may therefore say that they shut up between 11.30 and 1.30, though almost all between 12 and 1. I think that I could tell when it was 12 o'clock within half an hour by the lilies. One is about an hour about it. The petals gradually draw together, and the sepals raise themselves out of the water and follow. They do not shut up so tight but that a very little white appears at the apex. Sometimes a sepal is held back by a pad or other weed, leaving one side bare. Many fall over on their sides more or less, but none withdraw under water as some have said. The lilies reach from the water's edge, where they are raised two or three inches above the surface, out five or six rods to where the water is four feet deep, and there succeed the *small* yellow lily. . . .

I am surprised to see crossing my course in middle of Fair Haven Pond great yellowish devil's needles, flying from shore to shore, from Island to Baker's Farm and back, about a foot above the water, some against a head wind; also yellow butterflies, suggesting that these insects see the distant shore and resolve to visit it. In fact, they move much faster than I can toward it, yet as if they were conscious that they were on a journey, flying for the most part straight forward. It shows more enterprise and a wider range than I had suspected. It looks very bold. If devil's needles cross Fair Haven, then man may cross the Atlantic. . . .

* * *

1855

March 24. . . . P.M.—Up Assabet by boat. A cold and blustering afternoon after a flurry of snow which has not fairly whitened the ground. I see a painted tortoise at the bottom moving slowly over the meadow. They do not yet put their heads out, but merely begin to venture forth into their calmer element. It is almost as stationary, as inert, as the pads as yet.

Passing up the Assabet, by the Hemlocks, where there has been a slide and some rocks have slid down into the river, I think I see how rocks come to be found in the midst of rivers. Rivers are continually changing their channels—eating into one bank and adding their sediment to the other—so that frequently where there is a great bend you see a high and steep bank or hill on one side, which the river washes, and a broad meadow on the other. As the river eats into the hill, especially in freshets, it undermines the rocks, large and small, and they slide down, alone or with the sand and soil, to the water's edge. The river continues to eat into the hill, carrying away all the lighter parts [of] the sand and soil, to add to its meadows or islands somewhere, but leaves the rocks where they rested, and thus in course of time they occupy the middle of the stream and, later still, the middle of the meadow, perchance, though it may be buried under the mud. But this does not explain how so many rocks lying in streams have been split in the direction of the current. Again, rivers appear to have traveled back and worn into the meadows of their creating, and then they become more meandering than ever. Thus in the course of ages the rivers wriggle in their beds, till it feels comfortable under them. Time is cheap and rather insignificant. It matters not whether it is a river which changes from side to side in a geological period or an eel that wriggles past in an instant. . . .

June 14. *Thursday.* Up river.

See young red-wings; like grizzly-black vultures, they are still so bald. See many empty red-wing nests now amid the *Cornus scricca.* The bluebird's nest high in the black willow at Sassafras Shore has five eggs. The gold robin's nest, which I could pull down within reach, just beyond, has three eggs. I have one. I told C. to look into an old mortise hole in Wood's Bridge for a white-bellied swallow's nest, as we were paddling under; but he laughed, incredulous. I insisted, and when he climbed up he scared out the bird. Five eggs. "You see the feathers about, do you not?" "Yes," said he. . . .

It suddenly began to rain with great violence, and we in haste drew up our boat on the Clamshell shore, upset it, and got under, sitting on the paddles, and so were quite dry while our friends thought we were being wet to our skins. But we had as good a roof as they. It was very pleasant to lie there half an hour close to the edge of the water and see and hear the great drops patter on the river, each making a great bubble; the rain seemed much heavier for it. The swallows at once and numerously began to fly low over the water in the rain, as they had not before, and the toads' spray rang in it. After it began to hold up, the wind veered a little to the east and apparently blew back the rear of the cloud, and blew a second rain somewhat in upon us.

As soon as the rain was over I crawled out, straightened my legs, and stumbled at once upon a little patch of strawberries within a rod—the sward red with them. These we plucked while the last drops were thinly falling. . . .

Nov. 30. River skimmed over behind Dodd's and elsewhere. Got in my boat. River remained iced over all day. . . .

On the 27th, when I made my last voyage for the season, I found a large sound pine log about four feet long floating, and brought it home. Off the larger end I sawed two wheels, about a foot in diameter and seven or eight inches thick, and I fitted to them an axletree made of a joist, which also I found in the river, and thus I had a convenient pair of wheels on which to get my boat up and roll it about. The assessors called me into their office this year and said they wished to get an inventory of my property; asked if I had any real estate. No. Any notes at interest or railroad shares? No. Any taxable property? None that I knew of. "I own a boat," I said; and one of them thought that that might come under the head of a pleasure carriage, which is taxable. Now that I have wheels to it, it comes nearer to it. I was pleased to get my boat in by this means rather than on a borrowed wheelbarrow. It was fit that the river should furnish the material, and that in my last voyage on it, when the ice reminded me that it was time to put it in winter quarters. . . .

* * *

1856

April 22. It has rained two days and nights, and now the sun breaks out, but the wind is still easterly, and the storm probably is not over. In a few minutes the air is full of mizzling rain again.

8 A.M.—Go to my boat opposite Bittern Cliff. . . .

Soon after I turned about in Fair Haven Pond, it began to rain hard. The wind was but little south of east and therefore not very favorable for my voyage. I raised my sail and, cowering under my umbrella in the stern, wearing the umbrella like a cap and holding the handle between my knees, I steered and paddled, almost perfectly sheltered from the heavy rain. Yet my legs and arms were a little exposed sometimes, in my endeavors to keep well to windward so as to double certain capes ahead. For the wind occasionally drove me on to the western shore. From time to time, from under my umbrella, I could see the ducks spinning away before me, like great bees. For when they are flying low directly from you, you see hardly anything but their vanishing dark bodies, while the rapidly moving wings or paddles, seen edgewise, are almost invisible. At length, when the river turned more easterly, I was obliged to take down my sail and paddle slowly in the face of the rain, for the most part not seeing my course, with the umbrella slanted before me. But though my progress was slow and laborious, and at length I began to get a little wet, I enjoyed the adventure because it combined to some extent the advantages of being at home in my chamber and abroad in the storm at the same time.

It is highly important to invent a dress which will enable us to be abroad with impunity in the severest storms. We cannot be said to have fully invented clothing yet. In the meanwhile the rain water collects in the boat, and you must sit with your feet curled up on a paddle, and you expose yourself in taking down your mast and raising it again at the bridges. These rainstorms—this is the third day of one—characterize the season, and belong rather to winter than to summer. . . .

* * *

1857

May 3. Sunday. A remarkably warm and pleasant morning.
A.M.—To Battle-Ground by river.
I heard the ring of toads at 6 A.M. The flood on the meadows,

still high, is quite smooth, and many are out this still and suddenly very warm morning, pushing about in boats. Now, thinks many a one, is the time to paddle or push gently far up or down the river, along the still, warm meadow's edge, and perhaps we may see some large turtles, or muskrats, or otter, or rare fish or fowl. It will be a grand forenoon for a cruise, to explore these meadow shores and inundated maple swamps which we have never explored. Now we shall be recompensed for the week's confinement to shop or garden. We will spend our Sabbath exploring these smooth warm vernal waters. Up or down shall we go? To Fair Haven Bay and the Sudbury meadows, or to Ball's Hill and Carlisle Bridge? Along the meadow's edge, lined with willow and alders and maples, under the catkins of the early willow, and brushing those of the sweet-gale with our prow, where the sloping pasture and the plowed ground, submerged, are fast drinking up the flood. What fair isles, what remote coast shall we explore? What San Salvador or Bay of All Saints arrive at? All are tempted forth, like flies, into the sun. All isles seem fortunate and blessed today; all capes are of Good Hope. The same sun and calm that tempts the turtles out tempts the voyagers. It is an opportunity to explore their own natures, to float along their own shores. The woodpecker cackles and the crow blackbird utters his jarring chatter from the oaks and maples. All well men and women who are not restrained by superstitious custom come abroad this morning by land or water, and such as have boats launch them and put forth in search of adventure. Others, less free or, it may be, less fortunate, take their station on bridges, watching the rush of water through them and the motions of the departing voyagers, and listening to the notes of blackbirds from over the smooth water. They see a swimming snake, or a muskrat dive—airing and sunning themselves there until the first bell rings. . . .

* * *

1858

Aug. 22. P.M.—I have spliced my old sail to a new one, and now go out to try it in a sail to Baker Farm. It is a "square sail," some five feet by six. I like it much. It pulls like an ox, and makes me think there's more wind abroad than there is. The yard goes about with a pleasant force, almost enough, I would fain imagine, to knock me overboard. How sturdily it pulls, shooting us along, catching more wind than I knew to be wandering in this river valley! It suggests a new power in the sail, like a Grecian god. I can even worship it, after a heathen fashion. And then, how it becomes my boat and the river—a simple homely square sail, all for use not show, so low and broad! *Ajacean*. The boat is like a plow drawn by a winged bull. If I had had this a dozen years ago, my voyages would have been performed more quickly and easily. But then probably I should have lived less in them. . . .

* * *

Nathaniel Holmes Bishop
1837-1902

In successive years Bishop made two long-distance trips, one in a paper canoe, the other in a Barnegat Bay gunning skiff known locally as a sneak-box; and he wrote a full length book about each—books I have shortened very considerably.

Born in Medford, Massachusetts, he was thirty-seven when he set out; for some time before he had been a cranberry grower in Ocean County, New Jersey. His tremendous voyage in a paper canoe began in a quite different sort of craft—a wooden lapstrake decked canoe that with oars, rudder, mast and sail weighed three hundred pounds—so large that he had to take a boatman along to assist him. But he soon scrapped that ponderous arrangement, discharged the crew, and switched to a little thing made of laminated strips of heavy manila paper molded over a light wooden frame that he could manage alone. His canoe trip is surely one of the great small craft exploits. His voyage in a sneak-box was another. Here are two books that deserve to be better known.

VOYAGE OF THE PAPER CANOE

INTRODUCTION

The author left Quebec, Dominion of Canada, July 4, 1874, with a single assistant, in a wooden canoe eighteen feet in length, bound for the Gulf of Mexico. It was his intention to follow the natural and artificial connecting watercourses of the continent in the most direct line southward to the gulf coast of Folorida, making portages as seldom as possible, to show how few were the interruptions to a continuous waterway for vessels of light draught, from the chilly, foggy, and rocky regions of the Gulf of St. Lawrence in the north, to the semitropical waters of the great Southern Sea, the waves of which beat upon the sandy shores of the southernmost United States. Having proceeded about four hundred miles upon his voyage, the author reached Troy, on the Hudson River, New York State, where for several years E. Waters & Sons had been perfecting the construction of paper boats.

The advantages in using a boat of only fifty-eight pounds weight, the strength and durability of which had been well and satisfactorily tested, could not be questioned, and the author dismissed his assistant, and "paddled his own canoe" about two thousand miles to the end of the journey. Though frequently lost in the labyrinth of creeks and marshes which skirt the southern coast of his country, the author's difficulties were greatly lessened by the use of the valuable and elaborate charts of the United States Coast Survey Bureau, to the faithful executers of which he desires to give unqualified and grateful praise. . . .

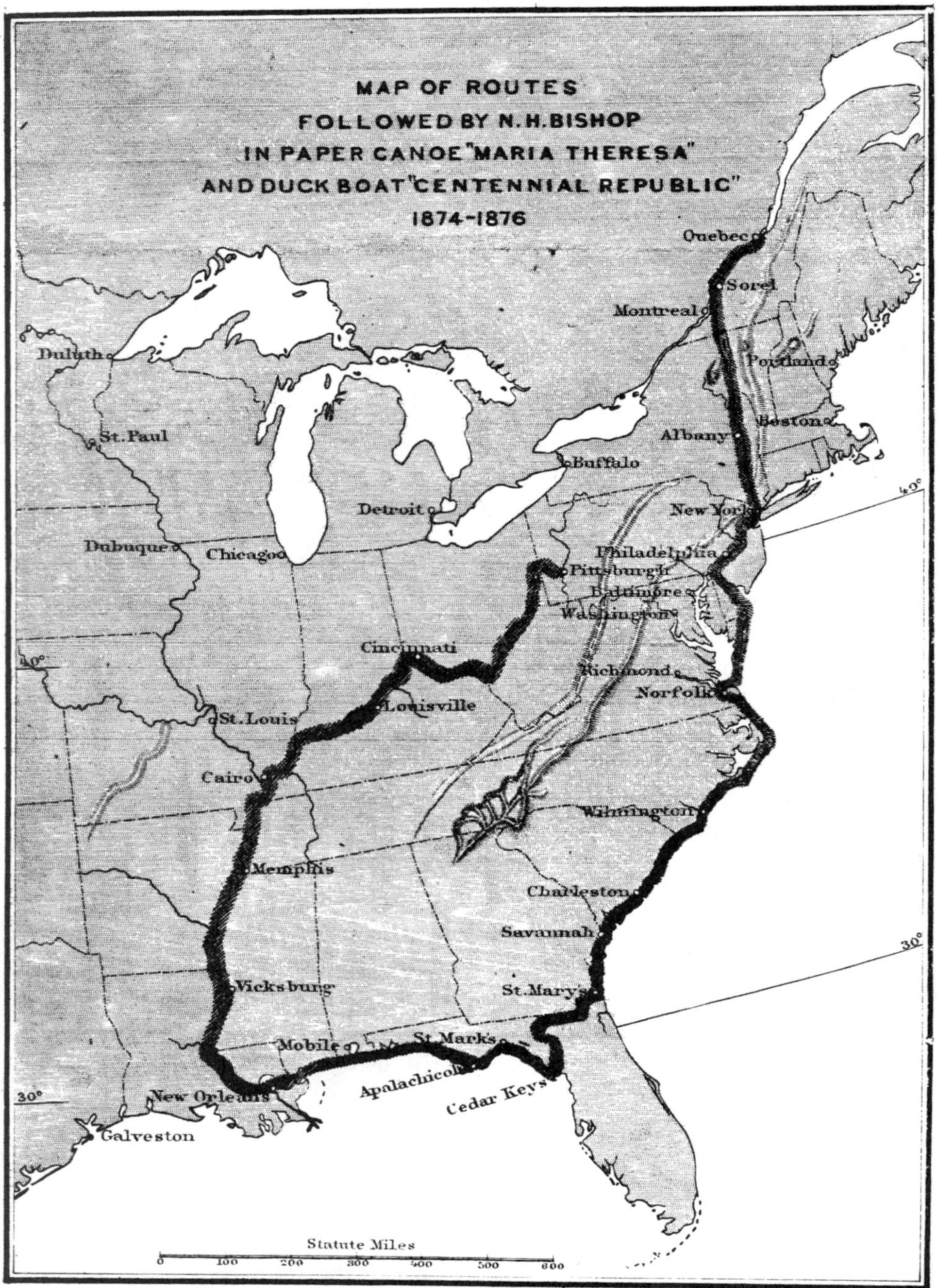
MAP OF ROUTES
FOLLOWED BY N. H. BISHOP
IN PAPER CANOE "MARIA THERESA"
AND DUCK BOAT "CENTENNIAL REPUBLIC"
1874-1876
Quebec
Sorel
Montreal
Portland
Boston
Albany
Duluth
St. Paul
Buffalo
Detroit
New York
Dubuque
Chicago
Philadelphia
Pittsburgh
Baltimore
Washington
Cincinnati
Richmond
Norfolk
Louisville
St. Louis
Cairo
Wilmington
Memphis
Charleston
Savannah
Vicksburg
St. Mary's
Mobile
St. Marks
Apalachicola
Cedar Keys
New Orleans
Galveston
40°
30°
Statute Miles
0
100
200
300
400
500
600

[Bishop's first four chapters describe the approaches to the continental waterway and his voyage from Quebec through the St. Lawrence to Lake Champlain, Lake George, and the Hudson River. His fifth chapter discusses the differences and relative merits of English and American canoes.]

TROY TO PHILADELPHIA

My canoe of the English "Nautilus" type was completed by the middle of October; and on the cold, drizzly morning of the twenty-first of the same month I embarked in my little fifty-eight pound craft from the landing of the paper-boat manufactory on the river Hudson, two miles above Troy. . . .

The dimensions of the *Maria Theresa* were: length, fourteen feet; beam, twenty-eight inches; depth, amidships, nine inches; height of bow from horizontal line, twenty-three inches; height of stern, twenty inches. The canoe was one-eighth of an inch in thickness, . . . She was fitted with a pair of steel outriggers, which could be easily unshipped and stowed away. The oars were of spruce, seven feet eight inches long, and weighed three pounds and a quarter each. The double paddle, which was seven feet six inches in length, weighed two pounds and a half. The mast and sail—which are of no service on such a miniature vessel, and were soon discarded—weighed six pounds. When I took on board at Philadelphia the canvas deck cover and the rubber strap which secured it in position, and the outfit—the cushion, sponge, provision basket, and a fifteen-pound case of charts—I found that, with my own weight included (one hundred and thirty pounds), the boat and her cargo, all told, provisioned for a long cruise, fell considerably short of the weight of three Saratoga trunks containing a very modest wardrobe for a lady's four weeks' visit at a fashionable watering place. . . .

A feeling of buoyancy and independence came over me as I glided on the current of this noble stream, with the consciousness that I now possessed the right boat for my enterprise. It had been a dream of my youth to become acquainted with the charms of this most romantic river of the American continent. Its sources are in the clouds of the Adirondacks, among the cold peaks of the northern wilderness; its ending may be said to be in the briny waters of the Atlantic, for its channel way has been sounded outside of the sandy beaches of New York harbor in the bosom of the restless ocean. . . .

While approaching the great city of New York, strong squalls of wind, blowing against the ebb tide, sent swashy waves into my open canoe, the sides of which, amidships, were only five or six inches above water; but the great buoyancy of the light craft and its very smooth exterior created but little friction in the water and made her very seaworthy, when carefully watched and handled, even without a deck of canvas or wood. While the canoe forged ahead through the troubled waters, and the breezes loaded with the saltness of the sea now near at hand struck my back, I confess that a longing to reach Philadelphia, where I could complete my outfit and increase the safety of my little craft, gave renewed vigor to my stroke as I exchanged the quiet atmosphere of the country for the smoke and noise of the city. Every instinct was now challenged, and every muscle brought into action, as I dodged tug boats, steamers, yachts, and vessels, while running the thoroughfare along the crowded wharves between New York on one side and Jersey City on the other. I found the slips between the piers most excellent ports of refuge at times, when the ferry boats, following each other in quick succession, made the river with its angry tide boil like a vortex. The task soon ended, and I left the Hudson at Castle Garden and entered the upper bay of New York harbor. As it was dark, I would gladly have gone ashore for the night, but a great city offers no inducement for a canoeist to land as a stranger at its wharves.

A much more pleasant reception awaited me down on Staten Island, a gentleman having notified me by mail that he would welcome the canoe and its owner. The ebb had ceased, and the incoming tide was being already felt close in shore; so with tide and wind against me, and the darkness of night settling down gloomily upon the wide bay, I pulled a strong oar for five miles to the entrance of Kill Van Kull Strait, which separates Staten Island from New Jersey and connects the upper bay with Raritan Bay.

The bright beams from the lighthouse on Robbin's Reef, which is one mile and a quarter off the entrance of the strait, guided me on my course. The head sea, in little, splashy waves, began to fill my canoe. The water soon reached the footrest; but there was no time to stop to bail out the boat, for a friendly current was near, and if once reached, my little craft would enter smoother waters. The flood which poured into the mouth of Kill Van Kull soon caught my boat, and the head tide was changed to a favorable current which carried me in its strong arms far into the saltwater strait, and I reached West New Brighton, along the high banks of which I found my haven of rest. Against the sky I traced the outlines of my landmark, three poplars, standing sentinellike before the house of the gentleman who had so kindly offered me his hospitality. The canoe was emptied of its shifting liquid ballast and carefully sponged dry. My host and his son carried it into the main hall of the mansion and placed it upon the floor, where the entire household gathered, an admiring group. . . .

October 31 was cool and gusty. The river route to Philadelphia is twenty-nine statute miles. The passage was made against a strong headwind, with swashy waves, which made me again regret that I did not have my canoe decking made at Troy, instead of at Philadelphia. . . .

At five o'clock I arrived at the city pier opposite the warehouse of Messrs. C. P. Knight & Brother, No. 114 South Delaware Avenue, where, after a struggle with wind and wave for eight hours, the canoe was landed and deposited with the above firm, . . .

PHILADELPHIA TO CAPE HENLOPEN

Monday, November 9, was a cold, wet day. Mr. Knight and the old, enthusiastic gunsmith-naturalist of the city, Mr. John Krider, assisted me to embark in my now decked, provisioned, and loaded canoe. The stock of condensed food would easily last me a month, while the blankets and other parts of the outfit were good for the hard usage of four or five months. My friends shouted adieu as the little craft shot out from the pier and rapidly descended the river with the strong ebb tide which for two hours was in her favor. The anchorage of the iron *Monitor* fleet at League Island was soon passed, and the great city sank into the gloom of its smoke and the clouds of rainy mist which enveloped it.

This pull was an exceedingly dreary one. The storms of winter were at hand, and even along the watercourses between Philadelphia and Norfolk, Virginia, thin ice would soon be forming in the shallow coves and creeks. . . . The canoe, though heavily laden, behaved well. I now enjoyed the advantages resulting from the possession of the new canvas deck cover, which, being fastened by buttons along each gunwale of the canoe, securely covered the boat, so that the occasional swash sent aboard by wicked tug boats and large schooners did not annoy me or wet my precious cargo.

By two o'clock the rain and wind caused me to seek shelter at Mr. J. C. Beach's cottage, at Markus Hook, some twenty miles below Philadelphia, and on the same side of the river. While Mr. Beach was varnishing the little craft, crowds of people came to *feel* of the canoe, giving it the usual punching with their finger-nails, "to see if it were truly paper." . . .

The next morning, in a dense fog, I followed the shores of the river, crossing the Pennsylvania and Delaware boundary line half a mile below the "Hook," and entered Delaware, . . . Reaching New Castle, . . . I pulled across to the New Jersey side of the river and skirted the marshy shore past the little Pea Patch Island, upon which rises in sullen dreariness Fort Delaware. . . .

After crossing Salem Cove, and passing its southern point, Elsinborough, five miles and a half below Fort Delaware, the inhospitable marshes became wide and desolate, warning me to secure a timely shelter for the night. Nearly two miles below Point Elsinborough the high reeds were divided by a little creek, into which I ran my canoe, for upon the muddy bank could be seen a deserted, doorless fish cabin, into which I moved my blankets and provisions, after cutting with my pocket knife an ample supply of dry reeds for a bed. Driftwood, which a friendly tide had deposited around the shanty, furnished the material for my fire, which lighted up the dismal hovel most cheerfully. And thus I kept house in a comfortable manner till morning, being well satisfied with the progress I had made that day in traversing the shores of three states. The booming of the guns of wild-fowl shooters out upon the water roused me before dawn, and I had ample time before the sun arose to prepare breakfast from the remnant of canned oxtail soup left over from last night's supper.

I was now in Delaware Bay, which was assuming noble proportions. From my camp I crossed to the west shore below Reedy Island, and, filling my water bottles at a farmhouse, kept upon that shore all day. The wind arose, stirring up a rough sea as I approached Bombay Hook, where the bay is eight miles wide. I tried to land upon the salt marshes, over the edges of which the long, low seas were breaking, but failed in several attempts. At last roller after roller, following in quick succession, carried the little craft on their crests to the land, and packed her in a thicket of high reeds.

I quickly disembarked, believing it useless to attempt to go further that day. About an eighth of a mile from the water, rising out of the salt grass and reeds, was a little mound, covered by trees and bushes, into which I conveyed my cargo by the backload, and then easily drew the light canoe over the level march to the camp. A bed of reeds was soon cut, into which the canoe was settled to prevent her from being strained by the occupant at night, for I was determined to test the strength of the boat as sleeping quarters. . . .

With the canvas deck cover and rubber blanket to keep off the heavy dews, the first night passed in such contracted lodgings was endurable, if not wholly convenient and agreeable. The river mists were not dispelled the next day until nine o'clock, when I quitted my warm nest in the reeds and rowed down the bay, which seemed to grow broader as I advanced. The bay was still bordered by extensive marshes, with here and there the habitation of man located upon some slight elevation of the surface. Having rowed twenty-six miles, and being off the mouth of Murderkill Creek, a squall struck the canoe and forced it on to an oyster reef, upon the sharp shells of which she was rocked for several minutes by the shallow breakers. Fearing that the paper shell was badly cut, though it was still early in the afternoon, I ascended the creek of ominous name and associations to the landing of an inn kept by Jacob Lavey, where I expected to overhaul my injured craft. To my surprise and great relief of mind there were found only a few superficial scratches upon the hornlike shellacked surface of the paper shell. To apply shellac with a heated iron to the wounds made by the oyster shells was the work of a few minutes, and my craft was as sound as ever. The gunner's resort, Bower's Beach Hotel, furnished an excellent supper of oyster fritters, panfish, and fried pork scrapple. . . .

Embarking the next day, I felt sure of ending my cruise on Delaware Bay before night, as the quiet morning exhibited no signs of rising winds. The little pilot town of Lewes, near Cape Delaware, and behind the Breakwater, is a port of refuge for storm-bound vessels. From this village I expected to make a portage of six miles to Love Creek, a tributary of Rehoboth Sound. The frosty nights were now exerting a sanitary influence over the malarial districts which I had entered, and the unacclimated canoeist of northern birth could safely pursue his journey, and sleep at night in the swamps along the fresh-water streams if protected from the dews by a rubber or canvas covering. My hopes of reaching the open sea that night were to be drowned, and in cold water too; for that day, which opened so calmly and with such smiling promises, was destined to prove a season of trial, and before its evening shadows closed around me, to witness a severe struggle for life in the cold waters of Delaware Bay.

An hour after leaving Murderkill Creek the wind came from the north in strong squalls. My little boat taking the blasts on her quarter, kept herself free of the swashy seas hour after hour. I kept as close to the sandy beach of the great marshes as possible, so as to be near the land in case an accident should happen. Mispillion Creek and a lighthouse on the north of its mouth were passed, when the wind and seas struck my boat on the port beam, and continually crowded her ashore. The water breaking on the hard, sandy beach of the marshy coast made it too much of a risk to attempt a landing, as the canoe would be smothered in the swashy seas if her headway was checked for a moment. Amidships the canoe was only a few inches out of water, but her great sheer, full bow, and smoothness of hull, with watchful management, kept her from swamping. I had struggled along for fourteen miles since morning, and was fatigued by the strain consequent upon the continued maneuvering of my boat through the rough waves. I reached a point on Slaughter Beach, where the bay has a width of nearly nineteen miles, when the tempest rose to such a pitch that the great raging seas threatened every moment to wash over my canoe, and to force me by their violence close into the beach. To my alarm, as the boat rose and fell on the waves, the heads of sharp-pointed stakes appeared and disappeared in the broken waters. They were the stakes of fishermen to which they attach their nets in the season of trout fishing. The danger of being impaled on one of these forced me off shore again.

There was no undertow; the seas being driven over shoals were irregular and broken. At last *my* sea came. It rolled up without a crest, square and formidable. I could not calculate where it would break, but I pulled for life away from it towards the beach upon which the sea was breaking with deafening sound. It was only for a moment that I beheld the great brown wave, which bore with it the mud of the shoal, bearing down upon me; for the next, it broke astern, sweeping completely over the canoe from stern to stem, filling it through the opening of the canvas round my body. Then for a while the watery area was almost smooth, so completely had the great wave levelled it. The canoe being waterlogged, settled below the surface, the high points of the ends occasionally emerging from the water. Other heavy seas followed the first, one of which striking me as high as my head and shoulders, turned both the canoe and canoeist upside down.

Kicking myself free of the canvas deck, I struck out from under the shell, and quickly rose to the surface. It was then that the words of an author of a European canoe manual came to my mind: "When you capsize, first right the canoe and get astride it over one end, keeping your legs in the water; when you have crawled to the well or cockpit, bail out the boat with your hat." Comforting as these instructions from an experienced canoe traveler seemed when reading them in my hermitage ashore, the present application of them . . . was in this emergency an impossibility; for my hat had disappeared with the seat cushion and one iron outrigger, while the oars were floating to leeward with the canoe.

The boat having turned keel up, her great sheer would have righted her had it not been for the cargo, which settled itself on the canvas deck cloth, and ballasted the craft in that position. So smooth were her polished sides that it was impossible to hold on to her, for she rolled about like a slippery porpoise in a tideway. Having tested and proved futile the kind suggestions of writers on marine disasters, and feeling very stiff in the icy water, I struck out in an almost exhausted condition for the shore. Now a new experience taught me an interesting lesson. The seas rolled over my head and shoulders in such rapid succession, that I found I could not get my head above water to breathe, while the sharp sand kept in suspension by the agitated water scratched my face, and filled my eyes, nostrils, and ears. While I felt this pressing down and burying tendency of the seas, as they broke upon my head and shoulders, I understood the reason why so many good swimmers are drowned in attempting to reach the shore from a wreck on a shoal, when the wind, though blowing heavily, is in the victim's favor. The land was not over an eighth of a mile away, and from it came the sullen roar of the breakers, pounding their heavy weight upon the sandy shingle. As its booming thunders or its angry, swashing sound increased, I knew I was rapidly nearing it, but, blinded by the boiling waters, I could see nothing.

At such a moment do not stop to make vows as to how you will treat your neighbor in future if once safely landed, but strike out, fight as you never fought before, swallowing as little water as possible, and never relaxing an energy or yielding a hope. The water shoaled; my feet felt the bottom, and I stood up, but a roller laid me flat on my face. Up again and down again, swimming and crawling, I emerged from the sea, . . .

Wearily dragging myself up the hard shingle, I stood and contemplated the little streams of water pouring from my woollen clothes. A new danger awaited me as the cold wind whistled down the barren beach and across the desolate marshes. I danced about to keep warm, and for a moment thought that my canoe voyage had come to an unfortunate termination. Then a buoyant feeling succeeded the moment's depression, and I felt that this was only the first of many trials which were necessary to prepare me for the successful completion of my undertaking. But where was the canoe, with its provisions that were to sustain me, and the charts which were to point out my way through the labyrinth of waters she was yet to traverse? She had drifted near the shore, but would not land. There was no time to consider the propriety of again entering the water. The struggle was a short though severe one, and I dragged my boat ashore.

Everything was wet excepting what was most needed—a flannel suit, carefully rolled in a waterproof cloth. I knew that I must change my wet clothes for dry ones, or perish. This was no easy task to perform, with hands benumbed and limbs paralyzed with the cold. O shade of Benjamin Franklin, did not one of thy kinsmen, in his wide experience as a traveler, foresee this very disaster, and did he not, when I left the City of Brotherly Love, force upon me an antidote, a sort of spiritual fire, which my New England temperance principles made me refuse to accept? "It is old, *very* old," he whispered, as he slipped the flask into my coatpocket, "and it may save your life. Don't be foolish. I have kept it well bottled. It is a pure article, and cost sixteen dollars per gallon. *I use it only for medicine.*" I found the flask; the *water* had not injured it. A small quantity was taken, when a most favorable change came over my entire system, mental as well as physical, and I was able to throw off one suit and put on another in the icy wind, that might, without the stimulant, have ended my voyage of life.

I had doctored myself homeopathically under the *old practice*. Filled with feelings of gratitude to the Great Giver of good, I reflected, as I carried my wet cargo into the marsh, upon the wonderful effects of my friend's medicine when taken *only as medicine*. Standing upon the cold beach and gazing into the sea, now lashed by the wild frenzy of the wind, I determined never again to do so mean a thing as to say a *bad* word against *good* brandy.

Having relieved my conscience by this just resolve, I transported the whole of my wet but still precious cargo to a persimmon grove, on a spot of firm land that rose out of the marsh, where I made a convenient windbreak by stretching rubber blankets between trees. On this knoll I built a fire, obtaining the matches to kindle it from a waterproof safe. . . .

Before dusk, all things not spoiled by the water were dried and secreted in the tall sedge of the marshes. The elevation which had given me friendly shelter is known as Hog Island. The few persimmon trees that grew upon it furnished an ample lunch, for the frosts had mellowed the plum-like fruit, making it sweet and edible. . . . The deepening gloom warned me to seek comfortable quarters for the night. . . .

[Bishop recounts his voyage from Cape Henlopen to Norfolk and on to Cape Hatteras—two chapters.]

FROM CAPE HATTERAS TO CAPE FEAR, NORTH CAROLINA

Cape Hatteras is the apex of a triangle. It is the easternmost part of the state of North Carolina, and it extends farther into the ocean than any Atlantic cape of the United States. It presents a low, broad, sandy point to the sea, and for several miles beyond it, in the ocean, are the dangerous Diamond Shoals, the dread of the mariner. . . .

A low range of hills commences at Cape Hatteras, . . . and extends nearly to Hatteras Inlet. This range is heavily wooded with live oaks, yellow pines, yaupons, cedars, and bayonet plants. The fishermen and wreckers live in rudely constructed houses, sheltered by this thicket, which is dense enough to protect them from the strong winds that blow from the ocean and the sound. . . .

On this Saturday night, spent at Hatteras Inlet, there broke upon us one of the fiercest tempests . . . For miles along the beach thousands of acres of land were soon submerged by the sea and by the torrents of water which fell from the clouds. . . . The sea pounded on the beach as if asking for admission to old Pamlico. It seemed to say, I demand a new inlet; and, as though trying to carry out its desire, sent great waves rolling up the shingle and over into the hollows among the hills, washing down the low sand dunes as if they also were in collusion with it to remove this frail barrier, this narrow strip of low land which separated the Atlantic from the wide interior sheet of water. . . .

Before morning the wind shifted, and by nine o'clock I . . . rowed down to Hatteras Inlet, which was reached a little past noon. Before attempting to cross this dangerous tidal gateway of the ocean I hugged the shore close to its edge, and paused to make myself familiar with the sandhills of the opposite side, a mile away, which were to serve as the guiding beacons in the passage. How often had I, lying awake at night, thought of and dreaded the crossing of this ill-omened inlet! It had given me much mental suffering. Now it was before me. Here on my right was the great sound, on my left the narrow beach island, and out through the portal of the open inlet surged and moaned under a leaden sky that old ocean which now seemed to frown at me, and to say: "Wait, my boy, until the inlet's waves deliver you to me, and I will put you among my other victims for your temerity."

As I gazed across the current I remarked that it did not seem very rough, though a strong ebb was running out to the sea, and if crossed immediately, before the wind arose, there could be no unreasonable risk. My canvas deck cover was carefully pulled close about my waist, and a rigid inspection of oars and rowlocks was made; then, with a desire to reserve my strength for any great demand that might be made upon it a little later, I rowed with a steady stroke out into Hatteras Inlet. There was no help nearer than Styron's, two miles away on the upper shore, while the beach I was approaching on the other side was uninhabited for nearly sixteen miles, to the village at its southern end, near Ocracoke Inlet. Upon entering the swash I thought of the sharks which the Hatteras fishermen had told me frequently seized their oars, snapping the thin blades in pieces, assuring me, at the same time, that mine would prove very attractive, being so white and glimmering in the water, and offering the same glittering fascination as a silver spoon bait does to a bluefish. These cheerful suggestions caused a peculiar creeping sensation to come over me, but I tried to quiet myself with the belief that the sharks had followed the bluefish into deeper water, to escape cold weather.

The canoe crossed the upper ebb, and entered an area where the ebb from the opposite side of the inlet struck the first one. While crossing the union of the two currents, a wind came in at the opening through the beach, and though not a strong one, it created a great agitation of the water. The dangerous experience at Watchapreague Inlet * had taught me that when in such a sea one must pull with all

---

* My canoe scraped its keel upon the shoals as I dodged the broken oyster reefs . . . while on the passage down to Watchapreague Inlet. The tide was very low, but the water deepened as the beach was approached. A northeaster was blowing freshly, and I was looking for a lee under the beach, when suddenly the canoe shot around a sandy point, and was tugging for life in the rough waters of the inlet. The tide was running in from the sea with the force of a rapid, and the short, quick puffs of wind tossed the

his strength, and that the increased momentum would give greater buoyancy to the shell; for while under this treatment she bounced from one irregular wave to another with a climbing action which greatly relieved my anxiety. The danger seemed to be decreasing, and I stole a furtive glance over my shoulder at the low dunes of the beach shore which I was approaching, to see how far into the inlet the tide had dragged me. The white water to leeward warned me of a shoal, and forced me to pull hard for the sound to escape being drawn into the breakers. This danger was hardly passed, when suddenly the waters around me seethed and foamed, and the short waves parted and closed, as great creatures rose from the deep into the air several feet, and then fell heavily into the sea. My tiny shell rocked and pitched about wildly as these animals appeared and disappeared, leaping from the waves all around me, diving under the boat and reappearing on the opposite side. They lashed the current with their strong tails, and snorted or blowed most dismally. For an instant surprise and alarm took such possession of me that not a muscle of my arms obeyed my will, and the canoe commenced to drift in the driving stream towards the open sea. This confusion was only momentary, for as soon as I discovered that my companions were porpoises and only old acquaintances, I determined to avoid them as soon as possible.

With a quick glance at my stern range, a sand hill on the shore of the inlet, and another look over my shoulder for the sand dunes of

waves wildly. It was useless to attempt to turn the canoe back to the beach in such rough water, but, intent on keeping the boat above the caps, I gave her all the momentum that muscular power could exert, as she was headed for the southern point of the beach, across the dangerous inlet.

Though it was only half a mile across, the passage of Watchapreague taxed me severely. Waves washed over my canoe, but the gallant little craft after each rebuff rose like a bird to the surface of the water, answering the slightest touch of my oar better than the best-trained steed. After entering the south-side swash, the wind struck me on the back, and seas came tumbling over and around the boat, fairly forcing me on to the beach. As we flew along, the tumultuous waters made my head swim; so, to prevent mental confusion, I kept my eyes only upon the oars, which, strange to say, never betrayed me into a false stroke.

As a heavy blast beat down the raging sea for a moment, I looked over my shoulder and beheld the low, sandy dunes of the southern shore of the inlet close at hand, and with a severe jolt the canoe grounded high on the strand. I leaped out and drew my precious craft away from the tide, breathing a prayer of thankfulness for my escape from danger, and mentally vowing that the canoe should cross all other treacherous inlets in a fisherman's sloop. . . . (from Chapter VIII. W. T.)

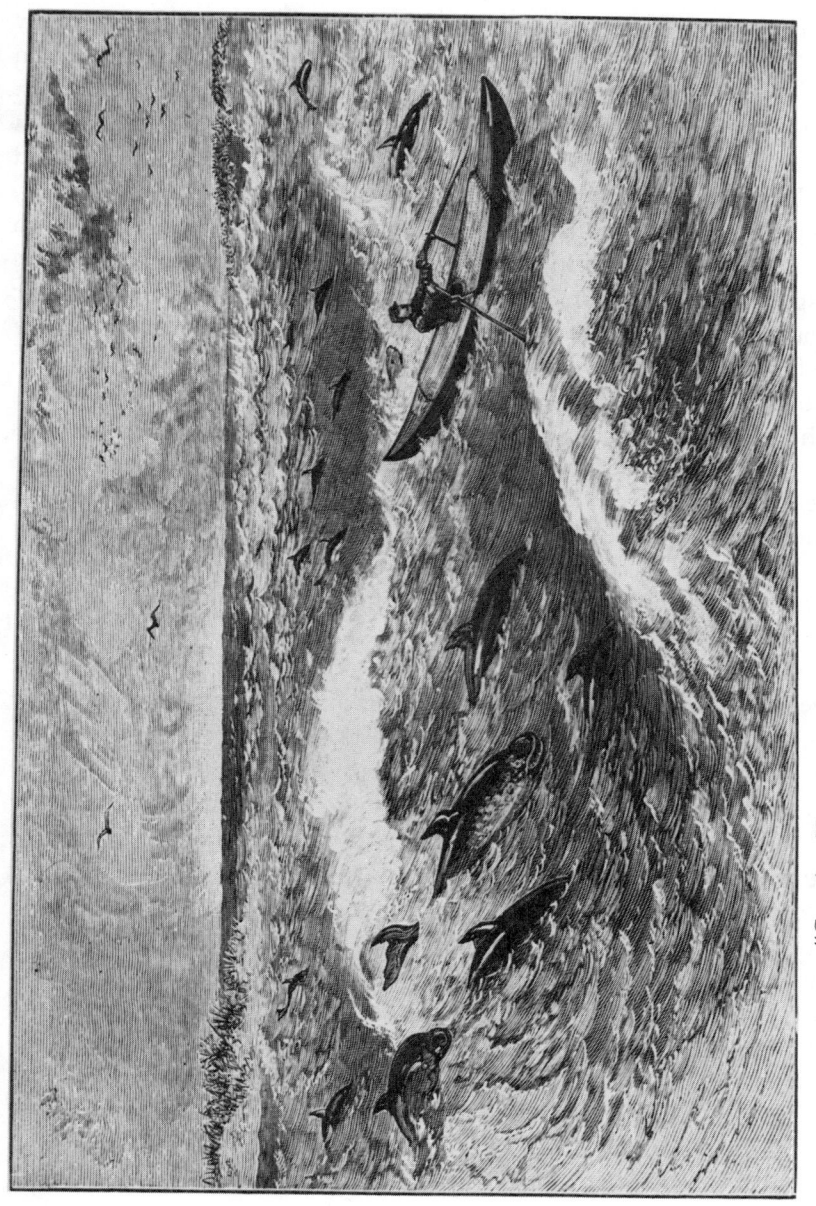

"Crossing Hatteras Inlet," from *Voyage of the Paper Canoe*

the other side, I exerted every muscle to reach the beach; but my frisky friends were in no mood to leave me, but continued their fun with increased energy as reinforcements came up from all directions. The faster I rowed the more they multiplied, ploughing the sea in erratic courses. They were from five to seven feet in length, and must have weighed from two hundred to four hundred pounds each. Though their attentions were kindly meant, their brusqueness on such an unsteady footing was unpardonable. I most feared the strong, shooting movements of their tails in the sudden dives under my canoe, for one sportive touch of such a *caudality* would have rolled me over, and furnished material for a tale the very anticipation of which was unpleasant.

The aquatic gambols of the porpoises lasted but a few minutes after they had called in all their neighbors, and had chased me into three feet depth of water. They then spouted a nasal farewell, which sounded more catarrhal than guitaral, and left me for the more profitable occupation of fishing in the tideway of the inlet, while I rowed into a shallow cove, out of the ebb, to rest, and to recover from the effects of my fright.

As I pulled along the beach the tide receded so rapidly that the canoe was constantly grounding, and wading became necessary, for I could not get within several feet of the shore. When five miles from Hatteras Inlet I espied an empty grass cabin, which the fishermen used in February while catching shad; and, as a southerly wind was now blowing from the sea, and rain was falling, it offered a night's shelter for the traveler. This Robinson Crusoe looking structure was located upon the low land near the sound, while bleak, sharp-pointed, treeless and grassless sand hills, blown into shape by the winds, arose in the background, and cut off a view of the ocean, which, judging from the low, melancholy moaning coming over the dunes, was in a sad mood.

The canoe was hauled into the bushes and tied securely for fear a deceptive tide might bear it away. The provisions, blankets, and so forth, were moved into the grass hut, which needed repairing. The holes in the south wall were soon thatched, and a bed easily prepared from the rushes of the marsh. It mattered not that they were wet, for a piece of painted canvas was spread over them, and the inviting couch finished.

As fresh water can usually be obtained on all these low beaches by digging two or three feet into the sand, I looked for a large clam shell, and my search being rewarded, I was soon engaged in digging a well near the cabin.

Upon looking up from my work a curious sight met my gaze. In some mysterious way every sharp-pointed sand hill had been covered by a black object, which swayed about and nodded up and down in a strange manner. As I watched the development of this startling phenomenon, the nodding, black objects grew in size until the head, body, and four legs of a horse were clearly cut against the sky. A little later every crest was surmounted by the comical figure of a marsh tacky. Then a few sheep came out of the hollows among the hills and browsed on the coarse grass near the cabin, as though they felt the loneliness of their situation so far removed from mankind. With the marsh ponies, the sheep, the wild fowls of the sound, and the sighing sea for companions, the night passed away. . . .

[From Cape Fear to Charleston, South Carolina—one chapter.]

FROM CHARLESTON TO SAVANNAH, GEORGIA

. . . I was now following one of the salt-water, steamboat passages through the great marshes of South Carolina. From Wappoo Creek I took the "Elliot Cut" into the broad Stono River, . . .

A little farther on the tides divided, one ebbing through the Stono to the sea, the other towards the North Edisto. "New Cut" connects Church Flats with Wadmelaw Sound, a sheet of water not over two miles in width and the same distance in length. From the sound the Wadmelaw River runs to the mouth of the Dahoo. . . .

For two miles along the Dahoo the porpoises gave me strong proof of their knowledge of the presence of the paper canoe by their rough gambols, but being now in quiet inland waters, I could laugh at these strange creatures as they broke from the water around the boat. At four o'clock the extensive marshes of Jehossee Island were reached, . . .

The surroundings were of a lovely nature during this day's journey. Here marshes, diversified by occasional hammocks of timber dotting their uninteresting wastes; there humble habitations of whites and blacks appearing at intervals in the forest growth. As I was destitute of a finished chart of the Coast Survey, after rowing along one side of Hutchinson's Island I became bewildered in the maze of creeks which penetrate the marshes that lie between Bennett's Point and the coast. . . .

While I was enveloped in reeds, and at a loss which way to go, the soft ripple of breaking waves struck my ear like sweet music. The sea was telling me of its proximity. Carefully balancing myself, I stood up in the cranky canoe, and peering over the grassy thickets, saw before me the broad waters of Helena Sound. The fresh salt breeze from the ocean struck upon my forehead, and nerved me to a renewal of my efforts to get within a region of higher land, and to a place of shelter.

The ebbing tide was yet high, and through the forest of vegetation, and over the submerged coast, I pushed the canoe into the sound. Now I rowed as though for my life, closely skirting the marshes, and soon entered waters covered by a chart in my possession. My course was to skirt the coast of the sound from where I had entered it, and cross the mouths of the Combahee and Bull rivers to the entrance of the broad Coosaw. This last river I would ascend seven miles to the first upland, and camp thereon until morning. The tide was now against me, and the night was growing darker, as the faithful craft was forced along the marshes four miles to the mouth of the Combahee River, which I had to ascend half a mile to get rid of a shoal of frisky porpoises, who were fishing in the current.

Then descending it on the opposite shore, I rowed two miles farther in the dark, but for half an hour previous to my reaching the wide debouchure of Bull River, some enormous blackfish surged about me in the tideway and sounded their nasal calls, while their more demonstrative porpoise neighbors leaped from the water in the misty atmosphere, and so alarmed me and occupied my attention, that instead of crossing to the Coosaw River, I unwittingly ascended the Bull, and was soon lost in the contours of the river.

As I hugged the marshy borders of the stream to escape the strong current of its channel, and rowed on and on in the gloom, eagerly scanning the high, sedge-fringed flats to find one little spot of firm upland upon which I might land my canoe and obtain a resting spot for myself for the night, the feeling that I was lost was not the most cheerful to be imagined. In the thin fog which arose from the warm water into the cool night air, objects on the marshes assumed fantastical shapes. A few reeds, taller than the rest, had the appearance of trees twenty feet high. So real did these unreal images seem, that I drove my canoe against the soft, muddy bank, repeatedly prompted to land in what seemed a copse of low trees, but in every instance I was deceived. Still I pulled up that mysterious river, ignorant at the time of even its name, praying only for one little spot of upland where I might camp.

While thus employed, I peered over my shoulder into the gloom, and beheld what seemed to be a vision; for, out of a cloud of mist rose the skeleton lines of a large ship, with all its sails furled to the yards. "A ship at anchor, and in this out-of-the-way place!" I ejaculated, scarcely believing my eyes; but when I pointed the canoe toward it, and again looked over my shoulder, the vision of hope was gone.

Again I saw tall masts cutting through the mists, but the ship's hull could not be distinguished, and as I rowed onwards the objects, first the lower masts disappeared, then the topmasts dissolved, and later, the topgallant and royal masts faded away. For half an hour I rowed and rowed for that mysterious vessel, which was veiled and unveiled to my sight. Never did so spectral an object haunt or thwart me. It seemed to change its position on the water, as well as in the atmosphere, and I was too busily employed in trying to reach it to discover in the darkness that the current, which I could not distinguish from smooth water, was whirling me down stream as fast as I would approach the weird vessel.

Drawing once more from the current, I followed the marsh until the canoe was opposite the anchorage of a real ship; then, with hearty pulls, I shot around its stern, and shouted: "Ship ahoy!"

No one answered the hail. The vessel looked like a man-of-war, but not of American build. Not a light gleamed from her ports, not a footfall came from her decks. She seemed to be deserted in the middle of the river, surrounded by a desolate waste of marshes. The current gurgled and sucked about her run, as the ebb tide washed her black hull on its way to the sea. The spectacle seemed now even more mysterious than when, miragelike, it peered forth from a cloud of mist. But it was real, and not fantastic. Another hail, louder than the first, went forth into the night air, and penetrated to the ship's forecastle, for a sailor answered my call, and reported to the captain in the cabin the presence of a boat at the ship's side.

A quick, firm tread sounded upon the deck; then, with a light bound, a powerfully built young man landed upon the high rail of the vessel. He peered down from his stately ship upon the little speck which floated upon the gurgling current; then, with a voice "filled with the fogs of the ocean," he thundered forth, as though he were hailing a man-of-war: "What boat's that?"

"Paper canoe *Maria Theresa*," I replied, in as foggy a voice as I could assume. . . .

"Ah, is it you?" cheerily responded the captain, suddenly dispensing with all his fogginess; "I've been looking for you this long time. Got a Charleston paper on board; your trip all in it. Come up, and break a bottle of wine with me."

"All hands" came from the forecastle, and Finland mates and Finland sailors, speaking both English and Russian, crowded to the rail to receive the paper canoe, . . .

The jolly crew lowered buntlines and clewlines, to which I attached my boat's stores. These were hoisted up the high sides of the ship, and, after bending on a line to the bow and stern rings of the canoe, I ascended by the ladder, while Captain Johs. Bergelund and his mates claimed the pleasure of landing the paper canoe on the deck of the *Rurik*. The tiny shell looked very small as she rested on the broad, white decks of the emperor of Russia's old steam yacht, . . .

FROM THE SAVANNAH RIVER TO FLORIDA

On February 24, the voyage was again resumed. My route lay through the coast islands of Georgia, as far south as the state boundary, Cumberland Sound, and the St. Mary's River. . . .

The weather was now delightful, and had I possessed a light tent I would not have sought shelter at night in a human habitation anywhere along the route. . . .

Monday, March 1, opened fair, but the wind arose when the canoe reached Three Mile Cut, which connects the Darien with the Altamaha River. I went through this narrow steamboat passage, and being prevented by the wind from entering the wide Altamaha, returned to the Darien River and ascended it to General's Cut, which, with Butler River, affords a passage to the Altamaha River. Before entering General's Cut, mistaking a large, half-submerged alligator for a log on a mud bank, the canoe nearly touched the saurian before he was roused from his nap to retire into the water. . . .

The calm weather greatly facilitated my progress, and had I not missed Jekyl Creek, which is the steamboat thoroughfare through the marshes to Jekyl and St. Andrew's Sound, that whole day's experience would have been a most happy one. The mouth of Jekyl Creek was a narrow entrance, and being off in the sound, I passed it as I approached the lowlands, which were skirted until a passage at Cedar Hammock through the marsh was found, some distance from the one I was seeking. Into this I entered, and winding about for some time over its tortuous course, at a late hour in the afternoon the canoe emerged into a broad watercourse, down which I could look across Jekyl Sound to the sea.

This broad stream was Jointer Creek, and I ascended it to find a spot of high ground upon which to camp. It was now low water, and the surface of the marshes was three or four feet above my head. After much anxious searching, and a great deal of rowing against the last of the ebb, a forest of pines and palmetto trees was reached on Colonel's Island, at a point about four miles—across the marshes and Brunswick River—from the interesting old town of Brunswick, Georgia.

The soft, muddy shores of the hammock were in one place enveloped in a thicket of reeds, and here I rested upon my oars to select a convenient landing place. The rustling of the reeds suddenly attracted my attention. Some animal was crawling through the thicket in the direction of the boat. My eyes became fixed upon the mysterious shaking and waving of the tops of the reeds, and my hearing was strained to detect the cause of the crackling of the dry rushes over which this unseen creature was moving. A moment later my curiosity was satisfied, for there emerged slowly from the covert an alligator nearly as large as my canoe. The brute's head was as long as a barrel; his rough coat of mail was besmeared with mud, and his dull eyes were fixed steadily upon me. I was so surprised and fascinated by the appearance of this huge reptile that I remained immovable in my boat, while he in a deliberate manner entered the water within a few feet of me. The hammock suddenly lost all its inviting aspect, and I pulled away from it faster than I had approached. In the gloom I observed two little hammocks, between Colonel's Island and the Brunswick River, which seemed to be near Jointer's Creek, so I followed the tortuous thoroughfares until I was within a quarter of a mile of one of them.

Pulling my canoe up a narrow creek toward the largest hammock, until the creek ended in the lowland, I was cheered by the sight of a small house in a grove of live oaks, to reach which I was obliged to abandon my canoe and attempt to cross the soft marsh. The tide was now rising rapidly, and it might be necessary for me to swim some inland creek before I could arrive at the upland.

An oar was driven into the soft mud of the marsh and the canoe tied to it, for I knew that the whole country, with the exception of the hammock near by, would be under water at floodtide. Floundering through mud and pressing aside the tall, wire-like grass of the lowland, which entangled my feet, frequently leaping natural ditches, and going down with a thud in the mud on the other side, I finally struck the firm ground of the largest Jointer Hammock, when the voice of its owner, Mr. R. F. Williams, sounded most cheerfully in my ears as he exclaimed: "Where *did* you come from? How did you get across the marsh?"

The unfortunate position of my boat was explained while the family gathered round me, after which we sat down to supper. Mr. Williams felt anxious about the cargo of my boat. "The coons," he said, "will scent your provisions, and tear everything to pieces in the boat. We must go look after it immediately." To go to the canoe we were obliged to follow a creek which swept past the side of the hammock, opposite to my landing place, and row two or three miles on Jointer Creek. At nine o'clock we reached the locality where I had abandoned the paper canoe. Everything had changed in appearance; the land was under water; not a landmark remained except the top of the oar, which rose out of the lake-like expanse of water, while near it gracefully floated my little companion. We towed her to the hammock; and after the tedious labor of divesting myself of the marsh mud, which clung to my clothes, had been crowned with success, the comfortable bed furnished by my host gave rest to limbs and nerves which had been severely overtaxed since sunset. . . .

ST. MARY'S RIVER AND THE SUWANEE WILDERNESS

I now ascended the beautiful St. Mary's River, which flows from the great Okefenokee Swamp. The state of Georgia was on my right hand, and Florida on my left. Pretty hammocks dotted the marshes, while the country presented peculiar and interesting characteristics. When four miles from Cumberland Sound, the little city of St. Mary's, situated on the Georgia side of the river, was before me, and I went ashore to make inquiries concerning the route of Okefenokee Swamp.

My object was to get information about the upper St. Mary's River, from which I proposed to make a portage of thirty-five or forty miles in a westerly direction to the Suwanee River, upon arriving at which I would descend to the Gulf of Mexico. . . .

. . . Messrs. Dutton & Rixford, northern gentlemen, who possessed large facilities for the manufacture of resin and turpentine at their new settlements of Dutton, six miles from the St. Mary's River, and at Rixford, near the Suwanee, kindly proposed that I should take my canoe by railroad from Cumberland Sound to Dutton. From that station Mr. Dutton offered to transport the boat through the wilderness to the St. Mary's River, which could be from that point easily descended to the sea. The Suwanee River, at Rixford, could be reached by rail, and the voyage would end at its debouchure on the marshy coast of the Gulf of Mexico. . . .

The turpentine distillery of Dutton was situated in a heavy forest of lofty pines. Major C. K. Dutton furnished a team of mules to haul the *Maria Theresa* to the St. Mary's River, the morning after my arrival by rail at Dutton Station. The warm sunshine shot aslant the tall pines as the teamster followed a faintly developed trail towards the swamps. Before noon the flashing waters of the stream were discernible, and a little later, with paddle in hand, I was urging the canoe towards the Atlantic coast. A luxurious growth of trees and shrubs fringed the low, and in some places submerged, river shores. Back, on the higher, sandy soils, the yellow pine forests, in almost primeval grandeur, arose, shutting out all view of the horizon. Low bluffs, with white, sandy beaches of a few rods in extent, offered excellent camping grounds.

When the cracker of Okefenokee Swamp is asked why he lives in so desolate a region, with only a few cattle and hogs for companions, with mosquitoes, fleas, and vermin about him, with alligators, catamounts, and owls on all sides, making night hideous, he usually replies, "Wal, stranger, wood and water is so *powerful* handy. Sich privileges ain't met with everywhar."

As I glided swiftly down the dark current I peered into the dense woods, hoping to be cheered by the sight of a settler's cabin; but in all that day's search not a clearing could be found, nor could I discern rising from the treetops of the solitary forest a little cloud of smoke issuing from the chimney of civilized man. I was alone in the vast wilds through which the beautiful river flowed noiselessly but swiftly to the sea. . . .

Swamps have their peculiar features. Those of the Waccamaw were indeed desolate, while the swamps of the St. Mary's were full of sunshine for the traveler. Soon after the canoe had commenced her river journey, a sharp sound, like that produced by a man striking the water with a broad, flat stick, reached my ears. As this sound was frequently repeated, and always in advance of my boat, it roused my curiosity. It proved to come from alligators. One after another slipped off the banks, striking the water with their tails as they took refuge in the river from the disturber of their peace. To observe the movements of these reptiles I ran the canoe within two rods of the left shore, and by rapid paddling was enabled to arrive opposite a creature as he entered the water. When thus confronted, the alligator would depress his ugly head, lash the water once with his tail, and dive under the canoe, a most thoroughly alarmed animal. All these alligators were mere babies, very few being over four feet long. Had they been as large as the one which greeted me at Colonel's Island, I should not have investigated their dispositions, but would have considered discretion the better part of valor, and left them undisturbed in their sun baths on the banks.

In all my experience with the hundreds of alligators I have seen in the southern rivers and swamps of North America, every one, both large and small, fled at the approach of man. . . . It is well to exercise care about camping at night close to the water infested with large saurians, as one of these strong fellows could easily seize a sleeping man by the leg and draw him into the river. They do not seem to fear a recumbent or bowed figure, but, like most wild animals, flee before the *upright* form of man.

Late in the afternoon I passed an island, made by a "cutoff" through a bend of the river, and, according to previous directions, counted fourteen bends or reaches in the river which was to guide me to Stewart's Ferry, the owner of which lived back in the woods, his cabin not being discernible from the river. Near this spot, which is occasionally visited by lumbermen and piney-woods settlers, I drew my canoe on to a sandy beach one rod in length. A little bluff, five or six feet above the water, furnished me with the broad leaves of the saw palmetto, a dwarfish sort of palm, which I arranged for a bed. The provision basket was placed at my head. A little fire of lightwood cheered me for a while, but its bright flame soon attracted winged insects in large numbers. Having made a cup of chocolate, and eaten some of Captain Akin's chipped beef and crackers, I continued my preparations for the night. Feeling somewhat nervous about large alligators, I covered myself with a piece of painted canvas, which was stiff and strong, and placed the little revolver, my only weapon, under my blanket.

As I fully realized the novelty of my strange position in this desolate region, it was some time before I could compose myself and sleep. It was a night of dreams. Sounds indistinct but numerous troubled my brain, until I was fully roused to wakefulness by horrible visions and doleful cries. The chuck-will's-widow, which in the south supplies the place of our whippoorwill, repeated his oft-told tale of "chuck-will's-widow, chuck-will's-widow," with untiring earnestness. The owls hooted wildly, with a chorus of cries from animals and reptiles not recognizable by me, excepting the snarling voices of the coons fighting in the forest. These last were old acquaintances, however, as they frequently gathered round my camp at night to pick up the remains of supper.

While I listened, there rose a cry so hideous in its character and so belligerent in its tone, that I trembled with fear upon my palm-leaf mattress. It resembled the bellowing of an infuriated bull, but was louder and more penetrating in its effect. The proximity of this animal was indeed unpleasant, for he had planted himself on the river's edge, near the little bluff upon which my camp had been constructed. The loud roar was answered by a similar bellow from the other side of the river, and for a long time did these two male alligators keep up their challenging cries, without coming to combat. Numerous woodmice attacked my provision basket, and even worked their way through the leaves of my palmetto mattress.

Thus with an endless variety of annoyances the night wore wearily away, . . .

DOWN UPON THE SUWANEE RIVER

. . . The Suwanee, which was swollen by some recent rains in the Okefenokee Swamp, was a wild, dark, turbulent current, which went coursing through the woods on its tortuous route with great rapidity. The luxuriant foliage of the riverbanks was remarkable. Maples were in blossom, beech trees in bloom, while the buckeye was covered with its heavy festoons of red flowers. Pines, willows, cottonwood, two kinds of hickory, water oak, live oak, sweet gum, magnolia, the red and white bay tree, a few red cedars, and haw bushes, with many species not known to me, made up a rich wall of verdure on either side, as I sped along with a light heart. . . . Wood ducks and egrets, in small flocks, inhabited the forest. The limestone banks of the river were not visible, as the water was eighteen feet above its low summer level.

I now passed under the railroad bridge which connects Live Oak with Savannah. After a steady row of some hours, my progress was checked by a great boom, stretched across the river to catch the logs which floated down from the upper country. I was obliged to disembark and haul the canoe around this obstacle, when, after passing a few clearings, the long bridge of the J. P. & M. Railroad came into view, stretching across the now wide river from one wilderness to the other. On the left bank was all that remained of the once flourishing town of Columbus, consisting now of a store, . . . and a few buildings. . . .

This far-famed river, . . . is a wild and lonely stream. Even in the most prosperous times there were but few plantations upon its shores. Wild animals roam its great forests, and vile reptiles infest the dense swamps. . . . The smooth but swift current rolled on its course like a sea of molten glass, as the soft sunlight trembled through the foliage and shimmered over its broad surface. . . . It was indeed a quiet, restful region, this great wilderness of the Suwanee.

March 26, . . . This day was to see the end of the voyage of the paper canoe, for my tiny craft was to arrive at the waters of the great southern sea before midnight. . . . The gulf port of Cedar Keys is but a few miles from the mouth of the Suwanee River. . . .

I made an attempt to examine more closely the character of the water moccasin—the *Trigono cephaluspiscivorus* of Lacepede—which I had more cause to fear than the alligators of the river. The water moccasin is about two feet in length, and has a circumference of five or six inches. The tail possesses a horny point about half an inch in length, which is harmless, though the crackers and Negroes stoutly affirm that when it strikes a tree the tree withers and dies, and when it enters the flesh of a man he is poisoned unto death. The color of the reptile is a dirty brown. Never found far from water, it is common in the swamps, and is the terror of the rice-field Negroes. The bite of the water moccasin is exceedingly venomous, and it is considered more poisonous than that of the rattlesnake, which warns man of his approach by sounding his rattle.

The moccasin does not, like the rattlesnake, wait to be attacked, but assumes the offensive whenever opportunity offers, striking with its fangs at every animated object in its vicinity. All other species of snakes flee from its presence. It is found as far north as the Peedee River of South Carolina, and is abundant in all low districts of the southern states. As the Suwanee had overflowed its banks below Old Town Hammock, the snakes had taken to the low limbs of the trees and to the tops of bushes, where they seemed to be sleeping in the warmth of the bright sunlight; but as I glided along the shore a few feet from their aerial beds, they discovered my presence, and dropped sluggishly into the water. . . .

. . . from the dark forest into the smooth savannas. The freshness of the sea air was exhilarating. The stars were shining softly, and the ripple of the tide, the call of the heron, or the whirr of the frightened duck, and the leaping of fishes from the water, were the only sounds nature offered. . . . It was like entering another world. In these lowlands, near the mouth of the river, there seemed to be but one place above the high-tide level. It was a little hammock, covered by a few trees, called Bradford's Island, and it rose like an oasis in the desert. The swift tide hurried along its shores, and a little farther on mingled the waters of the great wilderness with that of the sea. . . .

A glorious morning broke. . . . Behind . . . rose the compact wall of dark green of the heavy forests, and along the coast, from east to west, as far as the eye could reach, were the brownish-green savannalike lowlands, against which beat, in soft murmurs, the waves of that sea I had so longed to reach. From out the broad marshes arose low hammocks, green with pines and feathery with palmetto trees. Clouds of mist were rising, . . . The snow-clad north was now behind me. The *Maria Theresa* danced in the shimmering waters of the great southern sea, and my heart was light, for my voyage was over.

FOUR MONTHS IN A SNEAK-BOX

THE BOAT FOR THE VOYAGE

The reader who patiently followed the author in his long *Voyage of the Paper Canoe,* . . . may desire to know the reasons which impelled the canoeist to exchange his light, graceful, and swift paper craft for the comical-looking but more commodious and comfortable Barnegat sneak-box, or duckboat.

Having navigated more than eight thousand miles in sailboats, rowboats, and canoes, upon the fresh and salt watercourses of the North American continent (usually without a companion), a hard-earned experience has taught me that while the light, frail canoe is indispensable for exploring shallow streams, for shooting rapids, and for making long portages from one watercourse to another, the deeper and more continuous waterways may be more comfortably traversed in a stronger and heavier boat, which offers many of the advantages of a portable home.

To find such a boat—one that possessed many desirable points in a small hull—had been with me a study of years. I commenced to search for it in my boyhood—twenty-five years ago; and though I have carefully examined numerous small boats while traveling in seven foreign countries, and have studied the modes of miniature craft in museums, and at exhibitions of marine architecture, I failed to discover the object of my desire, until, on the seashore of New Jersey, I saw for the first time what is known among gunners as the Barnegat sneak-box. . . .

The sneak-box offered ample stowage capacity, while canoes built to hold one person were not large enough to carry the amount of baggage necessary for the voyage; for I was to avoid hotels and towns, to live in my boat day and night, to carry an ample stock of provisions, and to travel in as comfortable a manner as possible. In fact, I adopted a very homelike boat, which, though only twelve feet long, four feet wide, and thirteen inches deep, was strong, stiff, dry, and safe; a craft that could be sailed or rowed, as wind, weather, or inclination might dictate—the weight of which hardly exceeded two hundred pounds—and could be conveniently transported from one stream to another in an ordinary wagon. . . .

Experienced canoeists agree that a canoe of fourteen feet in length, which weighs only seventy pounds, if built of wood, bark, canvas, or paper, when out of the water and resting upon the ground, or even when bedded on some soft material, like grass or rushes, cannot support the sleeping weight of the canoeist for many successive nights without becoming strained.

Light indeed must be the weight and slender and elastic the form of the man who can sleep many nights comfortably in a seventy-pound canoe without injuring it. Cedar canoes, after being subjected to such use for some time, generally become leaky; so, to avoid this disaster, the canoeist, when threatened with wet weather, is forced to the disagreeable task of troubling some private householder for a shelter, or run the risk of injuring his boat by packing himself away in its narrow, coffin-like quarters and dreaming that he is a sardine, while his restless weight is every moment straining his delicate canoe, and visions of future leaks arise to disturb his tranquility.

The one great advantage possessed by a canoe is its lightness. Canoeists dwell upon the importance of the *light weight* of their canoes, and the ease with which they can be carried. If the canoeist is to sleep in his delicate craft while making a long journey, she must be made much heavier than the perfected models now in use in this country, many of which are under seventy-five pounds' weight. This additional weight is at once fatal to speed, and becomes burdensome when the canoeist is forced to carry his canoe upon his *own* shoulders over a portage. A sneak-box built to carry one person weighs about three times as much as a well-built cedar canoe. . . .

Captain Hazelton Seaman, of West Creek village, New Jersey, a boatbuilder and an expert shooter of wild fowl, about the year 1836 conceived the idea of constructing for his own use a low-decked boat, or gunning punt, in which, when its deck was covered

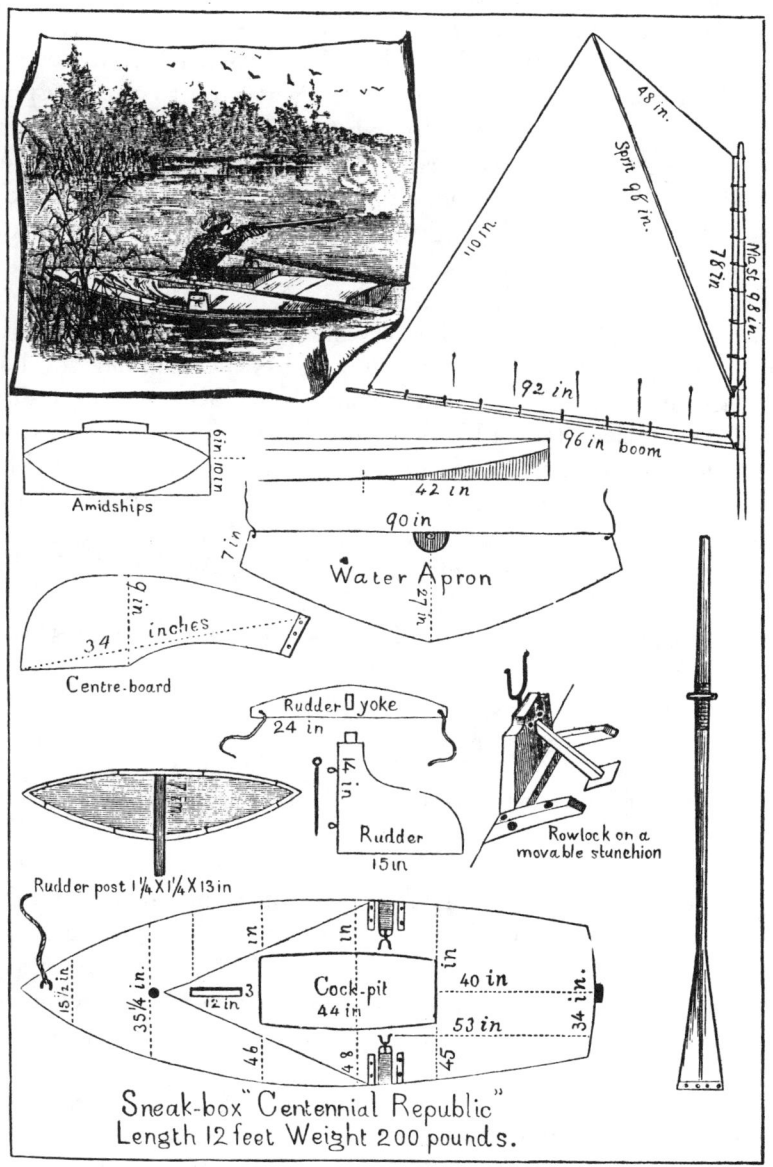

"Diagram of Parts of Boat," from *Four Months in a Sneak-Box*

with sedge, he could secrete himself from the wild fowl while gunning in Barnegat and Little Egg Harbor bays.

It was important that the boat should be sufficiently light to enable a single sportsman to pull her from the water on to the low points of the bay shores. During the winter months, when the great marshes were at times incrusted with snow, and the shallow creeks covered with ice—obstacles which must be crossed to reach the open waters of the sound—it would be necessary to use her as a sled, to effect which end a pair of light oaken strips were screwed to the bottom of the sneak-box, when she could be easily pushed by the gunner, and the transportation of the oars, sail, blankets, guns, ammunition, and provisions (all of which stowed under the hatch and locked up as snugly as if in a strong chest) became a very simple matter. While secreted in his boat, on the watch for fowl, with his craft hidden by a covering of grass or sedge, the gunner could approach within shooting distance of a flock of unsuspicious ducks; and this being done in a sneaking manner (though Mr. Seaman named the result of his first effort the "devil's coffin"), the bay men gave her the sobriquet of "sneak-box"; . . .

[In the succeeding chapter, Bishop writes of the sources of the Ohio River.]

FROM PITTSBURGH TO BLENNERHASSET'S ISLAND

Upon arriving at Pittsburgh, on the morning of December 2, 1875, after a dreary night's ride by rail from the Atlantic coast, I found my boat—it having preceded me—safely perched upon a pile of barrels in the freight house of the railroad company, which was conveniently situated within a few rods of the muddy waters of the Monongahela. . . .

The rains in the south had filled the gulches of the Virginia mountains, the sources of the Monongahela, and it now exhibited a great degree of turbulence. I was not then aware of the tumultuous state of the sister tributary, the Allegheny, on the other side of the city. . . . I expected to have an easy and uninterrupted passage down the river in advance of floating ice; and, so congratulating myself, I drew near to the confluence of the Monongahela and Allegheny, from the union of which the great Ohio has its birth, and rolls steadily across the country a thousand miles to the mightier Mississippi.

The current of the Monongahela, as it flowed from the south, covered with mists rising into the wintry air—for the temperature was but a few degrees above zero—had not a particle of ice upon its turbid bosom.

I rowed gayly on, pleased with the auspicious beginning of the voyage, hoping at the close of the month to be at the mouth of the river, and far enough south to escape any inconvenience from a sudden freezing of its surface, for along its course between its source at Pittsburgh and its debouchure at Cairo the Ohio makes only two hundred and twelve miles of southing, or a difference of about two and a half degrees of latitude. It is not surprising, therefore, that this river during exceedingly cold winters sometimes freezes over for a few days, from the state of Pennsylvania to its junction with the Mississippi.

In a few minutes my boat had passed nearly the whole length of the Pittsburgh shore, when suddenly, upon looking over my shoulder, I beheld the river covered with an ice raft, which was passing out of the Allegheny, and which completely blocked the Ohio from shore to shore. French Creek, Oil Creek, and all the other tributaries of the Allegheny, had burst from their icy barriers, thrown off the wintry coat of mail, and were pouring their combined wrath into the Ohio.

This unforeseen trouble had to be met without much time for calculating the results of entering the icepack. A light canoe would have been ground to pieces in the multitude of icy cakes, but the half-inch skin of soft but elastic white swamp cedar of the decked sneak-box, with its light oaken runner strips firmly screwed to its bottom, was fully able to cope with the difficulty; so I pressed the boat into the floating ice, and by dint of hard work forced her several rods beyond the eddies, and fairly into the steady flow of the strong current of the river.

There was nothing more to be done to expedite the journey, so I sat down in the little hold, and, wrapped comfortably in blankets, watched the progress made by the receding points of interest upon the high banks of the stream. Toward night some channel ways opened in the pack, and, seizing upon the opportunity, I rowed along the ice-bound lanes until dusk, when happily a chance was offered for leaving the frosty surroundings, and the duck boat was

"The Start—Head of the Ohio River," from *Four Months in a Sneak-Box*

soon resting on a shelving, pebbly strand on the left bank of the river, two miles above the little village of Freedom.

The rapid current had carried me twenty-two miles in four hours and a half.

Not having slept for thirty-six hours, or eaten since morning, I was well prepared physically to retire at an early hour. A few minutes sufficed to securely stake my boat, to prevent her being carried off by a sudden rise in the river during my slumbers; a few moments more were occupied in arranging the thin hair cushions and a thick cotton coverlet upon the floor of the boat. The bag which contained my wardrobe, consisting of a blue flannel suit, &c., served for a pillow. A heavy shawl and two thin blankets furnished sufficient covering for the bed. Bread and butter, with Shakers' peach sauce, and a generous slice of Wilson's compressed beef, a tin of water from the icy reservoir that flowed past my boat and within reach of my arm, all contributed to furnish a most satisfactory meal, and a half hour afterwards, when a soft, damp fog settled down upon the land, the atmosphere became so quiet that the rubbing of every ice cake against the shore could be distinctly heard as I sank into a sweeter slumber than I had ever experienced in the most luxurious bed of the daintiest of guest chambers, for my apartment, though small, was comfortable, and with the hatch securely closed, I was safe from invasion by man or beast, and enjoyed the well-earned repose with a full feeling of security. The owl softly winnowed the air with his feathery pinions as he searched for his prey along the beach, sending forth an occasional to-hoot! as he rested for a moment on the leafless branches of an old tree, reminding me to take a peep at the night, and to inquire "what its signs of promise" were. . . .

So the peaceful night wore away, and in the early dawn, enveloped in a thick fog, I hastily dispatched a cold breakfast, and at half-past eight pushed off into the floating ice, which became more and more disintegrated and less troublesome as the day advanced. The use of the soft bituminous coal in the towns along the river, and also by the steamboats navigating it, filled the valley with clouds of smoke. These clouds rested upon everything. Your five senses were fully aware of the presence of the disagreeable, impalpable *something* surrounding you. Eyes, ears, taste, touch, and smell, each felt the presence. Smoky towns along the banks gave smoky views. . . .

During the second day the current of the Ohio became less violent. I fought a passage among the ice cakes, and whenever openings appeared rowed briskly along the sides of the chilly raft, with the intent of getting below the frosty zone as soon as possible.

About half-past eight in the evening, when some distance above King's Creek, the struggling starlight enabled me to push my boat on to a muddy flat, destined soon to be overflowed, but offering me a secure resting place for a few hours. Upon peeping out of my warm nest under the hatch the next day, it was a cause of great satisfaction to note that a rise in the temperature had taken place, and that the ice was disappearing by degrees.

An open-air toilet, and a breakfast of about the temperature of a family refrigerator, with sundry other inconveniences, made me wish for just enough hot water to remove a little of the begriming results of the smoky atmosphere through which I had rowed.

At eleven o'clock, the first bridge that spans the Ohio River was passed. It was at Steubenville, and the property of the Pan-Handle Railroad.

Soon after four o'clock in the afternoon the busy manufacturing city of Wheeling, West Virginia, with its great suspension bridge crossing the river to the state of Ohio, loomed into sight.

This city of Wheeling, on the left bank of the river, some eighty miles from Pittsburgh, was the most impressive sight of that dreary day's row. Above its masses of brick walls hung a dense cloud of smoke, into which shot the flames emitted from the numerous chimneys of forges, glassworks, and factories, which made it the busy place it was. Ever and anon came the deafening sound of the triphammer, the rap-a-tap-tap of the rivetheaders' tools striking upon the heavy boiler plates; the screeching of steamwhistles; the babel of men's voices; the clanging of deep-toned bells. . . .

. . . I thought, as I brushed off the thin layer of soot with which the Wheeling cloud of enterprise had discolored the pure white deck of my little craft, that if this was civilization and enterprise, I should rather take a little less of those two commodities and a little more of cleanliness and quiet.

At Wheeling I left the last of the ice drifts, but now observed a new feature on the river's surface. It was a floating coat of oil from the petroleum regions, and it followed me many a mile down the stream.

The river being now free from ice, numerous crafts passed me, and among them many steamboats with their immense stern wheels beating the water, being so constructed for shallow streams. They were ascending the current, and pushing their "tows" of two, four, and six long, wide coal barges fastened in pairs in front of them. How the pilots of these stern-wheel freighters managed to guide their heavily loaded barges against the treacherous current was a mystery to me.

It suddenly grew dark, and wishing to be secure from molestation by steamboats, I ran into a narrow creek, with high, muddy banks, which were so steep and so slippery that my boat slid into the water as fast as I could haul her on to the shore. This difficulty was overcome by digging with my oar a bed for her to rest in, and she soon settled into the damp ooze, where she quietly remained until morning.

During this part of my journey particularly, the need of a small coal-oil stove was felt, as the usual custom of making a campfire could not be followed for many days on the upper Ohio River. The rains had wet the firewood, which in a settled and cultivated country is found only in small quantities on the banks of the stream. The driftwood thrown up by the river was almost saturated with water, and the damp, wild trees of the swamp afforded only green wood. . . .

For lack of one of these little blessings—which the prejudice of friends had inflenced me to leave behind—my daily meals for the first two or three weeks generally consisted of cold, cooked canned beef, bread and butter, canned fruits, and cold river water. The absence of hot coffee and other stimulants did not affect my appetite, nor the enjoyment of the morning and evening repasts, cold and untempting as they were. . . .

Sunday broke upon me a sunless day. The water of the creek was too muddy to drink, and the rain began to fall in torrents. I had anticipated a season of rest and quiet in camp, with a bright fire to cheer the lonely hours of my frosty sojourn on the Ohio, but there was not a piece of dry wood to be found, and it became necessary to change my position for a more propitious locality; so I rowed down the stream twelve miles, to Big Grave Creek, below which, and on the left bank of the Ohio, is the town of Moundsville. . . .

It would not interest the general reader to give a description of the few cities and many small villages that were passed during the descent of the Ohio. Few of these places possess even a local interest, and the eye soon wearies of the air of monotony found in them all. . . .

One feature may be, however, remarked in descending the Ohio, and that is the ambition displayed by the pioneers of civilization in the west in naming hamlets and towns—which, with few exceptions, are still of little importance—after the great cities of the older parts of the United States, and also of foreign lands. These names, which occupy such important positions on the maps, excite the imagination of the traveler, and when the reality comes into view, and he enters their narrow limits, the commonplace architecture and generally unattractive surroundings have a most depressing effect, and he sighs, "What's in a name?" . . .

FROM BLENNERHASSET'S ISLAND TO CINCINNATI

About this time the selection of resting places for the night became an important feature of the voyage. It was easy to draw the little craft out of the water on to a smooth, shelving beach, but such places did not always appear at the proper time for ending the day's rowing. The banks were frequently precipitous, and, destitute of beaches, frowned down upon the lonely voyager in anything but a hospitable manner. There were also present two elements antagonistic to my peace of mind. One was the night steamer, which, as it struggled up stream, coursing along shore to avoid the strong current, sent swashy waves to disturb my dreams by pitching my little craft about in the roughest manner. A light canoe could easily have been carried farther inland, out of reach of the unwelcome waves, and would, so far as that went, have made a more quiet resting place than the heavy duck boat; but then, on the other hand, a sleeping apartment in a canoe would have lacked the roominess and security of the sneak-box.

After the first few nights' camping on the Ohio, I naturally took to the channelless side of one of the numerous islands which dot the river's surface, or, what was still better, penetrated into the wild-looking creeks and rivers, more than one hundred of which enter the parent stream along the thousand miles of its course. Here, in these secluded nooks, I found security from the steamer's swash.

The second objectionable element on the Ohio was the presence of tramps, rough boatmen, and scoundrels of all kinds. In fact, the Ohio and Mississippi rivers are the grand highway of the West for a large class of vagabonds. One of these fellows will steal something of value from a farm near the river, seize the first bateau, or skiff, he can find, cross the stream, and descend it for fifty or a hundred miles. He will then abandon the stolen boat if he cannot sell it, ship as working hand upon the first steamer or coal ark he happens to meet, descend the river still further, and so escape detection.

To avoid these rough characters, as well as the drunken crews of shanty boats, it was necessary always to enter the night's camping ground unobserved; but when once secreted on the wooded shore of some friendly creek, covered by the dusky shades of night, I felt perfectly safe, and had no fear of a night attack from any one. Securely shut in my strong box, with a hatchet and a Colt's revolver by my side, and a double-barrelled gun, carefully charged, snugly stowed under the deck, the intruder would have been in danger, and not the occupant of the sneak-box.

The hatch, or cover, which rested upon the stern of the boat during rowing hours, was at night dropped over the hold, or well, in such a way as to give the hold plenty of ventilation, and still, at the same time, to be easily and instantly removed in case of need.

I must not fail here to mention one characteristic feature possessed by the sneak-box which gives it an advantage over every other boat I have examined. Its deck is nowhere level, and if a person attempts to step upon it while it is afloat, his foot touches the periphery of a circle, and the spoon-shaped, keelless, little craft flies out as if by magic from under the pressure of the foot, and without further warning the luckless intruder falls into the water. . . . When once inside of the sneak-box, it becomes the stiffest and steadiest of crafts. Two men can stand upright upon the flooring of the hold and paddle her along rapidly, with very little careening to right or left.

By far the most interesting and peculiar features of a winter's row down the Ohio are the life studies offered by the occupants of the numerous shanty boats daily encountered. They are sometimes called, and justly too, family boats, and serve as the winter homes

"Shanty Boats—the Champion Floaters of the West," from *Four Months in a Sneak-Box*

of a singular class of people, carrying their passengers and cargoes from the icy region of the Ohio to New Orleans. Their annual descent of the river resembles the migration of birds, . . .

The shanty boatman looks to the river not only for his life, but also for the means of making that life pleasant; so he fishes in the stream for floating lumber in the form of boards, planks, and scantling for framing to build his home. It is soon ready. A scow, or flatboat, about twenty feet long by ten or twelve wide, is roughly constructed. It is made of two-inch planks spiked together. These scows are calked with oakum and rags, and the seams are made water-tight with pitch or tar. A small, low house is built upon the boat, and covers about two-thirds of it, leaving a cockpit at each end, in which the crews work the sweeps, or oars, which govern the motions of the shanty boat. If the proprietor of the boat has a family, he puts its members on board—not forgetting the pet dogs and cats—with a small stock of salt pork, bacon, flour, potatoes, molasses, salt, and coffee. An old cooking stove is set up in the shanty, and its sheet-iron pipe, projecting through the roof, makes a chimney a superfluity. Rough bunks, or berths, are constructed for sleeping quarters; but if the family are the happy possessors of any furniture, it is put on board, and adds greatly to their respectability. A number of steel traps, with the usual double-barrelled gun, or rifle, and a good supply of ammunition, constitute the most important supplies of the shanty boat, and are never forgotten. Of these family boats alone I passed over two hundred on the Ohio.

Cobblers set afloat their establishments, calling attention to the fact by the creaking sign of a boot; and here on the rushing river a man can have his heel tapped as easily as on shore.

Tinsmiths, agents and repairers of sewing machines, grocers, saloonkeepers, barbers, and every trade indeed is here represented on these floating dens. I saw one circus boat with a ring twenty-five feet in diameter upon it, in which a troop of horsemen, acrobats, and flying trapeze artists performed while their boat was tied to a landing. . . .

After leaving my camp near Blennerhasset's Island, on December 9, the features of the landscape changed. The hills lost their altitude, and seemed farther back from the water, while the river itself appeared to widen. Snow squalls filled the air, and the thought of a comfortable camping ground for the night was a welcome one. About dusk I retired into the first creek above Letart's Landing, on the left bank of the Ohio, where I spent the night. The next forenoon I entered a region of salt wells, with a number of flourishing little towns scattered here and there upon the borders of the stream. One of these, called Hartford City, had a well eleven hundred and seventy feet in depth. From another well in the vicinity both oil and salt water were raised by means of a steam pump. These oil wells were half a mile back of the river. Coal mines were frequently passed in this neighborhood on both sides of the Ohio.

After dark I was fortunate enough to find a camping place in a low swamp on the right bank of the stream, in the vicinity of which was a gloomy looking, deserted house. I climbed the slippery bank with my cooking kit upon my back, and finding some refuse wood in what had once been a kitchen, made a fire, and enjoyed the first meal I had been able to cook in camp since the voyage was commenced.

Cold winds whistled round me all night, but the snug nest in my boat was warm and cheerful, for I lighted my candle, and by its clear flame made up my daily "log." There were, of course, some inconveniences in regard to lighting so low-studded a chamber. It was important to have a candle of not more than two inches in length, so that the flame should not go too near the roof of my domicile. Then the space being small, my literary labors were of necessity performed in a reclining position; while lying upon my side, my shoulder almost touched the carlines of the hatch above.

Saturday was as raw and blustering as the previous day, so hastily breakfasting upon the remains of my supper—*cold* chocolate, *cold* corned beef, and *cold* crackers—I determined to get into a milder region as soon as possible.

As I rowed down the stream, the peculiar appearance of the Barnegat sneak-box attracted the attention of the men on board the coal barges, shanty boats, etc., and they invariably crowded to the side I passed, besieging me with questions of every description, such as, "Say, stranger, where did you steal that pumpkin-seed looking boat from?" "How much did she cost, any way?" "Ain't ye afeard some steamboat will swash the life out of her?" On several occasions I raised the water apron, and explained how the little sneak-box shed the water that washed over her bows, . . .

The snow squalls now became so frequent, and the atmosphere was so chilly and penetrating, that I was driven from the swashy waves of the troubled Ohio, and eagerly sought refuge in Fourfold Creek, about a league below Huntington, where the high, wooded banks of the little tributary offered me protection and rest.

At an early hour the next morning I was conscious of a change of temperature. It was growing colder. A keen wind whistled through the treetops. I was alarmed at the prospect of having my boat fastened in the creek by the congealing of its waters, so I pushed out upon the Ohio and hastened towards a warmer climate as fast as oars, muscles, and a friendly current would carry me. The shanty boatmen had informed me that the Ohio might freeze up in a single night, *in places,* even as near its mouth as Cairo. I did not, however, feel so much alarmed in regard to the river as I did about its tributaries. The Ohio was not likely to remain sealed up for more than a few days at a time, but the creeks, my harbors of refuge, my lodging places, might remain frozen up for a long time, and put me to serious inconvenience.

About ten o'clock, the duck boat crossed the mouth of the Big Sandy River, the limit of Virginia, and I floated along the shores of the grand old state of Kentucky on the left, while the immense state of Ohio still skirted the right bank of the river.

The agricultural features of the Ohio valley had been increasing in attractiveness with the descent of the stream. The high bottom lands of the valley exhibited signs of careful cultivation, while substantial brick houses here and there dotted the landscape. Interspersed with these were the inevitable log cabins and dingy hovels, speaking plainly of the poverty . . . of some of the inhabitants.

At four P.M. I could endure the cold no longer, and when a beautiful creek with wooded shores, which divided fine farms, opened invitingly before me on the Kentucky side, I quickly entered it, and moored the sneak-box to an ancient sycamore whose trunk rose out of the water twelve feet from shore. I was not a moment too soon in leaving the wide river, for as I quietly supped on my cold bread and meat, which needed no better sauce than my daily increasing appetite to make it tempting, the wind increased to a tempest, and screeched and howled through the forest with such wintry blasts that I was glad to creep under my hatch before dark.

On Monday, December 13, the violent wind storm continuing, I remained all day in my box, writing letters and watching the scuds flying over the tops of high trees. At noon a party of hunters, with a small pack of hounds, came abruptly upon my camp. Though boys only, they carried shotguns, and expectorated enough tobacco juice to pass for the type of western manhood. They chatted pleasantly round my boat, though each sentence that fell from their lips was emphasized by its accompanying oath. I asked them the name of the creek, when one replied, "Why, boss, you don't call this a *creek,* do you? Why, there is twenty foot of water in it. It's the Tiger River, and comes a heap of a long way off." Another said, "Look here, cap'n, I wouldn't travel alone in that 'ere little skiff, for when you're in camp any feller might put a ball into you from a high bank." "Yes," added another, "there is plenty o' folks along the river that would do it, too."

As my camp had become known, I acted upon the friendly hint of the boy hunters, and took my departure the next day at an early hour, following the left bank of the river, which afforded me a lee shore. . . .

Two miles below Portsmouth, Ohio, I encountered a solitary voyager in a skiff, shooting mallards about the mouths of the creeks, and having discovered that he was a gentleman, I intrusted my mail to his keeping, and pushed on to a little creek beyond Rome, where, thanks to good fortune, some dry wood was discovered. A bright blaze was soon lighting up the darkness of the thicket into which I had drawn my boat, and the hot supper, now cooked in camp, and served without ceremony, was duly relished.

The deck of the boat was covered with a thin coating of ice, and as the wind went down the temperature continued to fall until six o'clock in the morning, when I considered it unsafe to linger a moment longer in the creek, the surface of which was already frozen over, and the ice becoming thicker every hour. An oar served to break a passageway from the creek to the Ohio, which I descended in a blustering wind, being frequently driven to seek shelter under the lee afforded by points of land.

At sunset I reached Maysville, where the celebrated Daniel Boone, the pioneer of Kentucky backwoods life, once lived; and as the wind began to fall, I pulled into a fine creek about four miles below the village, having made twenty-nine miles under most discouraging circumstances. The river was here, as elsewhere, lighted by small hand lanterns hung upon posts. The lights were, however, so dull and, where the channel was not devious, at such long intervals, that they only added to the gloom.

As the wind generally rose and fell with the sun, it became necessary to adopt a new plan to expedite my voyage, and the river being usually smooth at dawn of day, an early start was an imperative duty. At four o'clock in the morning the duck boat was under way, her captain cheered by the hope of arriving in Cincinnati, the great city of the Ohio valley, by sunset. I plied my oars vigorously all day, and when darkness settled upon the land, was rewarded for my exertions by having my little craft shoot under the first bridge that connects Cincinnati with Kentucky. Here steamers, coal barges, and river craft of every description lined the Ohio as well as the Kentucky shore. Iron cages filled with burning coals were suspended from cranes erected upon flatboats for the purpose of lighting the river, which was most effectually done, the unwonted brilliancy giving to the busy scene a strange weirdness, and making a picture never to be forgotten.

The swift current now carried me under the suspension bridge which connects Cincinnati and Covington, and my boat entered the dark area below, when suddenly the river was clouded in snow, as fierce squalls came up the stream, and I eagerly scanned the high, dark banks to find some inlet to serve as harbor for the night. It was very dark, and I hugged the Kentucky shore as closely as I dared. Suddenly a gleam of light, like a break in a fog bank, opened upon my craft, and the dim outlines of the sides of a gorge in the high coast caught my eye. It was not necessary to row into the cleft in the hillside, for a fierce blast of the tempest blew me into the little creek; nor was my progress stayed until the sneak-box was driven several rods into its dark interior, and entangled in the branches of a fallen tree.

In the blinding snowfall it was impossible to discern anything upon the steep banks of the little creek which had fairly forced its hospitality upon me; so, carefully fastening my painter to the fallen tree, I hastily disappeared below my hatch. During the night the mercury fell to six degrees above zero, but my quarters were so comfortable that little inconvenience from the cold was experienced until morning, when I attempted to make my toilet with an open hatch. Then I discovered the unpleasant fact that my boat was securely frozen up in the waters of the creek! Being without a stove, and finding that my canned provisions—not having been wrapped in several coverings like their owner, and having no power to convert oxygen into fuel for warmth—were solidifying, I locked my hatch, and scrambled up the high banks to seek the comforts of that civilization which I had so gladly left behind when I embarked at a point five hundred miles farther up the river, thinking as I went what a contrary mortal man was, myself among the number, for I was as eager now to find my human brother as I had been to turn my back upon him a short time before. The poetry of solitude was frozen into prose, and the low temperature around me made life under a roof seem attractive for the time being, though, judging from the general aspect of things, there was not much to look forward to, in either a social or comfortable light, in my immediate vicinity. . . .

FROM CINCINNATI TO THE MISSISSIPPI RIVER

. . . It was necessary to make an early start the next day, as I must run the falls of the Ohio at Louisville, Kentucky, or make a portage round them. The river was enveloped in fog; but I followed the shore closely, hour after hour, until the sun dispelled the mists, and my little duck boat ran in among the barges at the great Kentucky city. Here, at Louisville, is the only barrier to safe navigation on the Ohio River. These so-called *Falls* of the Ohio are in fact rapids which almost disappear when the river is at its full height. At such times, steamboats, with skillful pilots aboard, safely follow the channel, which avoids the rocks of the river. During the low stage of the water, navigation is entirely suspended. . . . I ascertained that the descent of the rapids could not be made without a pilot; and as the limited quarters of the sneak-box would not allow any addition to her passenger list, a portage round the falls became a necessity. The canal was not to be thought of, as it would have been a troublesome matter, without special passes from some official, to have obtained the privilege of passing through with so small a boat. . . . The portage was made in about an hour. At sunset the little boat was launched in the Ohio, and I felt that I had returned to an old friend. . . .

When night came on, and no friendly creek offered me shelter, I pushed the boat into a soft, muddy flat of willows, which fringed a portion of the Kentucky shore, where there was just enough water to float the sneak-box. The passing steamers during the night sent swashy waves into my lair, which kept me in constant fear of a ducking, and gave me anything but a peaceful night. This was, however, all forgotten the next morning, when the startling discovery was made that the river had fallen during the night and left me in a quagmire, from which it seemed at first impossible to extricate myself.

The boat was imbedded in the mud, which was so soft and slimy that it would not support my weight when I attempted to step upon it for the purpose of pushing my little craft into the water, which had receded only a few feet from my camp. I tried pushing with my oak oar; but it sank into the mire almost out of sight. Then a small watch tackle was rigged, one block fastened to the boat, the other to the limb of a willow which projected over the water. The result of this was a successful downward movement of the willow, but the boat remained *in statu quo,* the soft mud holding it as though it possessed the sucking powers of a cuttlefish.

I could not reach the firm shore, for the willow brush would not support my weight. There was no assistance to be looked for from fellow voyagers, as the river craft seemed to follow the channel of the opposite shore; and my camp could not be seen from the river, as I had taken pains to hide myself in the thicket of young willows from all curious eyes. There was no hope that my voice would penetrate to the other side of the stream, neither could I reach the water beyond the soft ooze. Being well provisioned, however, it would be an easy matter to await the rise of the river; and if no friendly freshet sent me the required assistance, the winds would harden the ooze in a few days so that it would bear my weight, and enable me to escape from my bonds of mud.

While partaking of a light breakfast, an idea suddenly presented itself to my mind. I had frequently built crossways over treacherous swamps. Why not mattress the muddy flat? Standing upon the deck of my boat, I grasped every twig and bough of willow I could reach, and making a mattress of them, about two feet square and a few inches thick, on the surface of the mud at the stern of my craft, I placed upon it the hatch-cover of my boat. Standing upon this, the sneak-box was relieved of my weight, and by dint of persevering effort the after part was successfully lifted, and the heavy burden slowly worked out of its tenacious bed, and moved two or three feet nearer the water. By shifting the willow mattress nearer the boat, which was now *on* the surface of the mud, and not *in* it, my floating home was soon again upon the current, and its captain had a new experience, which, though dearly bought, would teach him to avoid in future a camp on a soft flat when a river was falling.

A foggy day followed my departure from the unfortunate camp of willows; but through the mist I caught glimpses of the fine lands of the Kentucky farmers, with the grand old trees shading their comfortable homes. In the drizzle I had passed French's Creek, and after dark ran upon a stony beach, where, high and dry upon the bank, was a shanty boat, which had been converted into a landing house, and was occupied by two men who received the freight left there by passing steamers. The locality was six miles below Brandenburg, Kentucky, and was known as Richardson's Landing. Having rowed forty miles since morning, I turned in soon after drawing my boat upon the shelving strand, anticipating a quiet night.

At midnight a loud noise, accompanied with bright flashes of light, warned me of the approach of a steamboat. She soon after ran her bow hard on to the beach, within a few feet of my boat. Though the rain was falling in torrents, the passengers crowded upon the upper deck to examine the snow-white, peculiarly shaped craft, or "skiff" as they called it, which lay upon the banks, little suspecting that her owner was snugly stowed beneath her deck. I suddenly threw up the hatch and sat upright, while the strong glare of light from the steamer's furnaces brought out every detail of the boat's interior.

This sudden apparition struck the crowd with surprise, and, as is usual upon such an occasion in western America, the whole company showered a fire of raillery and "chaff" upon me, to which, on account of the heavy rain, I could not reply, but, dropping backward into my bed, drew the hatch into its place. The good-natured crowd would not permit me to escape so easily. Calling the entire ship's company from the staterooms and cabins to join them, they used every artifice in their power to induce me to show my head above the deck of my boat. One shouted, "Here, you deck hand, don't cut that man's rope; it's mean to steal a fellow's painter!" Another cried, "Don't put that heavy plank against that little skiff!" Suspecting their game, however, I kept under cover during the fifteen minutes' stay of the boat, when, moving off, they all shouted a jolly farewell, which mingled in the darkness with the hoarse whistle of the steamer, while the night air echoed with cries of, "Snug as a bug in a rug"; "I never seed the like afore"; "He'll git used to livin' in a coffin afore he needs one," etc.

The reader who may have looked heretofore upon swamps and gloomy creeks as too lonely for camping grounds, may now appreciate the necessity for selecting such places, and understand why a voyager prefers the security of the wilderness to the annoying curiosity of his fellow man.

The rains of the past two days had swollen the Kentucky River, which enters the Ohio above Louisville, as well as the Salt River, which I had passed twenty miles below that city, besides many other branches, so that the main stream was now rapidly rising. After leaving Richardson's Landing, the rain continued to fall, and as each tributary, affected by the freshet, poured logs, fallen trees, fence rails, stumps from clearings, and even occasionally a small frame shanty, into the Ohio, there was a floating raft of these materials miles in length. Sometimes an unlucky shanty boat was caught in an eddy by the mass of floating timber, and at once becoming an integral portion of the whole, would float with the great raft for two or three days. . . .

In the evening, a little creek below Alton was reached, which sheltered me during the night. Soon the rain ceased, and the stars shone kindly upon my lonely camp. I left the creek at half-past four in the morning. The water had risen two feet and a half in ten hours, and the broad river was in places covered from shore to shore with drift stuff, which made my course a devious one, and the little duck boat had many a narrow escape in my attempts to avoid the floating mass. The booming of guns along the shore reminded me that it was Chrismas, and, in imagination, I pictured to myself the many happy families in the valley enjoying their Christmas cheer. The contrast between their condition and mine was great, for I could not even find enough dry wood to cook my simple camp fare. . . .

The creeks were now so swollen from the heavy rains, and so full of driftwood, that my usual retreat into some creek seemed cut off; so I ran under the sheltered side of Three Mile Island, below Newburg, Indiana. The climate was daily improving, and I no longer feared an ice blockade; but a new difficulty arose. The heavy rafts of timber threatened to shut me in my camp. At dusk, all might be open water; but at break of day "a change came o'er the spirit of my dream," and heavy blockades of timber rafts made it no easy matter to escape. There were times when, shut in behind these barriers, I looked out upon the river with envious eyes at the steamboats steadily plodding upstream against the current, keeping free of the rafts by the skill of their pilots; . . .

The soft shores of alluvium were constantly caving and falling into the river, bringing down tons of earth and tall forest trees. The latter, after freeing their roots of the soil, would be swept out into the stream as contributions to the great floating raft of driftwood, a large portion of which was destined to a long voyage, for much of this floating forest is carried into the Gulf of Mexico, and travels over many hundreds of miles of salt water, until it is washed up on to the strands of the isles of the sea or the beaches of the continent.

Having tied up for the night to a low bank, with no thought of danger, it was startling, to say the least, to have an avalanche of earth from the bank above deposit itself upon my boat, so effectually sealing down my hatch cover that it seemed at first impossible to break from my prison. After repeated trials I succeeded in dislodging the mass, and, thankful to escape premature interment, at once pushed off in search of a better camp.

A creek soon appeared, but its entrance was barred by a large tree which had fallen across its mouth. My heavy hatchet now proved a friend in need, and putting my boat close to the tree, I went systematically to work, and soon cut out a section five feet in length. Entering through this gateway, my labors were rewarded by finding upon the bank some dry fence rails, with which a rude kitchen was soon constructed to protect me from the wind while preparing my meal. The unusual luxury of a fire brightened the weird scene, and the flames shot upward, cheering the lone voyager and frightening the owls and coons from their accustomed lairs. The strong current had been of great assistance, for that night my log registered sixty-two miles for the day's row. . . .

I entered a long reach in the river soon after nine o'clock on Friday morning, and could plainly see the town of Cairo, resting upon the flat prairies in the distance. . . . Across the southern apex of this prairie city could be seen the Father of Waters, its wide surface bounded on the west by the wilderness. A few moments more, and my little craft was whirled into its rapid, eddying current; and with the boat's prow now pointed southward, I commenced, as it were, a life of new experiences. . . .

The faithful sneak-box had carried me more than a thousand miles since I entered her at Pittsburgh. This, of course, includes the various detours made in searching for camping grounds, frequent crossings of the wide river to avoid drift stuff, etc. The descent of the Ohio had occupied about twenty-nine days, but many hours had been lost by storms keeping me in camp, and other unavoidable delays. As an offset to these stoppages, it must be remembered that the current, increased by freshets, was with me, and to it, as much as to the industrious arms of the rower, must be given the credit for the long route gone over in so short a time, by so small a boat.

DESCENT OF THE MISSISSIPPI RIVER

My floating home was now upon the broad Mississippi, . . . Its current was about one-third faster than that of its tributary, the Ohio. Its banks were covered with heavy forests, and for miles along its course the great wilderness was broken only by the half-tilled lands of the cotton planter. . . .

My entrance to the Mississippi River was marked by the advent of severe squalls of wind and rain, which drove me about noon to the shelter of Island No. 1, where I dined, and where in half an hour the sun came out in all its glory. Many peculiar features of the Mississippi attracted my notice. Sand bars appeared above the water, and large flocks of ducks and geese rested upon them. Later, the high Chickasaw Bluff, the first and highest of a series which rise at intervals, like islands out of the low bottoms as far south as Natchez, came into view on the left side of the river. . . .

A little lower down, and opposite Chalk Bluff, was a heavily wooded island, a part of the territory of the state of Illinois, and known as Wolf Island, or Island No. 5. At five o'clock in the afternoon I ran into a little thoroughfare on the eastern side of this island, and moored the duck boat under its muddy banks. The wind increased to a gale before morning, and kept me through the entire day, and until the following morning, an unwilling captive. Reading and cooking helped to while away the heavy hours, but having burned up all the dry wood I could find, I was forced to seek other quarters, which were found in a romantic stream that flowed out of a swamp and joined the Mississippi just one mile above Hickman, on the Kentucky side. Having passed a comfortable night, and making an early start without breakfast, I rowed rapidly over a smooth current to the stream called Bayou du Chien Creek, in which I made a very attractive camp among the giant sycamores, sweet gums, and cottonwoods. The warm sunshine penetrated into this sheltered spot, while the wind had fallen to a gentle zephyr, and came in refreshing puffs through the lofty trees. Here birds were numerous, and briskly hopped about my fire while I made an omelet and boiled some wheaten grits. . . .

Descending a long straight reach, after making a run of twenty-three miles, I crossed the limits of Kentucky, and, entering Tennessee, saw on its shore, in a deep bend of the river, the site of Fort Donaldson, while opposite to it lay the low Island No. 10. Both of these places were full of interest, being the scenes of conflict in our Civil War. The little white sneak-box glided down another long bend, over the wrecks of seven steamboats, and passed New Madrid, on the Missouri shore. The mouth of Reelfoot Bayou then opened before me, a creek which conducts the waters from the weird recesses of one of the most interesting lakes in America

—a lake which was the immediate result of a disastrous series of disturbances generally referred to as the New Madrid earthquakes, and which took place in 1811–13. . . .

At sunset I came upon Joe Eckel's Bar—not the fluvial establishment so much resorted to by people ashore—but a genuine Mississippi sandbar, or shoal, which was covered with two feet of water, and afforded lodgment for a heavy raft of trees that had floated upon it. The island was also partly submerged, but I found a cove with a sandy beach on its lower end; and running into the little bay, I staked the boat in one foot of water, much to the annoyance of flocks of wild fowl which circled about me at intervals all night. The current had been turbid during the day, and to supply myself with drinking water it was necessary to fill a can from the river and wait for the sediment to precipitate itself before it was fit for use. Fifty-six miles were logged for the day's row.

In the morning Joe Eckel's Bar was alive with geese and ducks, cackling a lusty farewell as I pushed through the drift stuff and resumed my voyage down the swelling river.

The reaches were usually five miles in length, though some of them were very much longer. Sometimes deposits of sand and vegetable matter will build up a small island adjacent to a large one, and then a dense thicket of cottonwood brush takes possession of it, and assists materially in resisting the encroachments of the current. These little, low islands, covered with thickets, are called towheads, and the maps of the Engineer Corps of the United States distinguish them from the originally numbered islands in the following manner: "Island No. 18," and "Tow Head of Island No. 18."

In addition to the numbered islands, which commence with Island No. 1, below the mouth of the Ohio, and end with Island No. 125, above the inlet to Bayou La Fourche, in Louisiana, there are many which have been named after their owners. . . .

This day's row carried me past heavily wooded shores, cotton fields with some of the cotton still unpicked; past the limits of Missouri on the left side, and into the wild state of Arkansas at Island No. 21. I finally camped on Island No. 26, in a half submerged thicket, after a row of fifty-eight miles.

As there were many flat and shanty boats floating southward, I adopted a plan by means of which my dinners were frequently cooked with little trouble to myself or others. About an hour before noon I gazed about within the narrow horizon for one of those floating habitations, and rowing alongside, engaged in conversation with its occupants. The men would tell what success they had had in collecting the skins of wild animals (though silent upon the subject of pig-stealing), while the women would talk of the homes they had left, and sigh for the refinements and comforts of "city life," by which they meant their former existence in some small town on the upper river. While we were exchanging our budgets of information I would obtain the consent of the presiding goddess of the boat to stew my ambrosia upon her stove, the sneak-box floating the while alongside its tub-like companion. Many a half hour was spent in this way; and, besides the comfort of a hot dinner, there were advantages afforded for the study of characters not to be found elsewhere.

These peculiar boats, so often encountered, found refuge in the frequent cutoffs behind the many islands of the river; for besides those islands which have been numbered, new ones are forming every year. At times, when the water is very high, the current will cut a new route across the low isthmus, or neck, of a peninsula, around which sweeps a long reach of the main channel, leaving the tortuous bend which it has deserted to be gradually filled up with snags, deposits of alluvium, and finally to be carpeted with a vegetable growth. In some cases, as the stream works away to the eastward or westward, it remains an inland crescent-shaped lake, numbers of which are to be found in the wilderness many miles from the parent stream. I have known the channel of the Mississippi to be shortened twenty miles during a freshet, and a steamboat which had followed the great ox-bow bend in ascending the river, on its return trip shot through the new cutoff of a few hundred feet in length, upon fifteen feet of water where a fortnight before a forest had been growing. . . .

[Bishop descends the Mississippi and spends some time in New Orleans—two chapters.]

ON THE GULF OF MEXICO

One of the chief charms in a boatman's life is its freedom, and what that freedom is no one knows until he throws aside the chains of everyday life, steps out of the worn ruts, and, with his kit beside him, his oar in his hand, feels himself master of his time, and *free*. There is one duty incumbent on the voyager, however, and that is to keep his face set upon his goal. Remembering this, I turned my back upon the beguiling city of New Orleans, with its orange groves and sweet flowers, its old buildings and modern civilization, its French cafés and bewitching oddities of every nature, . . .

My shortest route to the Gulf of Mexico was through New Basin Canal, six miles in length, into Lake Pontchartrain, and from there to the Gulf. . . . The first part of this canal runs through the city proper, and then through a low swampy region out into the shallow Lake Pontchartrain. At the terminus of New Basin Canal I found a small lighthouse, two or three hotels, and a few houses, making a little village.

A small fleet of schooners, which had brought lumber and firewood from Shieldsboro and other Gulf ports, was lying idly along the sides of the canal, awaiting a fair wind to assist them in making the return trip.

I rowed out of the canal on to the lake; but finding that the strong wind and rough waves were too much for my boat, I beat a hasty retreat into the port of refuge, and, securing my bowline to a pile, and my stern line to the bobstay of a wood schooner, the *Felicité,* I prepared to ride out the gale under her bow. The skippers of the little fleet were very civil men. Some of them were of French and some of Spanish origin, while one or two were Germans. My charts interested them greatly; for though they had navigated their vessels for years upon the Gulf of Mexico, they had never seen a chart; and their astonishment was unbounded when I described to them the bottom of the sea for five hundred miles to the eastward, over a route I had never traveled. . . .

During the day I was visited by a young northerner who had been for some time in New Orleans, but was very anxious to return to his home in Massachusetts. He had no money, but thought if I would allow him to accompany me as far as Florida he could ship as sailor from some port on a vessel bound for New York or Boston. Feeling sorry for the man who was homeless in a strange city, and finding he possessed some experience in salt-water navigation, I acceded to his request. Having purchased of the harbormaster, Captain M. H. Riddle, a light boat, which was sharp at both ends, and possessed the degree of sheer necessary for seaworthiness, the next thing in order was to make some important alterations in her, such as changing the thwarts, putting on half decks, etc. . . .

On Saturday evening, January 22, I completed the joining and provisioning of the new skiff, which was called, in honor of the harbormaster, the *Riddle*. . . .

The next day my shipmate, whom, for convenience, I will call Saddles, was not prepared to leave, as previously agreed upon, so I turned over to him the *Riddle,* her outfit, provisions, etc., and instructed him to follow the west shore of Lake Pontchartrain until he found me, . . . Saddles had hunted and fished upon the lake, and therefore felt confident he could easily find me the next day at Irish Bayou, two miles beyond the low Point aux Herbes Lighthouse.

An hour before noon, on Monday, January 24, I rowed out of the canal, . . . A heavy fog covered the lake while I felt my way along the shore, passing the Pontchartrain railroad pier. The shoal bottom was covered with stumps of trees, and the coast was low and swampy, with occasional short, sandy beaches. My progress was slow on account of the fog; and at five P.M. I went into camp, having first hauled the boat on to the land by means of a small watch tackle. The low country was covered in places with coarse grass, and, as I ate my supper by the campfire, swarms of mosquitoes attacked me with such impetuosity and bloodthirstiness that I was glad to seek refuge in my boat. This proved, however, only a temporary relief, for the tormentors soon entered at the ventilating space between the combing and hatch, . . . During this night of torture I heard in the distance the sound of oars moving in the oarlocks, and paused for an instant in the battle with the phlebotomists, thinking the *Riddle* might be coming, but all sound seemed hushed, and I returned to my dreary warfare.

Not waiting to prepare breakfast the next morning, I left the prairie shore, and rowed rapidly towards Point aux Herbes. At the lighthouse landing I found Saddles, with his boat drawn up on shore. He had followed me at four and a half P.M., and the evening being clear, he had easily reached the lighthouse at eleven P.M. on the same night. . . .

At eleven A.M., though a fog shut out all objects from our sight, I set a boat compass before me on the floor of my craft, and . . . we struck across the lake in a course which took us to a point below the Rigolets, a name given to the passages in the marshes through which a large portion of the water of Lake Pontchartrain flows into the Gulf of Mexico. The marshes, or low prairies, which confine the waters of Lake Pontchartrain, are extensive. The coarse grass grows to four or five feet in height, and in it coons, wildcats, minks, hogs, and even rabbits, find a home. In the bayous wild fowl abound. . . .

The Rigolets are at the eastern end of Lake Pontchartrain. Their northern side skirts the mainland, while their south side is bounded by marshy islands. As we rowed through this outlet of the lake, Fort Pike, with its grassy banks, arose picturesquely on our right from its site on a knoll of high ground. Outside of the Rigolets we entered an arm of the Gulf of Mexico, called Lake Borgne, the shores of which were desolate, and formed extensive marshes cut up by creeks and bayous into many small islands.

As it was late in the day, we ran our two boats into a bayou near the mouth of the Rigolets, and prepared, under the most trying circumstances, to rest for the night. The atmosphere was soft and mild, the evening was perfect. The great sheet of water extended far to the east. On the south it was bounded by marshes. A long, low prairie coast stretched away on the north; it was the southern end of the state of Mississippi. The lighthouses flashed their bright beacon lights over the water. All was tranquil save the ever-pervading, persistent mosquito. Thousands of these insects, of the largest size and of the most pertinacious character, came out of the high grass. . . . We had not provided ourselves with a tent, and no artifice on our part could protect us from these torments; . . .

Our sleepless night coming at last to an end, we rowed, at dawn, along the prairie shores of the northern coast toward the open Gulf of Mexico. Back of the prairies the forests rose like a green wall in the distance. A heavy fog settled down upon the water and drove us into camp upon the prairie, where we endured again the torture caused by the myriads of bloodthirsty mosquitoes, and were only too glad to make an early start the next morning. A steady pull at the oars brought us to the end of a long cape in the marshes. About a mile and a half east of the land's end we saw a marshy island, of three or four acres in extent, out of the grass of which arose a small wooden lighthouse, resting securely upon its bed of piles. There was a broad gallery around the low tower, and seeing the lightkeeper seated under the shadow of its roof, we pulled out to sea, hoping to obtain information from him as to the "lay of the land." It was the Light of St. Joseph, and here, isolated from their fellow men, lived Mr. H. G. Plunkett and his assistant lightkeeper. . . .

The keeper, standing on his gallery, pointed out the village of Shieldsboro, nine miles distant, on the north coast, and we plainly saw its white cottages glimmering among the green trees.

Mr. Plunkett advised us not to return to the coast which we had just left, as it would necessitate following a long contour of the shore to reach Shieldsboro, but assured us that we could row nine miles in a straight course across the open Gulf to the north coast without difficulty. He argued that the rising wind was a fair one for our boats; and that a two-hour strong pull at the oars would enable us to reach a good camping place on high ground, while if we took the safer but more roundabout route, it would be impossible to arrive at the desired port that night, and we would again be compelled to camp upon the low prairies. We knew what that meant; and to escape another sleepless night in the mosquito lowland, we were ready to take almost any risk.

Having critically examined our oarlocks, and carefully ballasted our boats, we pulled into the rough water. The lightkeeper shouted encouragingly to us from his high porch, "You'll get across all right, and will have a good camp tonight!" For a long time we worked carefully at our oars, our little shells now rising on the high crest of a combing sea, now sinking deep into the trough, when one of us could catch only a glimpse of his companion's head. As the wind increased, and the sea became white with caps, it required the greatest care to keep our boats from filling. The lightkeeper continued to watch us through his telescope, fearing his counsel had been ill-advised. At times we glanced over our shoulders at the white sandbanks and forest-crowned coasts of Shieldsboro and Bay St. Louis, which were gradually rising to our view, higher and higher above the tide. The piers of the summer watering places, some of them one thousand feet in length, ran out into shoal water. Against these the waves beat in fury, enveloping the abutments in clouds of white spray. When within a mile of Shieldsboro the ominous thundering of the surf, bounding upon the shelving beach of hard sand, warned us of the difficulty to be experienced in passing through the breakers to the land.

It was a very shoal coast, and the sea broke in long swashy waves upon it. If we succeeded in getting through the deeper surf, we would stick fast in six inches of water on the bottom, and would not be able to get much nearer than a quarter of a mile to the dry land. Then, if we grounded only for a moment, the breaking waves would wash completely over our boats.

Having no idea of being wrecked upon the shoals, I put the duck boat's bow, with apron set, towards the combining waves, and let her drift inshore stern foremost. The instant the heel of the boat touched the bottom, I pulled rapidly seaward, and in this way felt the approaches to land in various channels many times without shipping a sea.

Saddles kept in the offing, in readiness to come to my assistance if needed. It became evident that we could not land without filling our boats with water, so we hauled off to sea, and took the trough easterly, until we had passed the villages of Shieldsboro and Bay St. Louis, when, like a port of refuge, the bay of St. Louis opened its wide portals, which we entered with alacrity, and were soon snugly camped in a heavy grove of oaks and yellow pines. Here we found an ample supply of dry wood and fresh water, with wild ducks feeding within easy gunshot of our quarters. There were no mosquitoes, and that fact alone rewarded us for our exertions and anxieties. . . .

FROM BILOXI TO CAPE SAN BLAS

On the morning of February 8 we left Biloxi, and launching our boats, proceeded on our voyage to the eastward, skirting shores which were at times marshy, and again firm and sandy. At Oak Point, and Belle Fontaine Point, green magnolia trees, magnificent oaks, and large pines grew nearly to the water's edge. Beyond Belle Fontaine the waters of Graveline Bayou flow through a marshy flat to the sea, and offer an attractive territory to sportsmen in search of wild fowl. Beyond the bayou, between West and East Pascagoula, we found a delta of marshy islands, and an area of mud flats, . . .

At sunset we ran into the mouth of a creek near the village of East Pascagoula, and there slept in our boats, which were securely tied to stakes driven into the salt marsh. At eight o'clock the next morning, the tide being low, we waded out of the stream, towing our boats with lines into deeper water, and rowed past East Pascagoula, which, like the other watering places of the Gulf, seemed deserted in the winter. The coast was now a wilderness, with few habitations in the dense forests, which formed a massive dark green background to the wide and inhospitable marshes. As we proceeded upon our voyage wild fowl and fish became more and more abundant, but few fishermen's boats or coasting vessels were seen upon the smooth waters of the Gulf. About dusk we ascended a creek, marked upon our chart as Bayou Caden, and passing through marshes, over which swarmed myriads of mosquitoes, we landed upon the pebbly beach of a little hammock, and there pitched our tent.

This portable shelter, which we had made at Biloxi, proved indeed a luxury. It was only six feet square at its base, weighing but a few pounds, and when compactly folded occupying little space; but after the first night's peaceful sleep under its sheltering care it occupied a large place in our hearts; for, having driven out the mosquitoes and closely fastened the entrance, we bade defiance to our tormentors, and realized by comparison, as we never did before, the misery of voyaging without a tent.

Moving out of the Bayou Caden the next day, a lot of fine oysters was collected in shoal water, and by a lucky shot, a fat duck was added to the menu.

We were now on the coast of Alabama, . . .

The wind rose from the south, giving us a head sea, but we pulled across the shallow bay, through which ran a channel called Grant's Pass, it having been dredged out to enable vessels to pass from Mississippi Sound to Mobile Bay. This tedious pull ended by our safe arrival at Dauphine Island, . . .

The following day the wind stirred up the wide expanse of water about the island to such a degree of boisterousness that we could not launch our boats. Our position was somewhat peculiar. Between Dauphine Island and the beach of the mainland opposite was an open ocean inlet of three and a half miles in width, through which the tide flowed. Fort Gaines commanded the western side of this inlet, while Fort Morgan menaced the intruder on the opposite shore. North of this Gulf portal was the wide area of water of Mobile Bay, extending thirty miles to Mobile City, while to the south of it spread the Gulf of Mexico, bounded only by the dim horizon of the heavens. To the east, and inside the narrow beach territory of the eastern side of the inlet, was Bon Secours Bay, a sort of estuary of Mobile Bay, sixteen miles in length. The passage of the exposed inlet could be made in a small boat only during calm weather, otherwise the voyager might be blown out to sea, or be forced, at random, into the great sound inside the inlet. In either case the rough waves would be likely to fill the craft and drown its occupant. In case of accident the best swimmer would have little chance of escape in these semitropical waters, as the man-eating shark is always cruising about, waiting, Micawber-like, for something "to turn up."

The windy weather kept us prisoners on Dauphine Island for two days, but early on the morning of February 13 a calm prevailed, taking advantage of which, we hurried across the open expanse of water, not daring to linger. . . .

We now entered a wide expanse of bay and river, with shores clothed with solemn forests of dark green. The wide Perdido River, rising in this region of dismal pines, flows between Bear Point and Inerarity's Point, when, making a sharp turn to the eastward, it empties into the Gulf of Mexico. In crossing the river between the two points mentioned, we were only separated from the sea by a narrow strip of low land. The Perdido River is the boundary line between the states of Alabama and Florida. In a bend of the river, nearly three miles east of Inerarity's Point, we landed on a low shore, having passed the log cabins of several settlers scattered along in the woods.

It was now necessary to make a portage across the low country to the next interior watercourse, called Big Lagoon. It was a shallow tidal sheet of water seven miles in length by one in width, and separated from the sea by a very narrow strip of beach. We camped in our boats for the night, starting off hopefully in the morning for the little settlement, to procure a team to haul our boats three quarters of a mile to Big Lagoon. The settlers were all absent from their homes, hunting and fishing, so we returned to our camp depressed in spirits. There was nothing left for us but to attempt to haul our boats over the sandy neck of land; so we at once applied ourselves to the task. The boats were too heavy for us to carry, so we dragged the sneak-box on rollers, cut from a green pine tree, half way to the lagoon; and, making many journeys, the provisions, blankets, gun, oars, etc., were transported upon our shoulders to the half-way resting place.

So laborious was this portage that when night came upon us we had hauled one boat only, with our provisions, tent, and outfit, to the beach of Big Lagoon. The *Riddle* still rested upon the banks of the Perdido River. The tent was pitched to shelter us from mosquitoes, and partaking of a hearty supper, we rolled ourselves in our blankets and slept. The camp was in a desolate place, our only neighbors being the coons, and they enlivened the solitude by their snarling and fighting, having come down to the beach to fish in apparently no amiable mood.

Before midnight, that unmistakable cry so human in its agonizing tone, warned us of the approach of a panther. Coming closer and closer, the animal prowled round our tent, sounding his childlike wail. It was too dark to get a glimpse of him, though we watched, weapons in hand, for his nearer approach. Saddles had hunted the beast in his Louisiana lairs, and was eager to make him feel the weight of his lead. We succeeded in driving him off once, but he returned and skulked in the bushes near our camp for half an hour, when his cries grew fainter as he beat a retreat into the forest. . . .

The morning of the tenth of February was calm and beautiful, while the songs of mockingbirds filled the air. Across the inlet of Pensacola Bay was the western end of the low, sandy island of Santa Rosa, which stretches in an easterly direction for forty-eight miles to East Pass and Choctawhatchee Bay, and serves as a barrier to the sea. Behind this narrow beach island flow the waters of Santa Rosa Sound, the northern shores of which are covered with the same desolate forests of yellow pine that characterize the uplands of the Gulf coast. At the west end of Santa Rosa Island the walls of Fort Pickens rose gloomily out of the sands. It was the only structure inhabited by man on the long barren island, with the exception of one small cabin built on the site of Clapp's steam mill, four miles beyond the fort, and occupied by a Negro.

We crossed the bay to Fort Pickens, and followed the island shore of the sound until five o'clock, when we sought a camp on the beach at the foot of some conspicuous sand hills, the thick scrub of which seemed to be the abode of numerous coons. From the top of the principal sand dune there was a fine view of the boundless sea. Our position, however, had its inconveniences, the principal one being a scarcity of water, so we were obliged to break camp at an early hour the next day. . . .

On Monday morning we rowed through West Bay, across the southern end of North Bay, and skirted the north coast of the East Bay of St. Andrew's, with its picturesque groves of cabbage palms, for a few miles, when we turned southward into the inlet through which the tidal waters of the Gulf pass in and out of the sound.

We were now close to the sea, with a few narrow sandy islands only intervening between us and the Gulf of Mexico, and upon these ocean barriers we found breezy camping grounds. Our course was by the open sea for six or eight miles, when we reached a narrow beach thoroughfare, called Crooked Island Bay, through which we rowed, with Crooked Island on our right hand, until we arrived at the head of the bay, where we expected to find an outlet to the sea. Being overtaken by darkness, we staked our boats on the quiet sheet of water, and at sunrise pushed on to find the opening through the beach. Not a sign of human life had been seen since we had left the western end of the East Bay of St. Andrew's Sound, and we now discovered that no outlet to the sea existed, and that Crooked Island was not an island, but a long strip of beach land which was joined to the main coast by a narrow neck of sandy territory, and that the interior watercourse ended in a creek.

Our portage to the sea now loomed up as a laborious task. We needed at least one man to assist us, and we were fully half a day's row from the nearest cabin to the west of us, while we might look in vain to the eastward, where the uninhabited coastline stretched away with its shining sands and shimmering waters for thirty miles to Cape San Blas. There, upon a low sand bar, against which the waves lashed out their fury, rose a tall light tower, the only friend of the mariner in all this desolate region. We could not look to that distant light for help, however, and were thrown entirely upon our own feeble resources.

Going systematically to work, we surveyed the best route across Crooked Island, which was over the bed of an old inlet; for a hurricane, many years before, washed out a passage through the sand spit, and for years the tide flowed in and out of the interior bay. Another hurricane afterwards repaired the breach by filling up the new inlet with sand; so Crooked Island enjoyed but a short-lived notoriety, and again became an integral part of the continent.

Our survey of the portage gave encouraging results. The Gulf of Mexico was only four hundred feet from the bay, and the shortest route was the best one; so, starting energetically, we dragged the boats by main force across Crooked Island, and launched them in the surf without disaster. We then rowed as rapidly as the rough sea would permit along the coast toward the wide opening of St. Joseph's Bay, the wooded beaches of which rose like a cloud in the soft mists of a sunny day. The bay was entered at four o'clock in the afternoon, and, being out of water, we hauled our boats high on to the beach, and searched eagerly for signs of moisture in the soil.

Leaving Saddles to build a fire and prepare our evening meal, I proceeded to investigate our new domain, and soon discovered the remains of a cabin near a station, or signal staff, of the United States Coast Survey. Men do not camp for a number of days at a time in places destitute of water; and the fact of the cabin having been built on this spot proved conclusively to me that water must be found in the vicinity. After a careful and patient search, I discovered a depression in the high sandy coast, and although the sand was perfectly dry, I thought it possible that a supply of water had been obtained here for the use of the United States Coast Survey party—the same party which had erected the cabin and planted the signal near it.

Going quickly to the beach, I found the shell of an immense clam, with which I returned, and using it as a scoop, or shovel, removed two or three bushels of sand, when a moist stratum was reached, and my clam shovel struck the chime of a flour barrel. In my joy I called to Saddles, for I knew our parched throats would soon be relieved. It did not take long to empty the barrel of its contents, which task being finished, we had the pleasure of seeing the water slowly rise and fill the cistern so lately occupied by the sand. In half an hour the water became limpid, and we sat beside our well, drinking, from time to time, like topers, of the sweet water. Our water cans were filled, and no stint in the culinary department was allowed that evening. . . .

FROM CAPE SAN BLAS TO ST. MARKS

A portage now loomed in our horizon. The distance across the neck of land was one-third of a mile only, but the ascent of the hills of the Gulf beach would prove a formidable task. I proposed to Saddles that he should return to the boats, while I hurried down the beach to the point of the cape to find a man to assist us in their transportation from the bay to the sea.

While discussing the plan, a noise in the thicket caught my ear, and turning our eyes to the spot, we saw two men hurrying from their ambush into the forest. We at once started in pursuit of them. When overtaken, they looked confused, and acknowledged that the presence of strangers was so unusual in that region that they had been watching our movements critically from the moment we landed until we discovered them. These men wore the rough garb of cow hunters, and the older of the two informed me that his home was in Apalachicola. He was looking after his cattle, which had a very long range, and had been camping with his assistant along St. Joseph's Sound for many days, being now en route for his home. Two ponies were tied to a tree in a thicket, while a bed of palmetto leaves and dried grass showed where the hunters had slept the previous night.

These men assured us that the happiest life was that of the cow hunter, who could range the forest for miles upon his pony, and sleep where he pleased. The idea was, that the nearer one's instincts and mode of life approached to that of a cow, the happier the man: only another version, after all, of living close to nature. One of these wood philosophers, taking his creed from the animals in which all his hopes centered, said we should be as simple in our habits as an ox, as gentle as a cow, and do no more injury to our fellow man than a yearling. He was certain there would be less sin in the world if men were turned into cattle; was sure cattle were happier than men, and generally more useful.

Upon learning our dilemma, the good-natured fellows set at once to work to help us. We cut two pine poles, and placing one boat across them, each man grasped an end of a pole, and thus, upon a species of litter, we lifted the burden from the ground and bore it slowly across the land to the sea. Returning to the bay, we transported the second boat in the same manner; and making a third trip, carried away our provisions, blankets, etc.

It was now evening, and viewing with satisfaction our little boats resting upon the beautiful beach, we thanked our new friends heartily for their kindness. The owner of a thousand cattle gave us a warm invitation to visit his orange grove in Apalachicola, and then retired with his man to their nest in the woods, while we slept in our boats, with porpoises and blackfish sounding their nasal calls all night in the sea which beat upon the strand at our feet.

In the morning the wind arose and sent the waves tumbling far in upon the beach. . . .

The boisterous weather kept us on the beach until Friday, when we launched our boats and rowed along the coast three miles to a point opposite a lagoon which was separated from the sea by a narrow strip of land. While pulling along the beach, great blackfish, some of them weighing at least one thousand pounds, came up out of the sea and divided into four companies. The first ranged itself upon our right, the second upon our left, the third, forming a school, proceeded in advance, while the fourth brought up the rear. Unlike the frisky porpoises, these big fellows convoyed us in the most dignified manner, heaving their dark, shining, scaleless bodies half out of the water as they surged along within a few feet of our boats.

When we arrived at our point of disembarkation, and turned shoreward to run through the surf, our strange companions seemed loath to leave us, but rolled about in the offing, making their peculiar nasal sounds, and spouting, like whales, jets of spray into the air. A landing was accomplished without shipping much water, and we immediately hauled the boats across the beach, about three or four hundred feet, into a narrow lagoon, the western branch of St. Vincent's Sound. . . .

FROM ST. MARKS TO THE SUWANEE RIVER

. . . On Monday, March 13, we left St. Marks River, and, as the north wind blew, were forced to keep from one to two miles off the land on the open Gulf to find even two feet of water. In many places we found rough pieces of coral rocks upon the bottom, and in several instances grounded upon them. As the wind went down, the tide, which on this coast frequently rises only from eighteen inches to two feet, favored us with more water, and by night we were able to get close to the marshes, and enter a little creek west of the Ocilla River, where, staking our boats alongside the soft marsh, we supped on chocolate and dry bread, and slept comfortably in our little craft until morning.

We were now in an almost uninhabited region, where only an occasional fisherman or sponger is met; but as we pulled along the coast the day after our camp in the marshes, we were struck with the absence of any sign of the presence of man. . . .

My companion had not been well for several days, and he informed me at this late date that he was subject to malarial fever, or, as he called it, "swamp fever." It had been contracted by him while living on one of the bayous of southern Louisiana during a warm season. Swamp fever, when at its height, usually produces temporary insanity; and he alarmed me by stating that he had been deprived of his reason for days at a time during his attacks. The use of daily stimulants had kept up his constitutional vigor for several months; but as ours was a temperance diet, he gradually, after we left Biloxi and the regions where stimulants could be obtained, became nervous, lost his appetite, and was now suffering from chills and fever. He was much depressed after leaving St. Marks, and had long fits of sullenness, so that he would row for hours without speaking. I tried to cheer him, and on one occasion penetrated the forest a long distance to obtain some panacea with which to brace his unsettled nerves.

Saddles had deceived me as to the necessity of taking daily drams, which habit is, to say the least, a most inconvenient one for persons engaged in explorations of isolated parts of the coast, and voyaging in small boats; so we had both suffered much in consequence of his bad habit. To furnish one moderate drinker with the liquid stimulant necessary for a boat voyage from New Orleans to Cedar Keys, at least five gallons of whiskey, and a large and heavy demijohn in which to store it securely, must form a portion of the cargo. This bulk occupies important space in the confined quarters of a boat, every inch of which is needed for necessary articles, while the momentary and artificial strength given to the system is never, except as a remediable agent, productive of any real or lasting benefit. My unfortunate companion had become so accustomed to the daily use of liquor, and his shattered system had been so propped by it, that he had been like a man walking on stilts; and now that they were knocked away, his own feet failed to support him, and a reaction was the inevitable result.

After leaving Rock Island, and when about four miles beyond the Fenholloway River, while off a vast tract of marshes, poor Saddles broke down completely. He could not row another stroke. I towed his boat into a little cove, and was forced to leave him, with the fever raging in his blood, that I might search for a creek, and a hammock upon which to camp. Looking to the east, I saw a long, low point of marsh projecting its attenuated point southward, while upon it rose a signal staff of the United States Coast Survey. A black object seemed heaped against the base of the signal; and while I gazed at what looked like a bear, or a heap of dark soil, it began to move, breaking up into three or four fragments, each of which seemed to roll off into the grass, where they disappeared.

I pulled for the point as rapidly as possible, for I hoped, while hardly daring to believe, that this singular apparition might be human beings. The high grass formed an impenetrable barrier for my curious vision; but nearing the spot, voices were plainly audible on the other side of the narrow point, as though a party of men were in lively discussion. Rowing close to the land, and resting on my oars to gain time to reconnoitre either friends or foes, the deep but cultivated voice of a man fell upon my ear. . . .

At this point the company struggled through the high grass and invited me to land. Being seriously alarmed for my companion, who was lying helpless in his boat half a mile away, I quickly explained my situation, and was at once advised to ascend Spring Creek, on the east side of the point of marsh, to the swamp, where the orator said I would find his camp, and his partner in the fishing business, who would assist me to the best of his ability. The orator promised to follow us after making one more cast with his seine for redfish. I returned as fast as possible to Saddles, and trying to infuse his failing heart with courage, fastened his boat's painter to the stern of the duck boat, and followed the course indicated by the fishermen.

Upon entering Spring Creek, with my companion in tow, we were soon encompassed on all sides by the marshes; and as the boats slowly ascended the crooked stream, the fringes of the feathery-crested palms appeared close to the margins of the savanna. The land increased in height a few inches as I followed the reaches of the creek, and, when a mile from its mouth, entered the rank luxuriance of a swamp, where, in a thicket of red cedars, palmettos, and Spanish bayonets, I discovered two low huts, thatched with palm leaves, which afforded temporary shelter to Captain F., a planter from the interior, . . . The kind-hearted captain understood my companion's case at a glance, and when our tent was pitched, and a comfortable bed prepared, Saddles was put under his care.

He could not have fallen into better hands, for the planter had gone through many experiences in the treatment of fevers of all kinds. It was indeed a boon to find in the unpeopled wilds a shelter and a physician for the sick man; but the future loomed heavily before me, for though Saddles might improve, he would be pretty sure on the eighth day to have a return of his malady, and would probably again break down in a raving condition. . . .

. . . Saddles did not improve. He seemed to be suffering from a low form of intermittent fever, and looked like anything but a subject for a long row. Captain F. insisted upon sending the invalid in his wagon sixteen miles to his home, where he promised to nurse the unfortunate man until he was able to travel forty miles farther to a railroad station. On the 15th of March, the party, having made their final arrangements, were ready to make the start for home. It was our last day together.

Circumstances over which I had no control forced me to part from Saddles. I furnished him with a liberal supply of funds to enable him to reach Fernandina, Florida, by rail, and afterwards sent him a draft for an amount sufficient to pay his expenses from Cedar Keys to New Orleans, as he abandoned all his previous intentions of returning to his old home in the north.

The *Riddle* with its outfit, and about sixty pounds of shot and a large supply of powder, I presented to the good captain who had so generously offered to care for my unfortunate companion. As I was to traverse the most desolate part of the coast between Spring Creek and Cedar Keys alone, I deemed it prudent to divest myself of everything that could be spared from my boat's outfit, in order to lighten the hull. I had made an estimate of chances, and concluded that four or five days would carry me to the end of my voyage, if the weather continued favorable; so, on the evening of March 15, the little duck boat was prepared for future duty. . . .

My boat was tied alongside the bank of the creek, close to the palmetto huts. There were only two feet of water in the stream as I sat in the little sneak-box at midnight and went through the usual preparations for stowing myself away for the night. I touched the clear water with my hands as it laved the sides of my floating home, but my gaze could not penetrate the limpid current, for the heavy shades of the palms gave it a dark hue. I thought of the duties of the morrow, and also of poor Saddles, who was tossing uneasily upon the blankets in his tent nearby, when there was a mysterious movement in the water under the boat. Something unusual was there, for its presence was betrayed by the large bubbles of air which came up from the bottom and floated upon the surface of the water. Being too sleepy to make an investigation, I coiled myself in my nest, and drew the hatch cover over the hold.

The next morning my friends clustered on the bank, giving me a kind farewell as I pushed the duck boat gently into the channel of the creek. Suddenly Saddles, who had been gazing abstractedly into the water under my boat, hurried into the tent, and in an instant reappeared with the gun I had given him in his hands. He slowly pointed it at the spot in the water where my boat had been moored during the night, and drawing the trigger, an explosion followed, while the water flew upward in fine jets into the air. Then, to the astonished gaze of the party on the bank, an alligator as long as my boat arose to view, and, roused by the shock, hurried into deeper water.

It was now evident what the lodger under my boat had been, and I confess the thought of being separated from this fierce saurian by only half an inch of cedar sheathing during a long night, was not a pleasant one; and I shuddered while my imagination pictured the consequences of a nocturnal bath in which I might have indulged. . . .

The morning sun was shining brightly as I pulled steadily along the coast, passing Warrior Creek six miles from my starting point off the shores of Spring Creek. About this locality the rocky bottom was exchanged for one of sand. Having rowed eleven miles, a small sandy island, one-third of a mile from shore, offered a resting place at noon; and there I dined upon bread and cold canned beef. A mile further to the eastward a sandy point of the marsh extended into the Gulf. A dozen oaks, two palmettos, and a shanty in ruins, upon this bleak territory, were the distinctive features which marked it as Jug Island, though the firm ground is only an island rising out of the marshes. Sandy points jutting from the lowlands became more numerous as I progressed on my route. Four miles from Jug Island the wide debouchure of Blue Creek came into view, with an unoccupied fishing shanty on each side of its mouth.

Crossing at dusk to the east shore of the creek, I landed in shoal water on a sandy strand, when the wind arose to a tempest, driving the water on to the land; and had it not been for my watch tackle, the little duck boat must have sought other quarters. As it was, she was soon high and dry on a beach; and once beneath her sheltering hatch, I slept soundly, regardless of the screeching winds and dashing seas around me.

Before the sun had gilded the waters the next morning, the wind subsided, my breakfast was cooked and eaten, and the boat's prow pointed towards the desolate, almost uninhabited, wilderness of Deadman's Bay. The low tide annoyed me somewhat, but when the wind arose it was fair, and assisted all day in my progress. The marine grasses, upon which the turtles feed, covered the bottom; and many curious forms were moving about it in the clear water. Six miles from Blue Creek I found a low grassy island of several acres in extent, and while in its vicinity frequently grounded; but as the water was shoal, it was an easy matter to jump overboard and push the lightened boat over the reefs.

About noon the wind freshened, and forced me nearer to the shore. As I crossed channelways, between shoals, the porpoises, which were pursuing their prey, frequently got aground, and presented a curious appearance working their way over a submarine ridge by turning on their sides and squirming like eels. By two o'clock the wind forced me into the bight of Deadman's Bay. The gusts were so furious that prudence demanded a camp, and it was eagerly sought for in the region of ominous name and gloomy associations. . . .

My voyage of twenty-six hundred miles was nearly ended. The beautiful Suwanee River, from which I had emerged in my paper canoe one year before, . . . was only a few miles to the eastward. Upon reaching its debouchure on the Gulf coast, the termini of the two voyages would be united. . . .

Entering the swift current of the river, I gazed out upon the sea, which was bounded only by the distant horizon. The sun was slowly sinking into the green of the western wilderness. A huge saurian dragged his mail-clad body out of the water, and settled quietly in his oozy bed. The sea glimmered in the long, horizontal rays of light which clothed it in a sheen of silver and of gold. The wild sea gulls winnowed the air with their wings, as they settled in little flocks upon the smooth water, as though to enjoy the bath of soft sunlight that came from the west. The great forests behind the marshes grew dark as the sun slowly disappeared, while palm-crowned hammocks on the savannas stood out in bold relief like islets in a sea of green. The sun disappeared, and the soft air became heavy with the mists of night as I sank upon my hard bed with a feeling of gratitude to Him whose all-protecting arm had been with me in sunshine and in storm. . . .

Ralph K. Wing
c. 1923

Rising in the Allegheny Mountains in western Pennsylvania, the Genesee River flows northward about 150 miles through western New York State, cuts through the center of the city of Rochester and empties into Lake Ontario in the adjoining town of Irondequoit. Some say Irondequoit, a native American name, means "where the waters gasp and die"; others give the translation as "opening into the lake."

Wing, a student at the University of Rochester, had the curiosity (and the canoe) to explore the river and its well-known gorge upstream. Through dangerous seldom-traveled waters he navigated the grand canyon of the east. Perhaps if he had known more about canoeing he would not have attempted it.

CANOEING ON THE GENESEE *

It might be supposed that a canoe cruise through thickly populated western New York would not afford much material for description. To strangers, the Genesee, if ever heard of, is known either as furnishing the water power of Rochester, or for giving rise to the falls over which Sam Patch met his death.† Even the average inhabitant of Rochester is familiar with the river only in the six miles between the city and Lake Ontario. This distance being navigable to steamers, he travels on it to reach the lake summer resorts; but, as the river carries away all the refuse of the city, he receives such an impression of the Genesee as would make a further acquaintance undesirable. To him, for all practical purposes, the Genesee river rises in Rochester and empties in Lake Ontario. Residing in Rochester, my curiosity impelled me to explore this mystery. So, last fall, actuated by a desire for discovery, but imbued with the prevailing idea with regard to the river, I ascended a few miles in a canoe. Charmed and delighted by the beauty of the scenery and the contrast to expectations, we concluded that we need not go abroad for canoeing grounds.

We found the current very swift, and, after becoming further acquainted with the stream, decided that we would begin up the river, and descend. We—Edmunds and myself—started in May, to avail ourselves of high water. As information from no other source was obtainable, we put our canoe aboard the cars, and then ascer-

* *Outing,* December 1885.

† Celebrated daredevil, author of the once famous catch-phrase, "Some things can be done as well as others," Sam Patch lost his life in a jump from a wooden scaffold twenty-five feet above the one-hundred-foot height of the verge of the Upper Falls of the Genesee at Rochester, 13 November 1829. He was born in Rhode Island, it is said, about 1807. W. T.

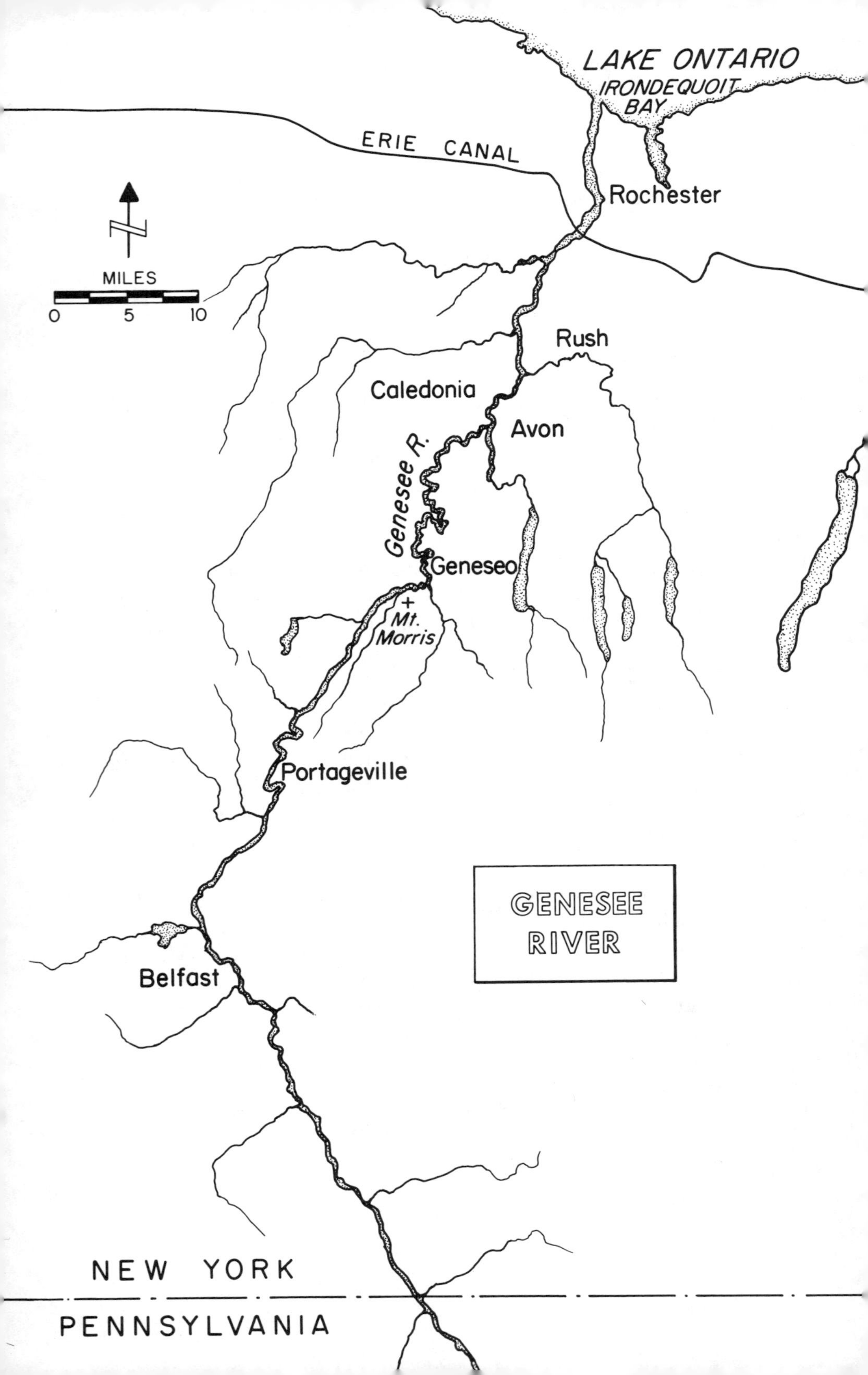
LAKE ONTARIO
IRONDEQUOIT BAY
ERIE CANAL
Rochester
MILES
0
5
10
Rush
Caledonia
Avon
Genesee R.
Geneseo
Mt. Morris
Portageville
GENESEE RIVER
Belfast
NEW YORK
PENNSYLVANIA

tained from the trainhands how far the river was navigable. From their advice we put in at Belfast, Allegany County, near the Pennsylvania line. We caught but few glimpses of the river from the cars, but these were such as to assure us that we would be amply repaid for our effort.

Belfast is country with the houses set a little closer together, that is all. To us, just from the city, it was well that we were initiated into rural life by staying overnight in this lesser country, otherwise the contrast might have been too great. We were entertained here by Prof. W——, a college friend. After making necessary purchases, and amid the best wishes of those assembled to see us off, we pushed out into the stream, of which we knew little.

We had had but little experience with swift water. Edmunds had never seen a rapid, except from the bank, and, although I had run several, I was little better than a novice; we noticed, therefore, with some trepidation, that the shores slipped past us faster than our exertions would seem to warrant. When, about half a mile below the village, we came upon a vigorous, full-grown rapid, our nervousness was turned into something like a panic; but we attacked it boldly, because that was the easiest thing to do, and struck when about half way down. We both jumped out and helped the canoe to float down, while I considered with some misgivings the probable effect to my fine cedar open canoe, if we had to use it to pound rocks for 200 miles. The next rapid was managed better. Each succeeding one seemed to treat us more tenderly, until, as our skill increased, we not only viewed the white water with equanimity, but looked forward to it with positive pleasure. We could soon tell, a hundred yards in advance of a rift, just where to go down; and if, because of a shoal extending all the way across the river, the passage was impracticable, we were able from the appearance of the water to take in the situation beforehand, press the bottom with the paddle to slacken the speed, and be in readiness to jump out before the canoe could strike. Now, in place of our former timidity, came a too great confidence, which nearly cost us dear. Late in the afternoon we reached a place where the river, covered with breakers and foam, rushed close to a high hill, and made a sharp bend. What this bend concealed we knew not—from the roar it might have been a fall. We ought to have landed and looked over the ground; but we did not, and we soon found ourselves on a down grade sufficient for coasting. Immense angular fragments of rock jutted up everywhere. By sharp turns to right and left we managed to get through, but upon inspecting the rapid from below it did not seem to afford an opening for a chip.

A mile farther down the river entered a gorge, and, by the dull thunder heard at a distance, we were forewarned that this must be our camping ground. To the eastward, the hills, covered with woods, overhang the water; on either side a flat ledge of rocks gently rises from the river's bed, and between them the Genesee plunges down several feet. Below, on the west, at the foot of the sloping bank, is a clean beach of shale. Here we camped. We had counted upon improvising a tent of rubber blankets and some cotton drilling we had bought for the purpose, but, alas for our hopes, the tent was a failure! However, we were well provided with clothing, and found that, as long as the rain held off, a tent was a superfluous luxury. All that night we saw the typical rapid; not this or that rapid encountered during the day, but *the* rapid. Instead of our canoe, the ground we were on, with its trees and stones, seemed to be floating, rolling, and plunging down a steep incline, to be lost in watery chaos.

The next day was Sunday. About a mile below, and back from the river, was a little village. We wished to enjoy the novel sensation of attending church at a place of whose name, history, inhabitants, and distance from any other place, we were totally ignorant. Between us and the village was a small fall, succeeded by a villainous rapid. We decided not to portage around these obstacles, and, on account of the shallowness, I went down alone. In an open canoe the paddler sits in the stern; with only one person in it, therefore, the canoe, in jumping a fall, with no more momentum than the current gives it, gets more than half over the brink before it leaves the horizontal. Add to its speed the headway given by the paddle and it will be seen that it does not make a vertical plunge, but takes its leap at only a slight incline. The main things to be observed are to select the deepest water and then give the boat as great a velocity as possible. I got over the falls in good shape, but, before losing my increased headway, ran sidewise upon a projecting rock. The water spurted in between the ribs, but the brave little craft recovered from the shock and passed down in safety.

That afternoon, for about three hours, we floated onward. Ours was, in truth, a "Sabbath-day's journey." We sat idly in the canoe, gliding swiftly and silently past green meadows with their curious herds; past forests just bursting into leaf; past hills that seemed now to advance, and now to recede from the river. So in sympathy with the peaceful scene did we feel that we appeared to lose our identity as spectators, and pass into, and form a part of, the landscape. Here and there an island would take its stand against the current. Into one of the narrow channels thus formed, we would sweep along under the cool shade of overhanging trees, to emerge with a rush into the broad vista where they again united, and feast our eyes upon the vivid green of spring. On one such occasion we found ourselves in a quiet pool, bordered in front and on the right by a hill. To the left the shore, from its dense vegetation, appeared to run down to the hill and cut off all avenue of escape, while behind us the two swift currents seemed to form tunnels in the all-pervading foliage. The turf at the water's edge and the fresh young leaves were so intensely, so acutely green, that, were it shown in a painting, the artist's fidelity to nature would be questioned.

That night we camped near a ford, within four miles of Portage. At Portage, as the name indicates, we had to make a carry, and for excellent reasons. The valley, some two miles broad, seems to terminate here. The river, after crossing from side to side, and doubling and turning, finally does a bold thing, and forces itself through an immensely deep gorge, over three falls. The first of these falls is the highest, sixty-nine feet. The others follow within three miles, and between them are heavy rapids and shoal water, while the banks, consisting of solid rock, rise vertically two or three hundred feet, with scarcely any interruption. Below this the gorge continues to Mt. Morris, thirty miles, with banks not so unbroken, but in some places even higher. We intended to descend this gorge—a feat seldom attempted.

We started early, to catch the eight o'clock train around the falls. We disembarked amid a curious and admiring company; for a canoe is a rare sight in New York, though common in Canada, and my costly and highly finished boat was enough to attract the attention even of canoemen. It was only a short carry to the station. Upon arrival, with an hour to spare, we took turns in going about the place and making our purchases, the one who remained being obliged, in order to satisfy the gaping rustic curiosity, to discourse upon the manner of construction, material, size, weight, cost, and other details regarding our canoe. About train time, among this motley crowd, appeared some ladies and a gentleman whom we thought were gotten up in a style out of keeping with the little hamlet. To our horror, upon second sight, we discovered them to be some city friends. Our first impulse was to flee and escape recognition; but we reflected that the canoe would explain our tramp-like appearance, and faced it out.

On the cars we again met the train hands with whom we had come up, and relied upon them, as before, for the best place to launch. They told us that Lewis's was the point. Since there are hardly any houses in this thirty-mile chasm, and as the knowledge of the stream can only be gained in the chasm, and it is very rarely that any one wishes to run the risk of going through it, information concerning the river is hard to obtain. We subsequently found that a knowledge of the mile or so of the gorge that can be seen from the railroad track was hardly sufficient to make a man a guide in a canoe trip from Portage to Mt. Morris.

With the cheery words of the expressman ringing in our ears, "I hope you'll get through all right, boys; drop me a postal when you reach Rochester;" and amid the waving of handkerchiefs, we were left beside the track. When we turned to telephone for an express wagon, we found the city to consist of one unpainted frame shanty. Upon inquiring there they told us they had no wagon, but neighbor B——, who lived about a mile up the hill, might accommodate us. Neighbor B——, after some persuasion, left his work in the field and harnessed up to a light, strong lumber wagon. A mile or so up the valley we could see where the river, after its last plunge, emerged from a deep black cleft in a solid wall of stone. From there, for a mile farther down than where we stood, the cliffs receded to give the river a chance to breathe ere it again sank into the darkness and turmoil of the deep defile. The only road for eight miles that leads into the ravine is at Lewis's. Down this we went, with many a jar and lurch, over places so steep that the wagon threatened to fall upon the horse.

We found the river to be very different from what it was above Portage. Instead of clay in the smooth places, and stones of a uniform size in the rapids, the river was paved with a bed of flat rocks in its quiet intervals, and in the rapids, scattered in promiscuous confusion, were boulders and jagged fragments which had fallen from the overhanging walls. The stream here lost the character of river, and became a mountain torrent. We had scarcely launched ere we came to as unprepossessing a rapid as any we had seen. It was a long steep rush, with breakers at the foot, the largest we had encountered. Edmunds went ahead by land, and then, with the speed of an express train, I sped down alone. In such a rapid one cannot wait till he sees the rocks through the water. If he waits, it is too late. He must be guided by their outward manifestations, the breakers. Wherever a big white-crested wave is visible, there is a rock just before it. In an instant I was dancing among the big waves at the foot; and, while I was congratulating myself that the worst was over, out of the river rose an island which projected itself before the boat. In an instant the choice of a channel was made, but, as I swept around the headland, I saw that a fall lay at the foot of the island. It was too late to retreat, and with a mighty effort I forced the canoe ahead. The stern struck with a great crash, the canoe halting a moment as if to turn broadside, but it did not, and then floundered over into the deep water below.

And now our attention was divided between thoughts for personal safety and the sublimity of our surroundings. At the end of the rapid just described we ran close to a wall that towered fully two hundred and fifty feet straight up from the river. On the opposite side was a narrow footing of land, which separated the river, by about a hundred feet, from the cliff. This strip of land, thickly covered with woods, possibly extended down on one side for a quarter of a mile; and then, as the river surged in and skirted the cliff, the fringe of land would reappear on the opposite side; and in this way it alternated for miles. How shall I describe the awful grandeur of the scene? High in air, on the verge of the precipice, a mass of virgin forest seeming to lie as lightly as clouds over the giddy space beneath; the beetling crags facing each other, showing the same strata, line for line, bare and black, scarred with deep seams, cut into bold points and promontories and grotesque shapes, the water flowing over the top in silvery cascades, to be dispersed in mist ere it reached the bottom, or issuing in springs to trickle down the sides; the thin strip of forest at the foot forming, with that above, living emerald layers, enclosing the dead, stony strata, while at the foot, echoing with roaring fury from point to point, the foam-crested river, rolling and tumbling down its rocky bed, all made a scene which it is mockery to attempt to express in words. . . .

But our thoughts were brought back to ourselves. After the first we ran, altogether, three rapids, without any accident aside from the big waves washing in; upon coming to the fifth, we saw that the river had broadened; all the way across, rocks appeared above the water, or lay just beneath the surface. The rocks became more numerous as we proceeded, and we slid up against one, at last, in a manner that threatened to tear the bottom out of the river, to say nothing of the canoe. Above Portage, as before stated, the rocks were generally small, and of uniform size, so that, with no shoes and stockings, it was easy enough to get out and keep dry. Below Portage, the rocks all being large and irregular, if one stepped from the rock he was on, he was as liable to find himself in four feet as in four inches of water. On this occasion, as Edmunds got out, the canoe floated broadside against him, threatening to shove him off the slippery surface into the deep water below. I relieved him, and although some distance from shore, since it was evident two could not go down, Edmunds told me to leave him. As I floated down, I looked round and saw him floundering nearly breast high in the swift current. Now began a mile of rapids in every way, to me, detestable. Every few feet I would strike, as I jumped from one stone to another, sometimes hip deep in the water, but always holding on to the canoe; and every minute I expected to have a hole made in the cedar, and our journey terminated here in the gorge where egress, except by water, seemed impossible. On one occasion, when I had an opportunity to look up, I saw Edmunds in the middle of the river making his way across. The strip of land on which he was walking had come to an end, and the only dry footing in the canyon was on the other side.

But at last this ended, and we found ourselves in a short stretch of still water. Here, on a beach of clean white sand, we cooked our dinner and rested from our labors. A short distance below there is a transverse gorge, equal in depth to the main one, throwing a clear, amber-colored stream into the river. Wading up this stream, for about a hundred feet, one finds himself at the bottom of a well-like hollow, almost covered at the top by the projecting branches of overhanging trees. At the left the stream comes down the cliff in two beautiful cascades, unseen and unheard from the river. The first cascade terminates in a deep basin, high above one's head. So wild was the picture, and so hidden from observation, that I felt like claiming the discovery of the spot.

Notwithstanding the improvement in the traveling I still floated alone. Another mile brought us to the only collection of houses in the canyon. This is the little hamlet of St. Helena, and is the place where *voyageurs* usually take to the river. We heard of but one instance of any one launching as near Portage as ourselves, and in that one case the boat was swamped, their camping kit lost, and their lives barely saved. Nevertheless, by far the finest scenery is between Portage and St. Helena. There is not a house or sign of human proximity in the entire distance; the cliffs are unbroken, and the gorge narrow; the cuts in the walls are finer and more varied. If one has a boat for which he does not care much, if he has plenty of time and patience to make carries, in order to avoid personal risk, I should unhesitatingly advise him to take in that part of the river between the lowest falls at Portage and St. Helena. From this place down to Rochester there was no difficulty in both occupying the canoe. Although these cliffs extend three-fourths of the distance between St. Helena and Mt. Morris, and the river is very swift, still the bottom land broadens, there are a few cultivated fields, and the river loses its torrent-like character.

We had hoped to reach Mt. Morris that night, and succeeded by good paddling. We arrived at seven in the evening, and wished there was no such place. There is a high dam here. All that can be seen of the town, from the river, is two houses on the east; by these houses is a road and a bridge across the Genesee, on which vehicles are constantly passing. There was no place near the river where the canoe could be kept, and the town lay back from it a mile and a half. It was now past twilight; but we could not stay there, and we did not wish to go back on our course for a camping ground; we therefore portaged around the dam, and took the risky expedient of running rapids in the dark. By the aid of the moon and instinct we got safely down two of them. We then pulled the canoe out among the trees and shrubbery on the bank; and, wrapping our bodies in blankets and our heads in rubber-goods, to keep off the mosquitos, slept until late in the morning.

The river, as we had known it, terminated at Mt. Morris. Here the Genesee receives a large creek. That is the way the map has it, but we should say that the Genesee flowed into the creek. The two streams are very dissimilar. The creek flows through a broad, alluvial valley; its banks being low, and the water quite turbid. Although the Genesee is the *river,* and has the larger amount of water, the creek stamps its character upon the stream, and thus seems to make it an affluent.

It took us some time to become used to our new surroundings, and we were never reconciled; still the novelty of the sudden change tempered our dislike for the disagreeable features. There was now plenty of water and, although rapids were not absent, no shallow places. So, without fear for the safety of canoe and cargo, we had leisure to observe. The most noticeable characteristic is the exceeding crookedness of the river's course; taking a conspicuous object, some distance from the water, we would be paddling straight for it, and the next minute our faces would be turned to an exactly opposite point of the compass. Hence the difficulty of ascertaining the distance between places. Few travel by the river, and the miles stated to reach a certain point, always given by land, stretch out into interminable leagues. By the road it is not ten miles from Mt. Morris to Geneseo, while I was informed by several that the distance by the river between those places was nearly forty miles!

We arrived at Geneseo early in the afternoon. Here there is a dam five or six feet high, over which the water poured in considerable volume. I had fully determined to run this; but as I sat there on the bank inspecting the fall while Edmunds was up town, the risk seemed too great and the advantage too little. Right below Geneseo, although the river is wide, two trees, on opposite sides of the Genesee, in longing for each other's company, regretting that they did not grow in the same soil, have stretched across the river and locked their leafy arms in loving embrace midway over the current. The stream is so wide, and the numerous other trees so straight, that it seems as if only an intelligent and concerted purpose could have brought about this strange coincidence. The trees all along here are grand. The banks of the river are not high, but sufficiently so, and so uniform as to prevent one's seeing what lies beyond. Along these banks is a fringe of trees that here and there widens into a stately grove, and has never been disturbed by the ax. These trees, consisting of elm, walnut, and hickory, are of the largest proportions, and frequently covered with a rich growth of wild grape or woodbine. The yielding alluvium is being constantly washed away, exposing an intricate network of fantastic roots, and, from time to time, toppling over into the stream the owners of these roots. The thickly crowded trees on the top of the banks, fresh and vigorous, shutting in the vision and keeping out the light; the trees nearer the water, undermined by the river, showing many dead branches, leaning upon each other in the utmost confusion; and down through the depths of the river the shadowy outlines of prostrated giants thrusting their white fingers up toward the surface, . . .

We were indifferent to the fishing, which had been one of the objects of our trip, for having found so much else to interest us we gave up the idea. In the upper waters of the river, and down to Geneseo, bass give the angler some fine sport; below this point pickerel abound, and the ordinary fresh-water fish can be caught. We carried no gun, but many times could have found use for one. The small fur-bearing animals are plentiful on the upper river, and time and again we startled ducks. From Piffard to Avon, ten miles, I amused myself with shooting with a revolver at everything I saw, while Edmunds paddled. The banks were lined with turtles just the color of the mud, and the first intimation one would have of their presence would be a splash in the water. A muskrat would stick his head above the surface to blink at us for an instant and disappear before he was fairly seen. Once, while chancing to look up, one of us discovered something swimming away below. The animal appeared as large as a dog, and whatever it was we wanted a shot. The discovery was mutual, the creature swimming desperately for the shore and we as vigorously paddling to prevent its landing. Just as we came tearing up it touched bottom. One shot made a big hole in the water; then another, and a poor little woodchuck lay dying on the beach. That was enough for me; the revolver was laid away and not disturbed again.

Upon rounding a bend two beautiful wood ducks rose before us and flew whistling out of sight. We had lost all thought of this incident, when two more ducks rose and bid us good-bye in the same hurried fashion. Several times this happened, and then we recognized these numerous couples to be but one. Very soon we struck up quite an acquaintance with the ducks. We would come upon them in the water. They would swim before us and herald our approach, till, as we came too near, they would go on again to await our arrival. Fully six miles we had their pleasant company; and, when at last some one frightened them from the river, we sadly missed the flash of their pretty mottled wings and their inspiring whistle. From a hunter's point of view we had to envy the next gunner who met those ducks. We had so tamed them that he would have easy work.

That night we reached the little hamlet of Rush. We pulled the canoe ashore and were immediately assailed by hordes of vagabond mosquitos. There was no hotel in the place, but we hastily decided that we must sleep under cover. We had become so accustomed to outdoor life that we could not bear to sleep in a regulation farmhouse room, with the windows nailed down, so we went to a rich-looking farmer's and asked permission to stay in his barn, which was readily granted. He tried to persuade us to stay in the house and have some supper; but no, we were roughing it, and had no occasion for such effeminate luxuries. Finally he brought out a lantern, and on the sweet hay, with the barn door wide open, we slept a dreamless sleep.

The next day, Thursday, was fuller of work than incident. We were within twenty-five miles (by river) of Rochester; Edmunds' time was up, and we wished to get back that day. As we proceeded, the river began to lose its sinuosities. A wind sprang up from the south, and we regretted that for which, before, we had often wished—a river that was straight. About six miles from the city houses began to appear. . . .

At two o'clock, by vigorous work, we had assured ourselves that we would reach the city in spite of the headwind. We then turned our thoughts to dinner. It was decided that this, our last meal on the Genesee, should be a feast. In keeping with this resolution we bought cream in place of the usual milk. After obtaining the cream we paddled on to find a suitable place for dinner. In fond anticipation we deluged our oatmeal with cream. Ugh! it was sour; the rough water had played us a scaly trick. This aroused Edmunds' slumbering genius, and he suggested that at that rate by the time we reached the city we would have butter. Not wishing to establish a dangerous precedent, and bring anything beside oleomargarine into Rochester, I decided to have the butter at once. Girding my loins I gave the tin pail a succession of vigorous shakes. Edmunds then relieved me, and so we alternated till success came to the rescue of our aching arms. That meal, with a good appetite, abundance of food, and, not least, butter of our own making, eaten on the soft turf after a hard day's work, will long linger in the memory.

Soon familiar landmarks appeared: the road close to the river; Mount Hope Cemetery, and the thickly clustering houses in the distance. Now we leave the river, and the canoe is put into the canal feeder. Down through the feeder, under bridges that are high enough, and over bridges that are too low; into the Erie Canal, past barges and houses and crowds of curious people; over the aqueduct, a carry through the dusty streets, and a voyage of pleasure and adventure is over.

Reuben Gold Thwaites
1853-1913

Rowing, paddling and camping out with his wife Jessie (W—— he called her in his narratives), Thwaites was a happy romantic, domestic canoeist. Born in Dorchester, Massachusetts, he grew up in Wisconsin, became secretary of the State Historical Society and in that capacity set out to trace the river routes of the early missionaries and explorers. What appealed to me, however, was not his historical commentary—I have deleted most of it—but his own observations as a voyager on the water. I especially liked the way he and his wife pulled together, their good nature in all kinds of spring and summer weather, their enjoyment of simple pleasures— wildflowers, riverside farms and villages and the everyday people they spoke with as they glided along.

HISTORIC WATERWAYS

PREFACE

There is a generally accepted notion that a brief summer vacation, if at all obtainable in this busy life of ours, must be spent in a flight as far afield as time will allow; that the popular resorts in the mountains, by the seaside, or on the margins of the upper lakes must be sought for rest and enjoyment; that neighborhood surroundings should, in the mad rush for change of air and scene, be left behind. The result is that your average vacationist—if I may be allowed to coin a needed word—knows less of his own state than of any other, and is inattentive to the delights of nature which await inspection within the limits of his horizon.

But let him mount his bicycle, his saddle horse, or his family carriage, and start out upon a gypsy tour of a week or two along the country roads, exploring the hills and plains and valleys of—say his congressional district; or, better by far, take his canoe, and with his best friend for a messmate explore the nearest river from source to mouth, and my word for it he will find novelty and fresh air enough to satisfy his utmost cravings; and when he comes to return to his counter, his desk, or his study, he will be conscious of having discovered charms in his own locality which he has in vain sought in the accustomed paths of the tourist. . . .

R. G. T.

Madison, Wis., December, 1887.

INTRODUCTION

Provided, reader, you have a goodly store of patience, stout muscles, a practiced fondness for the oars, a keen love of the picturesque and curious in nature, a capacity for remaining good-humored under the most adverse circumstances, together with a quiet love for that sort of gypsy life which we call "roughing it," canoeing may be safely recommended to you as one of the most delightful and healthful of outdoor recreations, as well as one of the cheapest.

The canoe need not be of birch bark or canvas, or of the Rob Roy or Racine pattern.* A plain, substantial, light, open clinker-build was what we used—thirteen feet in extreme length, with three-and-a-half feet beam. It was easily portaged, held two persons comfortably with seventy-five pounds of baggage, and drew but five inches—just enough to let us over the average shallows without bumping. It was serviceable, and stood the rough carries and innumerable bangs from sunken rocks and snags along its voyage of six hundred miles, without injury. It could carry a large spritsail, and, with an attachable keel, run close to the wind; while an awning, decided luxury on hot days, was readily hoisted on a pair of hoops attached to the gunwale on either side. . . .

The canoeist, from his lowly seat near the surface of the flood, sees the country practically as it was in pioneer days, in a state of unalloyed beauty. Each bend in the stream brings into view a new vista, and thus the bewitching scene changes as in a kaleidoscope. The people one meets, the variety of landscape one encounters, the simple adventures of the day, the sensation of being an explorer, the fresh air and simple diet, combined with that spirit of calm contentedness which overcomes the happy voyager who casts loose from care, are the never-failing attractions of such a trip. . . .

Some suggestions to those who may wish to undertake these or similar river trips may be advisable. Traveling alone will be found too dreary. None but a hermit could enjoy those long stretches of waterway, where one may float for a day without seeing man or animal on the forest-bounded shores, and where the oppression of

---

*The *Rob Roy,* a clinker-built cedar-decked canoe, was modeled after the craft in which the Scottish canoeist John "Rob Roy" McGregor (1825–1892) toured the rivers of Europe. His book, *A Thousand Miles in the Rob Roy Canoe,* appeared in 1866.

In the 1880s, the Racine Boat Company (Racine, Wisconsin) was considered one of the quality builders. W. T.

solitude is felt with such force that it requires but a slight stretch of imagination to carry oneself back in thought and feeling to the days when the black-robed members of the Company of Jesus first penetrated the gloomy wilderness. Upon the size of the party should depend the character of the preparations. If the plan is to spend the nights at farmhouses or village taverns, then a party of two will be as large as can secure comfortable quarters—especially at a farmhouse, where but one spare bed can usually be found, while many are the country inns where the accommodations are equally limited. If it is intended to tent on the banks, then the party should be larger; for two persons unused to this experience would find it exceedingly lonesome after nightfall, when visions of river tramps, dissolute fishermen, and inquisitive hogs and bulls, pass in review, and the weakness of the little camp against such formidable odds comes to be fully recognized. Often, too, the camping places are few and far between, and may involve a carry of luggage to higher lands beyond; on such occasions, the more assistance the merrier. But whatever the preparations for the night and breakfast, the mess box must be relied upon for dinners and suppers, for there is no dining car to be taken on along these water highways, and eating stations are unknown. Unless there are several towns on the route, of over one thousand inhabitants, it would be well to carry sufficient provisions of a simple sort for the entire trip, for supplies are difficult to obtain at small villages, and the quality is apt to be poor. Farmhouses can generally be depended on for eggs, butter, and milk—nothing more. For drinking water, obtainable from farm wells, carry an army canteen, if you can get one; if not, a stone jug will do. The river water is useful only for floating the canoe, and the offices of the bath. As to personal baggage, fly very light, . . .

Be prepared to find canoeing a rough sport. There is plenty of hard work about it, a good deal of sunburn and blister. You will be obliged to wear your old clothes, and may not be overpleased to meet critical friends in the river towns you visit. But if you have the true spirit of the canoeist, you will win for your pains an abundance of good air, good scenery, wholesome exercise, sound sleep, and something to think about all your life.

THE ROCK RIVER

It was a quarter to twelve, Monday morning, the twenty-third of May, 1887, when we took seats in our canoe at our own landing stage on Third Lake, at Madison, spread an awning over two hoops, as on a Chinese houseboat, pushed off, waved farewell to a little group of curious friends, and started on our way to explore the Rock River of Illinois. W—— wielded the paddle astern, while I took the oars amidships. Despite the one hundred pounds of baggage and the warmth emitted by the glowing sun—for the season was unusually advanced—we made excellent speed, as we well had need in order to reach the mouth, a distance of two hundred and eighty miles as the sinuous river runs, in the seven days we had allotted to the task.

It was a delightful run across the southern arm of the lake. There was a light breeze aft, which gave a graceful upward curvature to our low-set awning. The great elms and lindens at charming Lakeside—the home of the Wisconsin Chautauqua—droop over the boulder-studded banks, their masses of greenery almost sweeping the water. Down in the deep, cool shadows groups of bass and pickerel and perch lazily swish; swarms of "crazy bugs" ceaselessly swirl around and around, with no apparent object in life but this rhythmic motion, by which they wrinkle the mirror-like surface into concentric circles. Through occasional openings in the dense fringe of pendent boughs, glimpses can be had of park-like glades, studded with columnar oaks, and stretching upward to hazel-grown knolls, which rise in irregular succession beyond the bank. From the thickets comes the fussy chatter of thrushes and catbirds, . . .

A quarter of an hour sent us spinning across the mouth of Turvill's Bay. At Ott's Farm, just beyond, the bank rises with sheer ascent, in layers of crumbly sandstone, a dozen feet above the water's level. Close-cropped woodlawn pastures gently slope upward to storm-wracked orchards, and long, dark windbreaks of funereal spruce. Flocks of sheep, fresh from the shearing, trot along the banks, winding in and out between the trees, keeping us company on our way—their bleating lambs following at a lope—now and then stopping, in their eager, fearful curiosity, to view our craft, and assuming picturesque attitudes, worthy subjects for a painter's art.

A long, hard pull through close-grown patches of reeds and lily pads, encumbered by thick masses of green scum, brought us to the

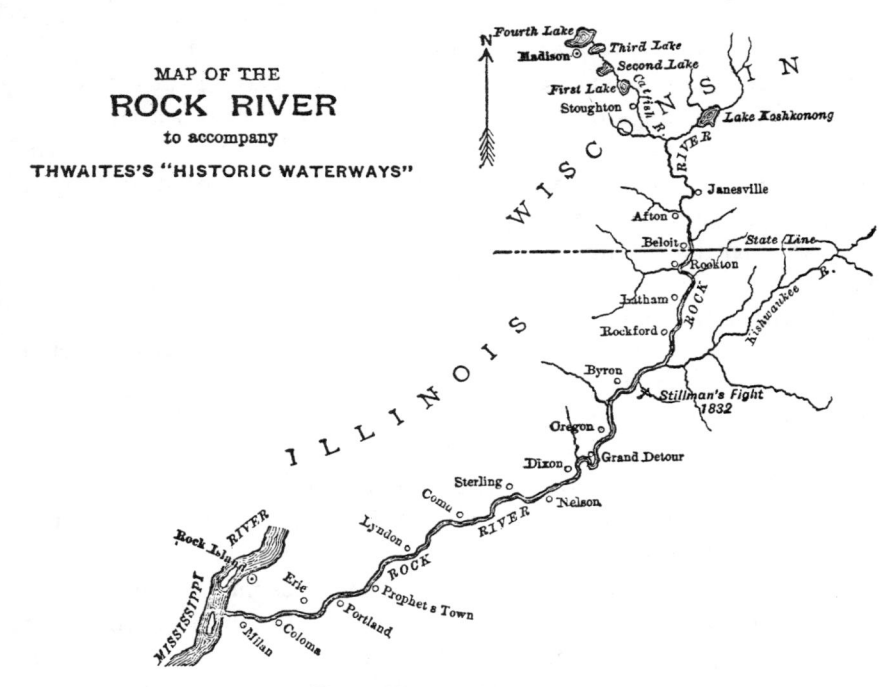

MAP OF THE
ROCK RIVER
to accompany
THWAITES'S "HISTORIC WATERWAYS"

From *Historic Waterways*

outlet of the lake and the head of that section of the Catfish River which is the medium through which Third Lake pours its overflow into Second. The four lakes of Madison are connected by the Catfish, the chief Wisconsin tributary of the Rock. Upon the map this relationship reminds one of beads strung upon a thread.

As the result of a protracted drought, the water in the little stream was low, and great clumps of aquatic weeds came very close to the surface, threatening, later in the season, an almost complete stoppage to navigation. But the effect of the current was at once perceptible. It was as if an additional rower had been taken on.

The river, the open stream of which is some three rods wide at this point, winds like a serpent between broad marshes, . . . In high water, even now, the marshes are converted into widespreads, where the dense tangle of wild rice, reeds, and rushes does not wholly prevent canoe navigation; while little mud-bottomed lakes, a quarter of a mile or so in diameter, are frequently met with at all stages. . . . In the widespreads, the progress is sluggish, the vegetable growth so crowding in upon the stream as to leave but a narrow and devious channel, requiring skill to pilot through; for in these labyrinthian turnings one is quite liable, if not closely watching the lazy flood, to push into some vexatious cul-de-sac, many rods in length, and be obliged to retrace, with the danger of mistaking a branch for the main channel.

In the depths of the tall reeds motherly mud hens are clucking, while their mates squat in the open water, in meditative groups, rising with a prolonged splash and a whirr as the canoe approaches within gunshot. Secluded among the rushes and cattails, nestled down in little clumps of stubble, are hundreds of the cup-shaped nests of the red-winged blackbird, or American starling; the females, in modest brown, take a rather pensive view of life, administering to the wants of their young; while the bright-hued, talkative males, perched on swaying stalks, fairly make the air hum with their cheery trills.

Water lilies abound everywhere. The blossoms of the yellow variety (*nuphar advena*) are here and there bursting in select groups, but as a rule the buds are still below the surface. In the mud lakes, the bottom is seen through the crystal water to be thickly studded with great rosettes, two and three feet in diameter, of corrugated ovate leaves, of golden russet shade, out of which are shot upward brilliant green stalks, some bearing arrow-shaped leaves, and others crowned with the tight-wrapped buds that will soon open upon the water level into saffron-hued flowers. The plate-like leaves of the white variety (*nymphaea tuberosa*) already dot the surface, but the buds are not yet visible. Anchored by delicate stems to the creeping root stalks, buried in the mud below, the leaves, when first emerging, are of a rich golden brown, but they are soon frayed by the waves, and soiled and eaten by myriads of water bugs, slugs, and spiders, who make their homes on these floating islands. Pluck a leaf, and the many-legged spiders, the roving buccaneers of these miniature seas, stalk off at high speed, while the slugs and leeches, in a spirit of stubborn patriotism, prefer meeting death upon their native heath to politic emigration.

By one o'clock we had reached the railway bridge at the head of Second Lake. Upon the trestlework were perched three boys and a man, fishing. They had that listless air and unkempt appearance which are so characteristic of the little groups of humanity often to be found on a fair day angling from piers, bridges, and railway embankments. Men who imagine the world is allied against them will loll away a dozen hours a day, throughout an entire summer season, sitting on the sun-heated girders of an iron bridge; yet they would strike against any system in the work-a-day world which compelled them to labor more than eight hours for ten hours' pay. In going down a long stretch of water highway, one comes to believe that about one quarter of the inhabitants, especially of the villages, spend their time chiefly in fishing. On a canoe voyage, the bridge fishermen and the birds are the classes of animated nature most frequently met with, the former presenting perhaps the most rare and varied specimens. There are fishermen and fishermen. I never could fancy Izaak Walton dangling his legs from a railroad bridge, soaking a worm at the end of a length of store twine, vainly hoping, as the hours went listlessly by, that a stray sucker or a diminutive catfish would pull the bob under and score a victory for patience. Now the use of a boat lifts this sort of thing to the dignity of a sport.

Second Lake is about three miles long by a mile in breadth. The shores are here and there marshy; but as a rule they are of good, firm land with occasional rocky bluffs from a dozen to twenty feet high, rising sheer from a narrow beach of gravel. As we crossed over to gain the lower Catfish, a calm prevailed for the most part, and the awning was a decided comfort. Now and then, however, a delightful puff came ruffling the water astern, swelling our canvas roof and noticeably helping us along. Light cloudage, blown swiftly before upper aerial currents, occasionally obscured the sun—black, gray, and white cumuli fantastically shaped and commingled, while through jagged and rapidly shifting gaps was to be seen with vivid effect, the deep blue ether beyond.

The bluffs and glades are well wooded. The former have escarpments of yellow clay and grayish sand and gravel; here and there have been landslides, where great trees have fallen with the débris and maintain but a slender hold amid their new surroundings, leaning far out over the water, easy victims for the next tornado. One monarch of the woods had been thus precipitated into the flood; on one side, its trunk and giant branches were water-soaked and slimy, while those above were dead and whitened by storm. As we approached, scores of turtles, sunning themselves on the unsubmerged portion, suddenly ducked their heads and slid off their perches amid a general splash, to hidden grottos below; while a solitary kingfisher from his vantage height on an upper bough, hurriedly rose, and screamed indignance at our rude entry upon his preserve.

A farmer's lad sitting squat upon his haunches on the beach, and another, leaning over a pasture fence, holding his head between his hands, exhibited lamb-like curiosity at the awning-decked canoe, as it glided past their bank. Through openings in the forest, we caught glimpses of rolling upland pastures, with sod close-cropped and smooth as a well-kept lawn; of gray-blue fields, recently seeded; of farmhouses, spacious barns, tobacco-curing sheds—for this is the heart of the Wisconsin tobacco region—and those inevitable signs of rural prosperity, windmills, spinning around by spurts, obedient to the breath of the intermittent May-day zephyr; while little bays opened up, on the most distant shore, enchanting vistas of blue-misted ridges.

At last, after a dreamy pull of two miles from the lakehead, we rounded a bold headland of some thirty feet in height, and entered Catfish Bay. Ice-pushed boulders strew the shore, which is here a gentle meadow slope, based by a gravel beach. A herd of cattle are contentedly browsing, their movements attuned to a symphony of cowbells dangling from the necks of the leaders. The scene is pre-eminently peaceful.

The Catfish, connecting Second Lake with First, has two entrances, a small flat willow island dividing them. Through the eastern channel, which is the deepest, the current goes down with a rush, the obstruction offered by numerous boulders churning it into noisy rapids; but the water tames down within a few rods, and the canoe comes gayly gliding into the united stream, which now has a placid current of two miles per hour—quite fast enough for canoeing purposes. This section of the Catfish is much more picturesque than the preceding; the shores are firmer; the parallel ridges sometimes closely shut it in, and the stream, here four or five rods wide, takes upon itself the characteristics of the conventional river. The weed- and vine-grown banks are oftentimes twenty feet in height, with as sharp an ascent as can be comfortably climbed; and the swift-rushing water is sometimes fringed with sumachs, elders, and hazel brush, with here and there willows, maples, lindens, and oaks. Occasionally the river apparently ends at the base of a steep, earthy bluff; but when that is reached there is a sudden swerve to the right or left, with another vista of banks—sometimes wood-grown to the water's edge, again with openings revealing purplish-brown fields, neatly harrowed, stretching up to some commanding, forest-crowned hilltop. The blossoms of the wild grape burden the air with sweet scent; . . .

There are charming rustic pictures at every turn—sleek herds of cattle, droves of fat hogs, flocks of sheep that have but recently doffed their winter suits, well-tended fields, trim-looking wire fences, neat farmhouses where rows of milk pans glisten upon sunny drying-benches, farmers and farmers' boys riding aristocratic-looking sulky drags and cultivators—everywhere an air of agricultural luxuriance, rather emphasized by occasional log houses, which repose as honored relics by the side of their pretentious successors, sharply contrasting the wide differences between pioneer life and that of to-day.

The marshes are few; and they in this dry season are luxuriant with coarse, glossy wild grass—the only hay crop the farmer will have this year—and dotted with clumps of dead willow trees, which present a ghostly appearance, waving their white, scarred limbs in the freshening breeze. . . .

Darting under a quaint rustic footbridge made of rough poles, which on its high trestles stalks over a wide expanse of reedy bog like a giant stick bug, we emerged into First Lake. The eastern shore, which we skirted, is a wide, sandy beach, backed by meadows. The opposite banks, two or three miles away, present more picturesque outlines. A stately wild swan kept us company for over a mile, just out of musket shot, and finally took advantage of a patch of rushes to stop and hide. A small sandstone quarry on the southeast shore, with a lone worker, attracted our attention. There was not a human habitation in sight, and it seemed odd to see a solitary man engaged in such labor apparently so far removed from the highways of commerce. The quarryman stuck his crowbar in a crack horizontally, to serve as a seat, and filled his pipe as we approached. We hailed him with inquiries, from the stone pier jutting into the lake at the foot of the bluff into which he was burrowing. He replied from his lofty perch, in rich Norsk brogue, that he shipped stone by barge to Stoughton, and good-humoredly added, as he struck a match and lit his bowl of weed, that he thought himself altogether too good company to ever get lonesome. We left the philosopher to enjoy his pipe in peace, and passed on around the headland. . . .

Three miles above Stoughton, we stopped for supper at the edge of a glade, near a quaint old bridge. . . .

We were off in the morning, after an early breakfast at the Stoughton inn. Our host kindly sent down his porter to help us over the milldam—our first and easiest portage, and one of the few in which we received assistance of any kind. Below this, as below all of the dams on the river, there are broad shallows. The water in the stream, being at a low stage, is mainly absorbed in the millrace, and the apron spreads the slight overflow evenly over the width of the bed, so that there is left a wide expanse of gravel and rocks below the chute, which is not covered sufficiently deep for navigating even our little craft, drawing but five inches when fully loaded. We soon grounded on the shallows and I was obliged to get out and tow the lightened boat to the tail of the race, where deeper water was henceforth assured. This experience became quite familiar before the end of the trip. I had fortunately brought a pair of rubbers in my satchel, and found them invaluable as wading shoes, where the river bottom is strewn with sharp gravel and slimy roundheads.

Below Stoughton the river winds along in most graceful curves, for the most part between banks from six to twenty feet high, with occasional pocket marshes, in which the skunk cabbage luxuriates. The stream is often thickly studded with lilypads, which the wind, blowing fresh astern, frequently ruffles so as to give the appearance of rapids ahead, inducing caution where none is necessary. But every half mile or so there are genuine little rapids, some of them requiring care to successfully shoot; in low water the canoe goes bumping along over the small moss-grown rocks, and now and then plumps solidly on a big one; when the stream is turbid—as often happens below a pasture, where the cattle stir up the bank mud—the danger of being overturned by scarcely submerged boulders is imminent.

There are some decidedly romantic spots, where little densely wooded and grape-tangled glens run off at right angles, leading up to the bases of commanding hillocks, which they drain; or where the noisy little river, five or six rods wide, goes swishing around the foot of a precipitous, bush-grown bluff. It is noticeable that in such beauty spots as these are generally to be found poverty-stricken cabins, the homes of small fishermen and hunters; while the more generous farmhouses seek the fertile but prosaic openings.

All of a sudden, around a lovely bend, a barbed-wire fence of four strands savagely disputed the passage. A vigorous backwater stroke alone saved us from going full tilt into the bayonets of the enemy. We landed, and there was a council of war. As every stream in Wisconsin capable of floating a saw log is "navigable" in the eye of the law, it is plain that this obstruction is an illegal one. Being an illegal fence, it follows that any canoeist is entitled to clip the wires, if he does not care to stop and prosecute the fencers for barring his way. The object of the structure is to prevent cattle from walking around through the shallow river into neighboring pastures. Along the upper Catfish, where boating is more frequently indulged in, farmers accomplish the same object by fencing in a few feet of the stream parallel with the shore. But below Stoughton, where canoeing is seldom practiced, the cattle owners run their fences directly across the river as a measure of economy. Taking into consideration the fact that the lower Catfish is seldom used as a highway, we concluded that we would be charitable and leave the fences intact, getting under or over them as best we might. I am afraid that had we known that twenty-one of these formidable barriers were before us, the council would not have agreed on so conciliatory a campaign.

Having taken in our awning and disposed of our baggage amidships, so that nothing remained above the gunwale, W——, kneeling, took the oars astern, while I knelt in the bow with the paddle borne like a battering-ram. Pushing off into the channel we bore down on the center of the works, which were strong and thickly posted, with wires drawn as tight as a drum-string. Catching the lower strand midway between two posts, on the blade end of the paddle, the speed of the canoe was checked. Then, seizing that strand with my right hand, so that the thick-strewn barbs came between my fingers, I forced it up to the second strand, and held the two rigidly together, thus making a slight arch. The canoe being crowded down into the water by sheer exercise of muscle, I crouched low in the bow, at the same time forcing the canoe under and forward through the arch. When half-way through, W—— was able similarly to clutch the wires, and perform the same office for the stern. This operation, ungraceful but effective, was frequently repeated during the day. When the current is swift and the wind fresh a special exertion is necessary on the part of the stern oar to keep the craft at right angles with the fence—the tendency being, as soon as the bow is snubbed, to drift alongside and become entangled in the wires, with the danger of being either badly scratched or upset. It is with a feeling of no slight relief that a canoeist emerges from a tussle with a barbed-wire fence; and if hands, clothing, and boat have escaped without a scratch, he may consider himself fortunate, indeed. Before the day was through, when our twenty-one fences had been conquered without any serious accident, it was unanimously voted that the exercise was not to be recommended to those weak in muscle or patience. . . .

A few miles downstream and we come to Stebbinsville. The water is backset by a milldam for two miles, forming a small lake. The course now changing, the wind came dead ahead, and we rowed down to the dam in a rolling sea, with much exertion. The river is six rods wide here, flowing between smooth, well-rounded, grass-grown banks, from fifteen to thirty feet in height, the fields on either side sloping up to wood-crowned ridges. There are a mill and two houses at Stebbinsville, and the country round about has a prosperous appearance. A tall, pleasant-spoken young miller came across the roadbridge and talked to us about the crops and the river, while we made a comfortable portage of five rods, up the grassy bank and through a close-cropped pasture, down to a sequestered little bay at the tail of an abandoned race, where the spray of the falls spattered us as we reloaded. We pushed off, with the joint opinion that Stebbinsville was a charming little place, with ideal riverside homes, that would be utterly spoiled by building the city on its site which the young man said his father had always hoped would be established there. A quarter of a mile below, around the bend, is a disused mill, thirty feet up, on the right bank. There is a suspended platform over a ravine, to one side of the building, and upon its handrail leaned two dusty millers, who had doubtless hastened across from the upper mill, to watch the progress down the little rapids here of what was indeed a novel craft to these waters. They waved their caps and gave us a cheery shout as we quickly disappeared around another curve; but while it still rang in our ears we were suddenly confronted by one of the tightest fences on the course, and had neither time nor disposition to return the salute.

And so we slid along, down rapids, through long stretches of quiet water and scraping over shallows, plying both oars and paddle, while now and then "making" a fence and comparing its savagery with that of the preceding one. Here and there the high vine-clad banks, from overshadowing us would irregularly recede, leaving little meadows full of painted cups, the wild rose-colored phlox and saxifrage, or bits of woodland in the dryer bottoms, radiant, amid the underbrush, with the daisy, cinquefoil, and puccoon. Kingfishers and blue herons abound. Great turtles, disturbed by the unwonted splash of oars, slide down high, sunny banks of sand, where they have been to lay their eggs, and amid a cloud of dust shuffle off into the water, their castle of safety. These eggs, so trustfully left to be hatched by the warmth of the sun, form toothsome food for coons and skunks, which in turn fall victims to farmers' lads—as witness the rows of pelts stretched inside out on shingles, and tacked up on the sunny sides of the barns and woodsheds along the river highway.

As we begin to approach the valley of the Rock, the hills grow higher, groups of red cedar appear, the banks of red clay often attain the height of fifty or sixty feet, broken by deep, staring gullies and wooded ravines, through which little brooklets run, the output of back-country springs, while the pocket meadows are less frequent, although more charmingly diversified as to color and background.

We had our midday lunch on a pleasant bank, that had been covered earlier in the season with hepatica, bloodroot, and dicentra, and was now replendent with Solomon's seal, the dark-purple waterleaf, and graceful maidenhair ferns, with here and there a dogwood in full bloom. Behind us were thick woods and an overlooking ridge; opposite, a meadow glade on which herds of cattle and black hogs grazed. A bell cow waded into the water, followed by several other members of the herd, and the train pensively proceeded in single file diagonally across the shallow stream to another feeding ground below. The leader's bell had a peculiarly mournful note, and the scene strongly reminded one of an ecclesiastical procession.

In the middle of the afternoon the little village of Fulton was reached. It is a dead-alive, moss-grown settlement, situated on a prairie, through which the river has cut a deep channel. There are a cheese factory, a gristmill, a church, a schoolhouse, three or four stores, and some twenty-five houses, with but a solitary boat in sight, and that of the punt variety. It was recess at the school as we rowed past, and boys and girls were chiefly engaged in climbing the trees which cluster in the little schoolhouse yard. A chorus of shouts and whistles greeted us from the leafy perches, in which we could distinguish "Shoot the roof!"—an exclamation called forth by the awning, which doubtless seemed the chief feature of our outfit, viewed from the top of the bank. . . .

Below Fulton, the stream is quite swift and the scenery more rugged, the evidences of disastrous spring overflows and backwater from the Rock being visible on every hand. At five o'clock, we came to a point where the river divides into three channels, there being a clump of four small islands. A barbed-wire fence, the last we were fated to meet, was stretched across each channel. Selecting the central mouth—for this is the delta of the Catfish—we shot down with a rush, but were soon lodged on a sandbank. It required wading and much pushing and twisting and towing before we were again off, but in the length of a few rods more we swung free into the Rock, which was to be our highway for over two hundred miles more of canoe travel.

The Rock River is nearly a quarter of a mile wide at this point, and comes down with a majestic sweep from the north, having its chief source in the gloomily picturesque Lake Koshkonong. The banks of the river at and below the mouth of the Catfish are quite imposing, rising into a succession of graceful, round-topped mounds, from fifty to one hundred feet high, and finely wooded except where cleared for pasture or as the site of farm buildings. While the immediate edges of the stream are generally firm and grass-grown, with occasional gravelly beaches, there are frequent narrow strips of marsh at the bases of the mounds, especially on the left bank where innumerable springs send forth trickling rills to feed the river. A stiff wind upstream had broken the surface into whitecaps, and more than counteracted the force of the lazy current, so that progress now depended upon vigorous exercise at the oars and paddle.

Three miles above Janesville is Pope's Springs, a pleasant summer resort, with white tents and gayly painted cottages commingled. It is situated in a park-like wood on the right bank, while directly opposite are some bold, rocky cliffs, or palisades, their feet laved in the stream. We spread our supper cloth on the edge of a wheatfield, in view of the pretty scene. The sun was setting behind a bank of roseate clouds, and shooting up broad, sharply defined bands of radiance nearly to the zenith. The wind was blowing cold, wraps were essential, and we were glad to be on our way once more, paddling along in the dying light, past palisades and fields and meadows, reaching prosperous Janesville, on her rolling prairie, just as dusk was thickening into dark.

We had an early start from the hotel next morning. A prospect of the situation at the upper Janesville dam, from a neighboring bridge, revealed the fact that the millrace along the left bank afforded the easiest portage. Reloading our craft at the boat renter's staging where it had passed the night, we darted across the river, under two low-hung bridges, keeping well out of the overflow current and entered the race, making our carry over a steep and rocky embankment.

Below, after passing through the center of the city, the river widens considerably, as it cuts a deep channel through the fertile prairie, and taking a sudden bend to the southwest, becomes a lake, formed by backwater from the lower dam. The wind was now dead ahead again, and fierce. Whitecaps came savagely rolling upstream. The pull down brought out the rowing muscles to their fullest tension. The canoe at times would appear to scarcely creep along, although oars and paddle would bend to their work.

The race of the carding mill, which we were now approaching, is by the left bank, the rest of the broad river—fully a third of a mile wide here—being stemmed by a ponderous, angling dam, the shorter leg of which comes dangerously close to the entrance of the race, which it nearly parallels. Overhead, fifty feet skyward, a great railway bridge spans the chasm. The disposition of its piers leaves a rowing channel but two rods wide, next the shore. Through this a deep, swift current flows, impelling itself for the most part over the short leg of the chute, with a deafening roar. Its backset, however, is caught in the yawning mouth of the race. It so happens then that from either side of an ugly whirling strip of doubting water, parallel with the shorter chute, the flood bursts forth—to the left plunging impetuously over the apron to be dashed to vapor at its foot; to the right madly rushing into the narrow race, to turn the wheels of the carding mill half a mile below. This narrow channel, under the bridge and next the shore, of which I have spoken, is the only practicable entrance to the race.

We had landed above and taken a panoramic view of the situation from the deck of the bridge; afterward had descended to the floodgates at the entrance of the race, for detailed inspection and measurements. One of the set of three gates was partly raised, the bottom being but three feet above the boiling surface, while the great vertical iron beams along which the cogwheels work were not over four feet apart. It would require steady hands to guide the canoe to the right of the whirl, where the flood hesitated between two destinations, and finally to shoot under the uplifted gate, which barely gave room in either height or breadth for the passage of the boat. But we arrived at the conclusion that the shoot was far more dangerous in appearance than in reality, and that it was preferable to a long and exceedingly irksome portage.

So we determined to make the attempt, and walked back to the canoe. Disposing our baggage in the center, as in the barbed-wire experience of the day before, W—— again took the oars astern and I the paddle at the bow. A knot of men on the bridge had been watching our movements with interest, and waved their hats at us as we came cautiously creeping along the shore. We went under the bridge with a swoop, waited till we were within three rods of the brink of the thundering fall, and then strained every muscle in sending the canoe shooting off at an angle into the waters bound for the race. We went down to the gate as if shot out of a cannon, but the little craft was easily controlled, quickly obeying every stroke of the paddle. Catching a projecting timber, it was easy to guide ourselves to the opening. We lay down in the bottom of the boat and with uplifted hands clutched the slimy gate; slowly, hand over hand, we passed through under the many internal beams and rods of the structure, with the boiling flood under us, making an echoing roar, amid which we were obliged to fairly shout our directions to each other. In the last section the release was given; we were fairly hurled into daylight on the surface of the mad torrent, and were many a rod down the race before we could recover our seats. The men on the bridge, joined by others, now fairly yelled themselves hoarse over the successful close of what was apparently a hazardous venture, and we waved acknowledgments with the paddle, as we glided away under the willows which overhang the long and narrow canal. At the isolated mill, where there is one of the easiest portages on the route, the hands came flocking by dozens to the windows to see the craft which had invaded their quiet domain. . . .

The dam at Rockton was reached in a two hours' pull. It was being repaired, stone for the purpose being quarried on a neighboring bank and transported to the scene of action on a flatboat. We had been told that we could save several miles by going down the race, which cuts the base of a long detour. But the boss of the dam menders assured us that the race was not safe, and that we would "get in a trap" if we attempted it. Deeming discretion the better part of valor, with much difficulty we lifted the canoe over the high, jagged, stone embankment and through a bit of tangled swamp to the right, and took the longest way around. It was four or five miles by the bend to the village of Rockton, whose spires we could see at the dam, rising above a belt of intervening trees. It being our first detour of note, we were somewhat discouraged at having had so long a pull for so short a vantage; but we became well used to such experiences long before our journey was over. It was not altogether consoling to be informed at Rockton . . . that the race was perfectly practicable for canoes, and the tail portage easy. . . .

The spin down to Roscoe next morning was delightful in every respect. The air was just sharp enough for vigorous exercise. These were the pleasantest hours we had yet spent. The blisters that had troubled us for the first three days were hardening into calluses, and arm and back muscles, which at first were sore from the unusually heavy strain upon them, at last were strengthened to their work. Thereafter we felt no physical inconvenience from our self-imposed task. At night, after a pull of eleven or twelve hours, relieved only by the time spent in lunching, in which we hourly alternated at the oars and paddle, slumber came as a most welcome visitation, while the morning ever found us as fresh as at the start. Let those afflicted with insomnia try this sort of life. My word for it, they will not be troubled so long as the canoeing continues. Every muscle of the body moves responsive to each pull of the oars or sweep of the paddle; while the mental faculties are kept continually on the alert, watching for shallows, snags, and rapids, in which operation a few days' experience will render one quite expert, though none the less cautious.

As we get farther down into the Illinois country, the herds of livestock increase in size and number. Cattle may be seen by hundreds at one view, dotted all over the neighboring hills and meadows, or dreamily standing in the cooling stream at sultry noonday. Sheep, in immense flocks, bleat in deafening unison, the ewes and their young being particularly demonstrative at our appearance, and sometimes excitedly following us along the banks. Droves of black hogs and shoats are ploughing the sward in their search for sweet roots, or lying half buried in the wet sand. Horses, in familiar groups, quickly lift their heads in startled wonder as the canopied canoe glides silently by—then suddenly wheel, kick up their heels, sound a snort of alarm, and dash off at a thundering gallop, clods of turf filling the air behind them. There are charming groves and parks and treeless downs, and the river cuts through the alluvial soil to a depth of eight and ten feet, throwing up broad beaches on either side.

At Roscoe, three or four miles below our morning's starting point, there is a collection of three or four neat farmhouses, each with its spinning windmill.

Latham Station, nine miles below Rockton, was reached at ten o'clock. . . .

At Latham Station we encountered the first ferryboat on our

>
> FARE.
>
> Foot Passengere . . 10 cts.
> Man & Horse . . . 15 ct.
> single Carriage . . . 10 c.
> double   " . . . 15 c
> each Passinger . . . .5 c
>
> Night Raites . . Double Fare.
>
> All persons
> Are cautioned
> Againts useing
> this Boat with Out
> Permistion from
> the Owners

trip—a flat-bottomed scow with side rails, attached by ropes and pulleys to a suspended wire cable, and working diagonally, with the force of the current. A sign conspicuously displayed on the craft bore the above legend.

From the time we had entered Illinois, the large, graceful, white blossoms of the Pennsylvanian anemone and the pink and white fringe of the erigeron Canadense had appeared in great abundance upon the river banks, while the wild prairie rose lent a delicate beauty and fragrance to the scene. On sandy knolls, where in early spring the anemone patens and crowfoot violets had thrived in profusion, were now to be seen the geum triflorum and the showy yellow puccoon; the long-flowered puccoon, with its delicate pale yellow, crepe-like blossom, was just putting in an appearance; and little white, star-shaped flowers, which were strangers to us of Wisconsin, fairly dotted the green hillsides, mingled in striking contrast with dwarf blue mint. Bevies of great black crows, sitting in the tops of dead willow trees or circling around them, rent the air with sepulchral squawks. Men and boys were cultivating in the cornfields, the prevalent drought painfully evidenced by the clouds of gray dust which enveloped them and their teams as they stirred up the brittle earth.

There was now a fine breeze astern, and the awning, abandoned during the headwinds of the day before, was again welcomed as the sun mounted to the zenith. At 2:30 P.M., we were in busy Rockford, where the banks are twenty or twenty-five feet high, with rolling prairies stretching backward to the horizon, except where here and there a wooded ridge intervenes. Rockford is the metropolis of the valley of the Rock. . . .

There are numerous mills and factories along both sides of the river, and a protracted inspection of the portage facilities was necessary before we could decide on which bank to make our carry. The right was chosen. The portage was somewhat over two ordinary city blocks in length, up a step incline and through a roadway tunnel under a great flouring mill. We had made nearly half the distance, and were resting for a moment, when a mill driver kindly offered the use of his wagon, which was gratefully accepted. We were soon spinning down the tail of the race, a half-dozen millers waving a "Chautauqua salute" * with as many dusty flour bags, and in ten minutes more had left Rockford out of sight.

Several miles below, there are a half-dozen forested islands in a bunch, some of them four or five acres in extent, and we puzzled over which channel to take—the best of them abounding in shallows. The one down which the current seemed to set the strongest was selected, but we had not proceeded over half a mile before the trees on the banks began to meet in arches overhead, and it was evident that we were ascending a tributary. It proved to be the Cherry River, emptying into the main stream from the east. The wind, now almost due west, had driven the waves into the mouth of the Cherry, so that we mistook this surface movement for the current. Coming to a railway bridge, which we knew from our map did not cross the Rock, our course was retraced, and after some difficulty with snags and gravel spits, we were once more upon our proper highway, trending to the southwest.

Supper was eaten upon the edge of a large island, several miles farther down stream, in the shade of two wide-spreading locusts. . . .

. . . The atmosphere was bracing; and there being a favoring

* Chautauqua salute, according to *A Dictionary of Americanisms,* meant waving a white handkerchief. W. T.

northwest breeze, our awning was stretched over a hoop for a sail. The banks were now steep inclines of white sand and gravel. It was like going through a railroad cut. But in ascending the sides, as we did occasionally, to secure supplies from farmhouses or refill our canteen with fresh water, there were found broad expanses of rolling prairie. The farm establishments increase in number and prosperity. Windmills may be counted by the scores, the cultivation of enormous cornfields is everywhere in progress, and cattle are more numerous than ever.

Three or four miles above Oregon the banks rise to the dignity of hills, which come sweeping down "with verdure clad" to the very water's edge, and present an inspiring picture, quite resembling some of the most charming stretches of the Hudson. At the entrance to this lovely vista we encountered a logy little pleasure steamer anchored in the midst of the stream, which is here nearly half a mile wide, for the river now perceptibly broadens. The captain, a ponderous old sea dog, wearing a cowboy's hat and having the face of an operatic pirate, with a huge pipe between his black teeth, sat lounging on the bulwark, watching the force of the current, into which he would listlessly expectorate. He was at first inclined to be surly, as we hauled alongside and checked our course; but gradually softened down as we drew him out in conversation, and confided to us that he had in earlier days "sailed the salt water," a circumstance of which he seemed very proud. . . .

Oregon was reached just before noon. . . . The portage on the east side, around a flouring-mill dam, involved a hard pull up the gravelly bank thirty feet high, and a haul of two blocks' length along a dusty street.

There was a fine stretch of eroded palisades in front of the island on which we lunched. The color effect was admirable—patches of gray, brown, white, and old gold, much corroded with iron. Vines of many varieties dangle from earth-filled crevices, and swallows by the hundreds occupy the dimples neatly hollowed by the action of the water in some ancient period when the stream was far broader and deeper than now.

But at times, even in our day, the Rock is a raging torrent. The condition of the trees along the river banks and on the thickly strewn island pastures shows that not many months before it must have been on a wild rampage, for the great trunks are barked by the ice to the height of fifteen feet above the present water level. Everywhere, on banks and islands, are the evidences of disastrous floods, and the ponderous icebreakers above the bridges give one an awesome notion of the condition of affairs at such a time. . . . We were amply convinced, by the thousands of broken trees which littered our route, the snags, the mud-baked islands, the frequent stretches of sadly demoralized bank that had not yet had time to reweave its charitable mantle of verdure, that the Rock, on such a spring "tear," must indeed be a picture of chaos broken loose. This explained why these hundreds of beautiful and spacious islands—many of them with charming combinations of forest and hillock and meadow, and occasionally enclosing pretty ponds blushing with water-lilies—are none of them inhabited, but devoted to the pasture of cattle, who swim or ford the intervening channels, according to the stage of the flood; also why the picturesque bottoms on the main shore are chiefly occupied by the poorest class of farmers, who eke out their meager incomes with the spoils of the gun and line. . . .

. . . Our course still lay among large, densely wooded islands—many of them wholly given up to maples and willows—and deep cuts through sun-baked mudbanks, the color of adobe; but occasionally there are low, gloomy bottoms, heavily forested, and strewn with flood wood, while beyond the land rises gradually into prairie stretches. In the bottoms the trees are filled with flocks of birds—crows, hawks, blackbirds, with stately blue herons and agile plovers foraging on the long gravel spits which frequently jut far into the stream; ducks are frequently seen sailing near the shores, while divers silently dart and plunge ahead of the canoe, safely out of gunshot reach. A head wind this morning made rowing more difficult, by counteracting the influence of the current.

We were at Lyndon at eleven o'clock. There is a population of about two hundred, clustered around a red paper mill. The latter made a pretty picture standing out on the bold bank, backed by a number of huge stacks of golden straw. We met here the first rapids worthy of record; also an old, abandoned milldam, in the last stages of decay, stretching its whitened skeleton across the stream, a harbor for driftwood. Near the south bank the framework has been entirely swept away for a space several rods in width, and through this opening the pent-up current fiercely sweeps. We went through the center of the channel thus made, with a swoop that gave us an impetus which soon carried our vessel out of sight of Lyndon and its paper mill and strawstacks.

Prophetstown, five miles below, is prettily situated in an oak grove on the southern bank. Only the gables of a few houses can be seen from the river, whose banks of yellow clay and brown mud are here twenty-five feet high. . . .

There are rapids, almost continually, from a mile above Prophetstown to Erie, ten miles below. The river bed here has a sharper descent than customary, and is thickly strewn with boulders; many of them were visible above the surface, at the low stage of water which we found, but for the greater part they were covered for two or three inches. What with these impediments, the snags that had been left as the legacy of last spring's flood, and the frequent sandbanks and gravel spits, navigation was attended by many difficulties and some dangers.

Four or five miles below Prophetstown, a lone fisherman, engaged in examining a "trautline" stretched between one of the numerous gloomy islands and the mainland, kindly informed us of a mile-long cutoff, the mouth of which was now in view, that would save us several miles of rowing. Here the high banks had receded, with several miles of heavily wooded, boggy bottoms intervening. Floods had held high carnival, and the aspect of the country was wild and deserted. The cutoff was an ugly looking channel; but where our informant had gone through, with his unwieldy hulk, we considered it safe to venture with a canoe, so readily responsive to the slightest paddle stroke. The current had torn for itself a jagged bed through the heart of a dense and moss-grown forest. It was a scene of howling desolation, rack and ruin upon every hand. The muddy torrent, at a velocity of fully eight miles an hour, went eddying and whirling and darting and roaring among the gnarled and blackened stumps, the prostrate trees, the twisted roots, the huge boulders which studded its course. The stream was not wide enough for the oars; the paddle was the sole reliance. With eyes strained for obstructions, we turned and twisted through the labyrinth, jumping along at a breakneck speed; and, when we finally rejoined the main river below, were grateful enough, for the run had been filled with continuous possibilities of a disastrous smashup, miles away from any human habitation.

The thunderstorm which had been threatening since early morning, soon burst upon us with a preliminary wind blast, followed by drenching rain. Running ashore on the lee bank, we wrapped the canvas awning around the baggage, and made for a thick clump of trees on the top of an island mudbank, where we stood buttoned to the neck in rubber coats. A vigorous "Halloo!" came sounding over the water. Looking up, we saw for the first time a small tent on the opposite shore, a quarter of a mile away, in front of which was a man shouting to us and beckoning us over. It was getting uncomfortably muddy under the trees, which had not long sufficed as an umbrella, and the rubber coats were not warranted to withstand a deluge, so we accepted the invitation with alacrity and paddled over through the pelting storm.

Our host was a young fisherman, who helped us and our luggage up the slimy bank to his canvas quarters, which we found to be dry, although odorous of fish. . . .

Within an hour and a half the storm had apparently passed over, and we continued our journey. But after supper another shower and a stiff head wind came up, and we were well bedraggled by the time a ferry landing near the little village of Erie was reached. . . .

The following day opened brightly. . . .

The river continues to widen as we approach the junction with the Mississippi—thirty-nine miles below Erie—and to assume the characteristics of the great river into which it pours its flood. The islands increase in number and in size, some of them being over a mile in length by a quarter of a mile in breadth; the bottoms frequently resolve themselves into wide morasses, thickly studded with great elms, maples, and cottonwoods, among which the spring flood has wrought direful destruction. The scene becomes peculiarly desolate and mournful, often giving one the impression of being far removed from civilization, threading the course of some hitherto unexplored stream. Penetrate the deep fringe of forest and morass on foot, however, and smiling prairies are found beyond, stretching to the horizon and cut up into prosperous farms. The river is here from a half to three quarters of a mile broad, but the shallows and snags are as numerous as ever and navigation is continually attended with some danger of being either grounded or capsized.

Now and then the banks become firmer, with charming vistas of high, wooded hills coming down to the water's edge; broad savannas intervene, decked out with variegated flora, prominent being the elsewhere rare *atragene Americana,* the spiderwort, the little blue lobelia, and the cupweed. These savannas are apparently overflowed in times of exceptionally high water; and there are evidences that the stream has occasionally changed its course, through the sun-baked banks of ashy-gray mud, in years long past.

At Cleveland, a staid little village on an open plain, which we reached soon after the dinner hour, there is an unused milldam going to decay. In the center, the main current has washed out a breadth of three or four rods, through which the pent-up stream rushes with a roar and a hundred whirlpools. It is an ugly crevasse, but a careful examination showed the passage to be feasible, so we retreated an eighth of a mile upstream, took our bearings, and went through with a speed that nearly took our breath away and appeared to greatly astonish a half-dozen fishermen idly angling from the dilapidated apron on either side. It was like going through Cleveland on the fast mail.

Fourteen miles above the mouth of the Rock is the Chicago, Burlington and Quincy railroad bridge, with Carbon Cliff on the north and Coloma on the south, each one mile from the river. The day had been dark, with occasional slight showers and a stiff head wind, so that progress had been slow. We began to deem it worth while to inquire about the condition of affairs at the mouth. Under the bridge, sitting on a boulder at the base of the north abutment, an intelligent-appearing man in a yellow oiled-cloth suit, accompanied by a bright-eyed lad, peacefully fished. Stopping to question them, we found them both well informed as to the railway time-tables of the vicinity and the topography of the lower river. They told us that the scenery for the next fourteen miles was similar, in its dark desolation, to that which we had passed through during the day; also that owing to the great number of islands and the labyrinth of channels both in the Rock and on the east side of the Mississippi, we should find it practically impossible to know when we had reached the latter; we should doubtless proceed several miles below the mouth of the Rock before we noticed that the current was setting persistently south, and then would have an exceedingly difficult task in retracing our course and pulling upstream to our destination, Rock Island, which is six miles north of the delta of the Rock. They strongly advised our going into Rock Island by rail. The present landing was the last chance to strike a railway, except at Milan, twelve miles below. It was now so late that we could not hope to reach Milan before dark; there were no stopping-places en route, and Milan was farther from Rock Island than either Carbon Cliff or Coloma, with less frequent railway service.

For these and other reasons, we decided to accept this advice, and to ship from Coloma. Taking a final spurt down to a ferry landing a quarter of a mile beyond, on the south bank, we beached our canoe at 5:05 P.M., having voyaged two hundred and sixty-seven miles in somewhat less than seven days and a half. Leaving W—— to gossip with the ferryman's wife, who came down to the bank with an armful of smiling twins to view a craft so strange to her vision, I went up into the country to engage a team to take our boat upon its last portage. After having been gruffly refused by a churlish farmer, who doubtless recognized no difference between a canoeist and a tramp, I struck a bargain with a Negro cultivating a cornfield with a span of coal-black mules, and in half an hour he was at the ferry landing with a wagon. Washing out the canoe and chaining in the oars and paddle, we lifted it into the wagon box, piled our baggage on top, and set off over the hills and fields to Coloma, W—— and I trudging behind the dray, ankle deep in mud, for the late rains had well moistened the black prairie soil. It was a unique and picturesque procession. . . .

John Boyle O'Reilly
1844 - 1890

Poet, journalist, and athlete—a swimmer, boxer, and former cavalryman in the British Army—O'Reilly canoed hard and wrote well. Born in Ireland, imprisoned for Fenian activities and transported to Australia, he escaped to the United States, became an American citizen, and a contributor to the literature of his adopted country. His narratives open our mouths (almost) to the taste of clear water, our eyes to its glories and wonders.

Walt Whitman knew O'Reilly. "Boyle's charm," he said, "came out of his tremendous fiery personality: he had lived through tremendous experiences which were always appearing somehow reflected in his speech and in his dress and in his attitudes of body and mind." * And why not add "in his canoeing" as well for he loved it with passion—intensely—and seemed to find it his cure-all for troubles and ills.

* Horace Traubel, *With Walt Whitman in Camden,* vol. 3 (New York: Mitchell Kennerley, 1914), p. 17.

ATHLETICS AND MANLY SPORT

CANOEING ON THE CONNECTICUT

The canoe is the American boat of the past and of the future. It suits the American mind: it is light, swift, safe, graceful, easily moved; and the occupant looks in the direction he is going, instead of behind, as in the stupid old tubs that have held the world up to this time.

Who, among the hard workers of our eastern cities, needs two months' vacation, and can only get away from the desk or office for two weeks?

Who feels the confined work tell on his lungs, or his eyes, or shudders at that tremulousness of the shoulders and arms which precedes the breaking down from overwork?

All this can be cured by the sun and the wind and the delicious splash of the river on face and breast and arms. Those are they to whom a canoe is a godsend. They can get more health and strength and memorable joy out of a two-weeks' canoe trip than from a lazy, expensive and seasick voyage to Europe, or three months' dawdle at a fashionable watering place.

Boats are for work; canoes are for pleasure. Boats are artificial; canoes are natural. In a boat you are always an oar's length and a gunwale's height away from Nature. In a canoe you can steal up to her bower and peep into her very bosom.

What memories are stored away in the canoeist's mind! My friend, Dr. Ramon Guiteras, and I have canoed together in many rivers, in the same little Racine boat (though we now believe that it is preferable to have only one man to a canoe), and we can enjoy rare hours of reminiscence, recalling delightful scenes and amusing incidents from this or that excursion. And let two canoeists, strangers, meet: their talk is an endlessly pleasant comparison.

Going on this trip on the Connecticut, when we took our boat to

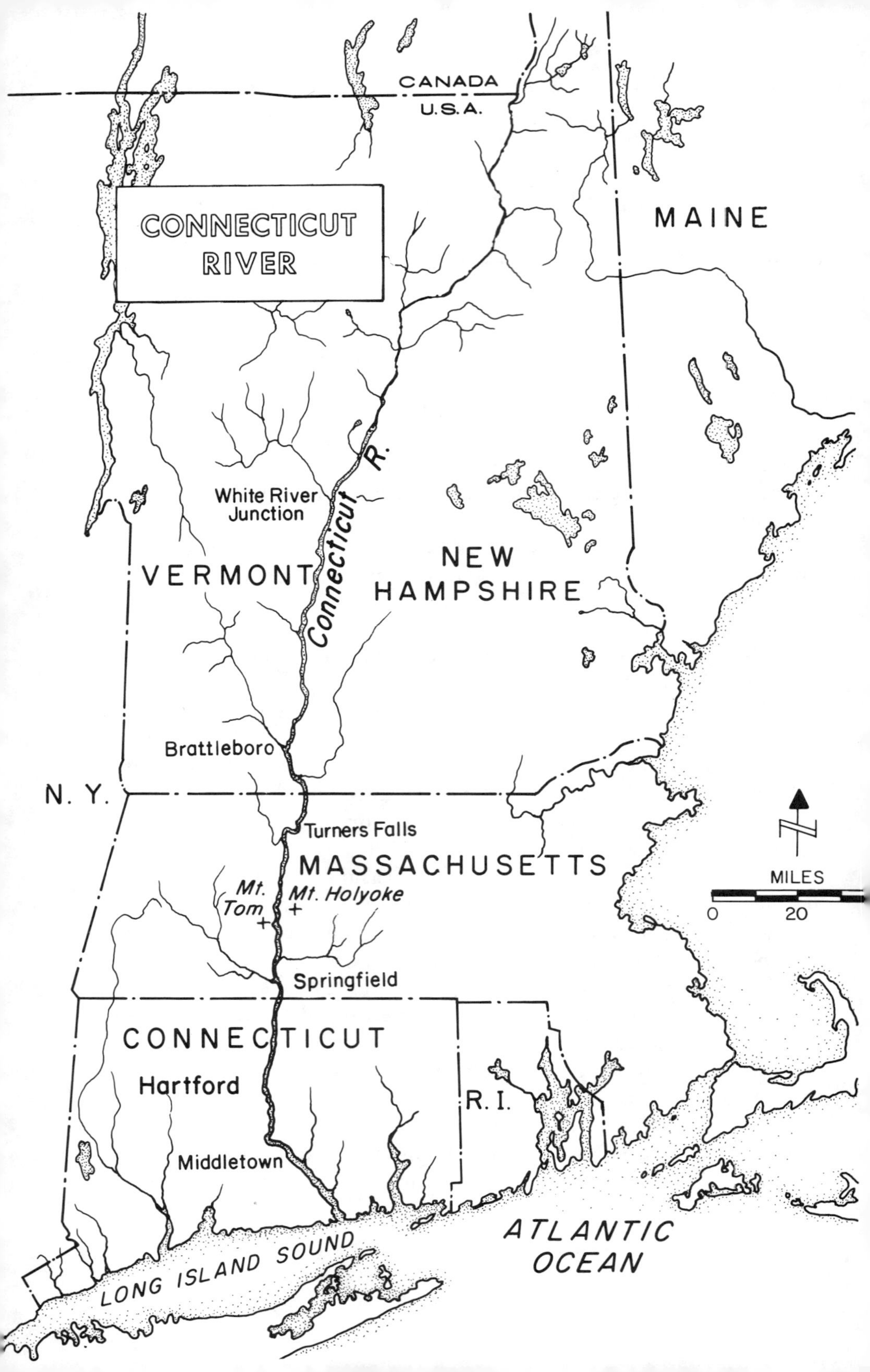
CONNECTICUT
RIVER
CANADA
U.S.A.
MAINE
White River
Junction
Connecticut R.
VERMONT
NEW
HAMPSHIRE
Brattleboro
N. Y.
Turners Falls
MASSACHUSETTS
MILES
0
20
Mt.
Tom
Mt. Holyoke
Springfield
CONNECTICUT
Hartford
R. I.
Middletown
ATLANTIC
OCEAN
LONG ISLAND SOUND

the Boston and Maine depot, in Boston, we found another canoe in the baggage car. I happened to know one of the gentlemen who was tying it up, Mr. Morris Meredith, an experienced canoeman; and with him was a veteran of many rivers, Mr. Frank Hubbard, of Boston. What a chat of hours we had! What rapids we ran over again! What tender touches of memory when some river scene familiar to all was brought up! And how unselfishly these two canoemen (who were going on a two-weeks' cruise on Lake Champlain) tore their chart in two, and gave us that part which included the Connecticut River.

When Dr. Guiteras and I started from Boston, we intended to take water at White River Junction; but, when we reached that place, we found the river full of logs—the largest quantity ever cut in one year going down this season. But the "end of the logs" was only a few miles above the White River; and we were told that, by going farther up, we should have it all clear as we came down, and might follow the logs to Holyoke.

So we took our little boat farther up, till we came to a favorable spot for launching, and there we slid her into the river from a marvelous white sandbank, which ran into the deep, slow stream, and from which we took our first glorious "header" into the Connecticut.

All along the river, down to Middletown, hundreds of miles away, we found, at intervals, this remarkable kind of sandbank on which one may take a race, and dive directly into deep water. And yet the bank is not straight, under water, but a rapid incline, easy and pleasant for landing.

What need of details? Miles in a voyage are of no more account than years in a life: they may be filled with commonplace. Men live by events, and so they paddle.

We had ten, fifteen, twenty days ahead, if necessary! We were rich in this. Hundreds of miles of beautiful water, splendid days, a new moon, a well-stored locker, and a boat that danced under us like a duck! So we started, dripping from the embrace of the sweet water.

We paddled about fifteen miles, when we saw a tempting nook, a pine grove above a sandbank, with a dashing stream; and, not far withdrawn, a comfortable farmhouse, where we might buy milk and eggs and bread. As we had started late, we landed for the night, and one set off for the farmhouse, while the other made ready for supper.

We had a copious larder. We carried too many things, observers said. So we did; but we both liked many things when we stopped for meals. Our table was the sandbank, with a rubber blanket spread. Olives, cheese, sardines, bacon, Liebig's extract of beef—these looked well. Then came the farm supplies—quarts of rich milk, a dozen eggs, two loaves of bread, and a lot of cooked green peas, thrown in by the farmer's wife; a bottle of good claret. What a dinner and supper in one! Then coffee, then a cigar, then the philosophies—quiet talk as we sat looking at the river with the darkness coming down, the frogs sounding resonant notes over on the New Hampshire side, and the white light of the young moon trembling up over the dark pine hills. Then we wrapped ourselves in our blankets, and slept till morning.

We had no tent; we two had discovered that we needed no tent in July or August, though we do not advise others to follow our example. Fortunately for us, we wake in the early morning with the same feeling of refreshment—our lungs full of the delicious air, and our faces wet with dew. On this first morning, I leaped up at sunrise, shouting, "This is the way Nature meant men to live and sleep and wake!"

I shall never forget that first glorious morning. For an hour before rising, I had lain awake looking out at the river, and listening to the strange country sounds around me. All over the grass and low bushes the spider's webs were stretched, glistening with dew. What a wonderful night's industry! Those webs were nearly all, or quite all, new. The little night toilers had woven them over our olive bottle, over the gun, over ourselves. The field above us was white as snow with this incomparable cloth-of-silver.

As I lay and looked at one of those webs close to my face, I saw a strange thing. A little gray-and-black spider ran up a tall grass blade, rested a moment, and then ran off, through empty air, to another blade, six inches off. I looked closer; surely he must have a fine line stretched between those points, I thought. No; the closest scrutiny could find none. I watched him; he was soon off again, straight for another point, a foot above the ground, running on clear space, and turning down and hanging to it, like a monkey, but still going ahead. I called Guiteras, and he came and saw and examined, and smiled in his wise way when he doesn't know. We could not see the little fellow's cable, or railway, or bridge. He was as much finer than we as we are finer than mastodons.

And the birds, in that first rich morning speech of theirs, full of soft, bubbling joy, not singing, but softly and almost silently overflowing. Two little fellows flew rapidly down to a twig near us, and began bubble-bubbling as if in a great flutter and hurry; and immediately they flew far and high, as for a long journey; at which my philosophic friend moralized:

"Those little fellows are like some canoeists who wake up, and don't wait for breakfast; but bubble-bubble, hurry-hurry, get-afloat, we-have-a-long-way-to-go! Now, *we* don't do that."

Indeed, we do not. This is what we do. We light our little alcohol stove, and boil two quarts of the rich milk, into which we put our prepared coffee (Sanford's—a great and precious compound, which we heartily recommend to all men fond of outing). Then we plunge into the river for a good swim, getting the first of the sun as he comes over the hill. The sandbank is soft to land on; and so up we go to the meadow above, for a four-round bout with boxing gloves; and, when this is done, we are in good trim for breakfast.

Here let me say that we were never sorry when we selected a white sandbank or a pine grove to sleep in; the latter to be preferred, on account of the soft pine needles, the healthy fragrance, and the absence of mosquitoes. If the sandbank is chosen, first scoop out a hollow for the hips and shoulders; spread the rubber blanket, and then the woollen blanket; turn the latter bag-like up from the feet, and draw the rubber over all. Then your couch is as soft as a feather bed, and a hundred times healthier.

After breakfast, two hours of easy paddling, during which we keep the gun ready, and usually kill about a half dozen birds to enrich our dinner. Then follow two hours of hard paddling, which prepares us for dinner and a rest. After this, two hours of easy paddling, and two hours of hard paddling. Then supper; after which, a slow and easy, meditative paddle in search of pine grove or sandbank. This was our regular daily program, and its worth was shown by our excellent condition when we reached the end of the river.

Events by the way—how shall I recall them, crowded as they are? We were upset: it was in this way. We had carried our boat round a fall, where the logs ran so furiously that nothing else had a chance to run. At about eight o'clock in the evening we floated her, below the falls, intending just to paddle down till we found a place to sleep. We did not know, from the dusk, that the rapids extended for miles below the falls. We soon found the water extremely strong and swift, full of eddies and whirls, and mixed up with tumbling and pushing logs. It was the ugliest race we had seen or did see on all the river. We swept down like an arrow for about half a mile, and then a thunderstorm of extraordinary violence and continuity burst. The night became pitch dark. We could only see the black river, running like a wolf at the gunwale, and the lightning zigzagging the night above. Suddenly we realized that the logs on our left were stationary, while those in the stream on our right were tearing down like battering rams. So long as you go *with* the logs they are gentle as friendly savages, just rubbing you softly like living things, and movable with a finger. But get fast, and let them come down on you, and the ribs of a boat will smash like a matchbox under their brutal drive and the jagged fibers of their tapered butt ends. The logs on our left were stationary; but the rapid water boiled up between them. We ran swiftly along two great logs—then suddenly stopped. An immense log had been forced up and across its fellows, and as its farther end was driven swiftly forward, its heavy butt came straight for the canoe. Dr. Guiteras got the first blow, on the head and shoulder, which rather keeled us. Then the log took me fairly on the chest, and over and down we went. For some seconds, Guiteras's feet having got fast somehow in the boat forward, he was in a bad way; but he soon kicked free, and we swam at our ease with the boat down the river.

To men who can swim well enough not to lose their presence of mind by a sudden upset, there is little danger in canoeing—probably no more than in riding. It is well, though, to know what to do when you find yourself rolling into the water. When you come up, the canoe is, of course, bottom-side up. By catching hold of her keel, she is easily righted. If there be two swimmers, they should take the two sides, holding her with one hand and swimming with the other. They can pass through any kind of sea in this fashion, safely, and even with pleasure. If there be only one in the canoe, he ought to hold her by the stern or painter ring with one hand, and swim with the other. If he attempt to hold her by the side he will surely upset her again. It is good drill to upset your canoe in safe water half a dozen times, and get used to it, as we did on the day following our ducking.

We lost, strange to say, only a few insignificant articles. Everything in the locker was safe, and even dry, including our watches. The gun had not rolled out.

To go into further detail would give the affair more weight than it deserves. I shall only say that in our difficulty we were kindly and courageously helped by Mr. Woodman, a farmer on the shore, for whom we shall long keep a friendly feeling.

This was our only mishap of a serious nature. Of course, we got into many tight places; canoeists must expect it. But we emerged without turning a hair, and we paid for all our troubles with endless interest and enjoyment.

We laughed at all things that came: at a memory of last year; at simple questions by the country lads, who sat with us at times while we feasted, but who never would join us, being shy and proud; at a certain stupid kind of bird that waited every day to be shot; we laughed infinitely at the logs, when we learned their ways; we named them, patted their rough backs, or rubbed the old bald ones; we leaped out and rode on them, and tried to walk on them like the logmen, and always tumbled in, and came up blowing and laughing. . . .

We had another queer experience with an antagonist who "took it out of us," at least for a day—the sun. We make a point of wearing as little covering as possible—no hats, no sleeves, no shoes while in the boat. Healthy men are never sunstruck. Alcohol stroke or toilstroke or stomachstroke is the real name of sunstroke. If the bare head feels warm in a boat, moisten it and it becomes deliciously cool.

But sunburn is another thing, and it must be looked to until the skin toughens. It must not be cooled with water, for every drop becomes a burning lens, to score a deeper mark. On our fourth day out we were badly sunburnt. Guiteras on that day had swum from 10 A.M. to 5 P.M., making about fifteen miles. The sun had taken hold of our shoulders, arms and face, and next day we were both feverish and crossgrained. Every movement was painful. We stopped at a village and bought half a pound of bicarbonate of soda (common baking soda). That night we made a thick solution, poured it over the burnt parts and put on tight cotton shirts with long sleeves. In the morning the pain was gone, though the blistered flesh remained.

Here is an experience of "cures" for sunburn; we tried many remedies, some on one arm, some on another; some on our faces, and others on our necks. We tried Nature's remedy—*let it alone*—and the burns treated in this way were the first to get well. Moral: do nothing for a sunburn but to take it out of the sun for a day or two.

As we came down the river one thing was noticeable and very enjoyable—the courtesy and kindness of every one on the banks. At Brattleboro we found two gentlemen who owned canoes . . . who lent us a pair of single paddles, and who were otherwise exceedingly kind.

At Springfield we stopped long enough for me to lecture in the evening (by previous arrangement). There was a large audience, and Guiteras sat on the platform, brown as an Indian, and fell asleep. Fortunately he was shielded by a large tropical plant. . . .

We had been told that the beauty of the Connecticut ended at Springfield; but it is not so. Indeed, one of the loveliest stretches lies between Hartford and Middletown, though the river under Mt. Tom and Mt. Holyoke is surpassingly beautiful. I never saw more delightful scenery than in the river valley just above and below Northampton. . . .

From Hartford to Middletown is one of the finest stretches of the Connecticut, and it is by no means low-banked or monotonous. One of the peculiarities of the river is that it is almost as wide and apparently as deep at Hanover as in this latest reach.

It is not necessary to go a great distance up the Connecticut to find splendid canoeing water. If one had only a week's time, and entered the river at Brattleboro, or below Turner's Falls, he would find enough beauty to remember for a lifetime.

The distances on the river appear to be quite unknown to residents on the banks, who evidently judge by road measurement. We found, in most cases, that the river distance was at least a third to a half longer than the road.

One of our rarest pleasures came from paddling for a few miles up the smaller rivers that run into the Connecticut. They are invariably beautiful, and the smaller ones are indescribable as fairyland.

One stream, particularly (I think it is a short distance below White River Junction, on the New Hampshire side), called Bromidon, was, in all respects, an ideal brook. It had the merriest voice; the brownest and most sun-flecked shallows; the darkest little nooks of deep, leafy pools; the most happy-looking, creeper-covered homesteads on its banks. We could hardly paddle into it, it was so shallow; or out of it, it was so beautiful. Guiteras wanted to write a poem about it. "The name is a poem in itself," he said; "any one could write a poem about such a stream." All the way down the river his muttered "Bromidon!" was like the self-satisfied bubble-bubble of the morning birds.

This leads me to say that, in the rapid growth of canoeing, which is surely coming, it is to be hoped that the paddle will be the legitimate means of propulsion, and not the sail. If men want to sail, let them get keel boats and open water. The canoe was meant for lesser surfaces. Indeed, the smaller the river, the more enjoyable the canoeing. A few feet of surface is wide enough. With the quiet paddle, one can steal under the overhanging boughs, drift silently into the deep morning and afternoon shadows; study the ever-changing banks, birds, even the splendid dragonflies and butterflies among the reeds and rushes.

As an athletic exercise, paddling is one of the best, or can easily be made so. A canoe trip of a couple of weeks, diversified by two good swims daily, will bring the whole muscular system into thorough working condition. Dr. Guiteras, who has had unusual experience in athletic training, and has given it special attention, is of the opinion that *no other* exercises are so excellent as paddling and swimming in conjunction.

A word about the logs. They are not so bad as they look, nor as their general reputation. We should, of course, prefer a river without them; and canoeists on the Connecticut can easily avoid them by finding out when they start and cease running. But they always keep in the current; they people the river with odd and interesting fellow voyagers, and they are as harmless as sheep in a meadow when you know how to handle them.

Since this trip on the Connecticut, we have canoed many other rivers, some of them streams of much greater volume. We had in these the width of water, the calm greatness of the flow, the splendid reaches unbroken by falls and rapids and dams; but we often missed the overhanging branches, the flash and twitter among the leaves, the shadows that made the river look deep as the sky, and the murmur of the little brown brooks that are lost in the great stream, leaving only their names, like Bromidon, clinging to the water like naiads.

DOWN THE SUSQUEHANNA IN A CANOE

"This river runs palpably down hill!" said my friend in the other boat, as our two canoes rounded a sweeping curve, and ran down an unbroken slope of half a mile.

So it did. Beautiful! That first airborne sensation of a sheer slide was not beaten on the next hundred miles of river. The water was not three feet deep; clear as air—every pebble seen on the bottom, and none larger than your hand; and the whole wide river slipping and sliding like a great sheet of glass out of its frame! At the foot of the sloping water was a little rapid, our first on the Susquehanna, which is even more truly a river of rapids than a river of bends, though the latter is the meaning of its melodious Indian name.

We had stopped paddling on the "palpable hill," and we let the stream carry our canoes into the noisy rapid at its foot. Zigzag it crossed the river; and as I led into a well-defined rushing V, aiming at the angle, I felt the first grumble of a rock along the keel. Next moment we were pitching on sharp little whitecaps below the rush, and scooting down toward the swift, deep water.

We had launched our canoes at Binghamton, J. Smith and I, because the river above is too low in September. Shame that it should

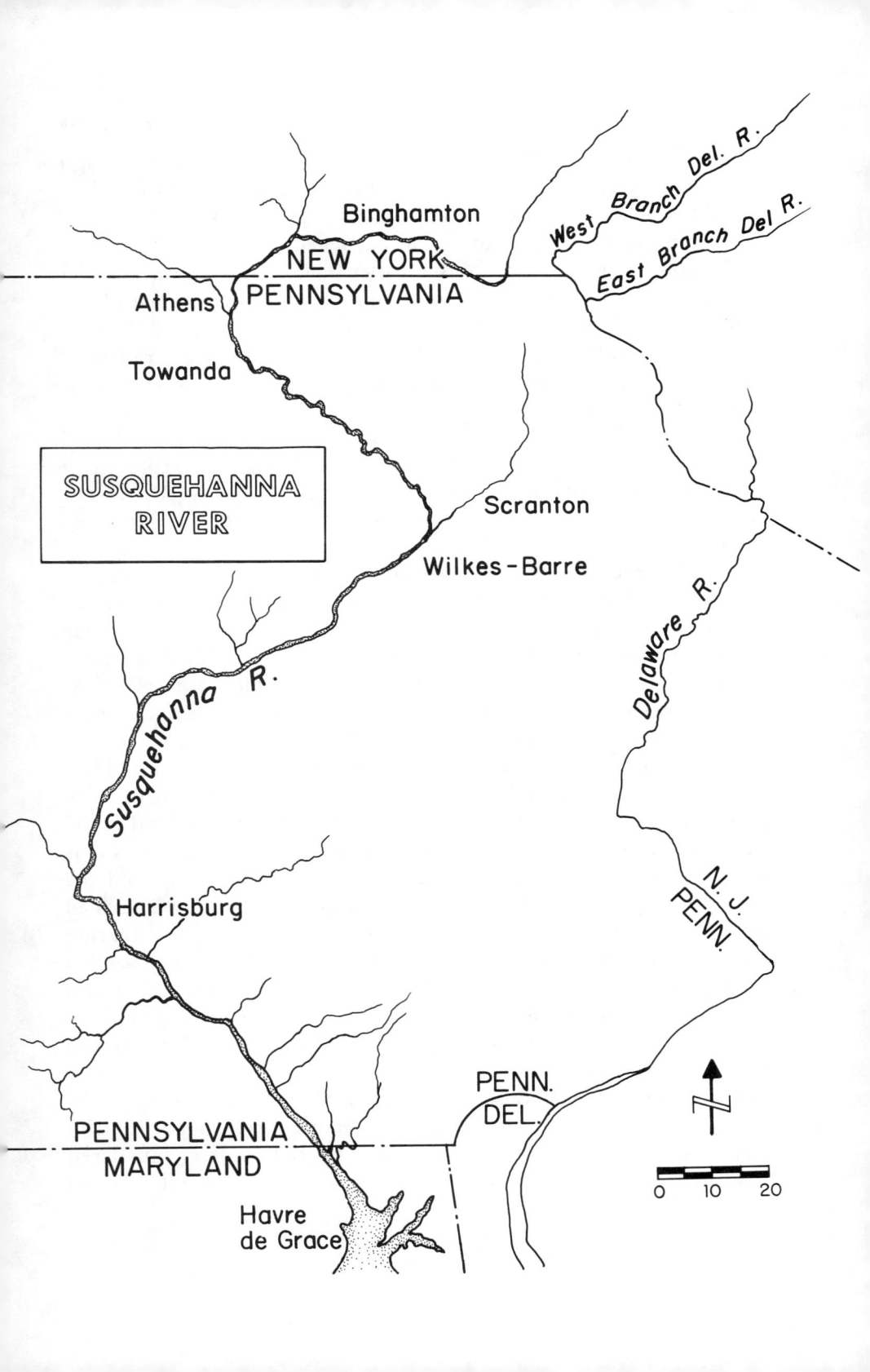

SUSQUEHANNA RIVER

be so! The beautiful hills above Binghamton, that a few years ago were clothed with rich foliage for unbroken leagues, are shorn like a stubble field. The naked stumps are white and unsightly on the mountains, like the bones of an old battlefield.

A monster has crept up the valley and devoured the strong young trees. Every trunk has been swallowed; and the maw of the dragon is belching for more. On both sides of the river, and through many of the valleys that open back to the farmlands, the railroads wind like serpents; and every foot-long joint in their vertebrae is the trunk of a twenty-year-old tree. The hills stand up in the sun, cropped and debased . . . their beauty and mystery and shadowed sacredness torn from them; their silence and loneliness replaced by the selfish chirp of the grasshopper among the dry weeds. Never did the hard utility of civilization appear less disguised and less lovely. . . .

But the injured hills, like all old and strong children of nature, curse their destroyer as they die. The railroads have killed the trees, and the death of the trees is as surely killing the river. Year by year its life blood decreases; it grows narrower, shallower, yet more fitfully dangerous. Scores and hundreds of miles it runs, drinking in the volume of the streams; but in all this distance its own volume does not increase.

Marvelous and shocking! The Susquehanna is no deeper at Harrisburg than at Towanda. Its evaporation equals its growth. The shorn hills can hold no moisture. The rain and dew are dried in the morning sun like a breath on a mirror. But when the heavy clouds roll in and rain for weeks, there are no thirsty roots to hold the water, no myriad-leafed miles to be drenched before a rill is formed below. Then the dried veins are suddenly and madly filled, tearing down to the lowlands with unchecked violence. The river, swollen with drunken fury, becomes the brute that civilization is always making—leaping at the bridges, devouring the fields, deluging farmhouses and streets, until its fury is glutted on the blind selfishness that gave it birth.

Pittsburgh riots and Susquehanna devastations are children of the same parents—Greed and Ignorance. Beautiful trees and beautiful souls, steeped in the coalpits, scorched by the cinders, thundered over by the roaring wheels that carry treasures to the cultured and luxurious, there is a curse in your defilement and mutilation. Yet our moralists and socialists will not listen and understand.

But who shall be didactic in a canoe on a river that laughs into little rapids every few hundred yards? It was delightful to see Smith take his first rapid. He had only canoed before in still water. A few miles below Binghamton we heard the break of the water, and saw the zigzag line ahead. Not knowing the nature of the thing, whether it was a dam, an eel rack, a woodshoot, or a natural shoal, I paddled ahead, and took a look at it. There was just one place in the line, about three feet wide, where the water rushed down like a sluiceway; and we must go in there. On one side of this passage, a thin spur of black stone rose above the surface, and made a good mark to steer by; but on the other side of the sluice was a great round stone, covered with about six inches of rushing water. I paddled back and asked Smith to observe exactly where my boat entered; and, turning her head, I let her go in "with the swim." It was a delightful little shoot of about fifty yards, and when I had reached the smooth water, I turned to see my friend coming down. He neared the rapids, not letting his boat drift, but paddling with all his force, and moving at tremendous speed down the swift water. He was not heading for the opening, but was coming straight for the big stone at the right side. No use shouting; the din of the water drowned all other sound. I expected to see him strike and swing round, and probably get upset and rolled over; but instead of that, the bow of his plucky little boat rose at the stone like a steeplechaser, till I saw half her keel in the air—and then over she came, without a scratch, and buried her nose in the deep water below the stone, while the canoeist sat straight, laughing with excitement, and dripping with the shower of spray from the plunge.

"How did it feel?" I asked.

"Glorious!" he shouted.

He thought he had come down *secundum artem*. But before night he knew all about it, for the river was so low that every shallow had an angry brawl. Next day, with a steady hand and cool head, he found the way out for me when I had got into a bad place.

It was in this way: I had gone in first on rather a long and rough descent. There was a bend on the rapid, and in going round I struck heavily and unexpectedly, and swung right athwart the race, amidships fast on a huge brown shelf rock. The divided water caught bow and stern, and held the canoe against the stone. I got one foot out against the rock and stopped her trembling; and there I was, fast. I could hold her steady, but could do no more. The stone was so shaped that I could not stand on it. The water ran deep and strong, and if I pushed off altogether I should be apt to go down broadside or stern first. So I sat thinking for a second or two; and then I looked back to wave to Smith to keep off. I saw his boat, but not him. He was swimming, "accoutred as he was," right across the river above, to give me a hand. His judgment had told him that I was badly placed. In a few minutes he had reached the head of the rapid, stepped from stone to stone till he caught hold of my painter, and next moment my bow came round to the race, and down I shot like a rocket. In a few minutes he followed in the same course.

Just below that rapid we had an unpleasant experience—the only one on our whole voyage. We fell in with a sordid lout, and up to this day I am sorry we did not thrash him or duck him in the river. We had gone up to a farmhouse on the bluff to buy milk and eggs for dinner. Two old women had very kindly served us, and we were coming away when the lout appeared. He was evidently the master of the place: a big, rawboned, ragged-whiskered, and dirty-skinned brute. He had just caught a snake, about two feet long, and he held it wriggling in his hand, while he laughed a vile chuckle, and opened his filthy mouth in derision as the older woman, his mother, probably, fled, almost screaming with terror. Then he came toward us, and seeing Smith's bare ankles he deliberately put the snake down to bite them, chuckling all the time, and mumbling: "You hain't got the sand! He won't bite. *I* ain't afeard. *I've* got the sand. *I* ain't afeard o' snakes," and so on.

We stepped away from him, and at last told him, in a tone he minded, to drop the snake. He did so at once. His mother said to him from the door: "If you did that to me, and I was a man, *I'd kill you!*". . .

It took us some hours to forget the barbarian. A handsome young trapper, logman, and railroad worker, lower down, who knew him well, told us that the lout was known along the river as a coward, a braggart, and "a man that was no good, anyhow."

The Susquehanna is, in one respect, quite unlike any other river on which I have canoed. There is an endless recurrence of half-mile and mile-long deep stretches, and then a brawling rapid. The river rarely makes a bend without shoaling to a foot or two of water; and this is invariably ended by a bar, with a swift descent beyond. These shallow places have been utilized as eel racks, by driving stakes or piling stones in a zigzag line across the river. From Towanda down to Wilkes-Barre, with a bold, wooded hill, or "mountain," always on one side, and sometimes on both, the deep stretches become deeper and longer; but in a very few places is the "slow water" more than two or three miles in length.

We had brought a small tent with us, and we carried some provisions—prepared coffee, Liebig's extract of beef, a jar of delicious butter (which we broke and lost on the third day), a can of corned beef, some hardtack, and some bacon. We had tin cups, a little alcohol stove, and a bottle of very old Jamaica (for the malaria).

We had two canoes of the "Shadow" model, Mr. Smith's, a Rushton,* decked and hatched; mine without hatches, and built by Partelow, of Riverside, Mass.—both good boats of their kind, from good builders. But the "Shadow" is not a good kind of canoe for river work. Her keel is to long and too deep. This makes her heavy in turning sharp curves; and, when she runs on a stone—even a round or flat one—the keel throws her on one side; and this is really a canoe's unpardonable sin. A canoe should have no keel. The "Shadow" model is really not a canoe at all, but simply a light boat.

The Indian round-bottomed, birch-bark canoe is the best model for American rivers; and it is a pity that our builders do not keep it as their radical study. It should be modified and improved, of course; narrowed for double paddling, and shortened and lightened for portage; but its first principle, of a bottom that can run on or over a stone without capsizing, ought never to be forgotten. In my opinion, paper will win against lapstreak in the canoe of the future; all that is needed to insure this is a method of patching the wound on a paper bottom.

Never have I seen river water so clear and wholesome as the

* John Henry Rushton (1843–1906) of Canton, New York, watercraft designer and builder, is the subject of a well-illustrated study by Atwood Manley, *Rushton and His Times in American Canoeing,* Syracuse University Press, 1968, 203 pp. W. T.

Susquehanna. One of our daily pleasures was to dip our bright tin cups into the river, drink a mouthful, and pour the rest into our mouths without swallowing.

The sun flamed on the water every day of our trip; the records ashore made it the hottest fortnight of the year. So we lovingly hugged the banks when there was any shade; and, unexpectedly, this habit led us into the two greatest pleasures of our voyage.

The first occurred a few miles above the village of Appalaken. We left the main river to run to the left of an island, where the stream was only twenty feet wide. The island was perhaps three quarters of a mile long, and the trees on both sides reached over, interlaced, and made the stream as dark as late evening. There was a turbulent little rapid at the entrance, as we swung in from the big river and the noonday blaze; and the water all down the narrow stream ran with incredible rapidity. When we felt ourselves carried along in this silent cool shadow, and looked up at the light sifting through the dense foliage, we both exclaimed, "This is too lovely to be repeated!" And the word was true. Such a superlative canoe ride one could hardly ever expect to enjoy twice. We laid down our paddles, only fearing to come to the end of our marvelous green archway, with its dark gleaming floor; and when, at last, we did sweep out into the broad glare of the river, we sighed and looked back wistfully, as men will. Ten minutes later we were wading over a shallow place and hauling our canoes by the painter.

The other peak of our enjoyment was reached about four miles below the town of Athens. Ah, me! how we did enjoy our evening in that little town! But let the tale bide a little. We had gone down some miles below the bridge at Athens, where the river widened out and grew consumedly slow and commonplace. There was an island, with a narrow opening to the left and a rough little rapid at the entrance—almost a repetition of the Appalaken archway. After that other experience we did not hesitate, but turned from the big sheet of water, and shot into the narrow turmoil, to the left of the island. Again we dashed into a splendid sweep, but about three times as wide as the Appalaken archway. The water was about four feet deep all the way down, and the bottom was of small pebbles, every one as clearly seen as if laid on a mirror. Once more our paddles were crossed before us, and we sat in profound enjoyment of water, wood, and sky, as we were swept along by the current. . . .

And here we made a discovery that will redound to the fame of Athens, . . .

Halfway down between the island and the shore we plunged into the swift current, intending to float after the canoes, holding on by the painter—a most enjoyable and interesting thing to do. When you lie at utter rest in the water and watch the shore go by, it seems too delicious for waking life; but this is not the best. Let your whole body and head sink well under the surface, keeping your eyes open; the river becomes an aquarium—you see the weeds, the stones, and the fishes as clearly almost as if they were in the air. This is because you have no motion except the motion of the water itself; your eyes are fixed in a crystalline medium, and nothing can express the sense of ease, of utter luxury, which the supporting fluid gives to every limb. You are lolling on or in an air cushion without surface or friction. The mere swimmer can never feel this, nor even he who is *towed* after a boat—though that is an ideal method of taking an invigorating bath. To see the river's inner life, and to enjoy this complete luxury of resting in the water, you must float in and with the stream, without effort or motion, supported by the painter of your boat.

But our discovery waits: halfway down this lovely and lonely island passage we plunged in, as I have many times said; and we had no sooner struck bottom than Smith uttered a strange shout and threw up his hands. I was startled till I looked at his face; and then I was puzzled beyond measure by his motions and expressions. With his hands above his head, he seemed to be dancing on the bottom of the river, and with every step he gave a shout of pleasure. While I looked at him, astonished, I began to feel the infection of his strange conduct. A thrill like soft music ran through me, and seemed to tingle in my ears and under my tongue; and every movement I made brought a repetition of the inexpressible sound, for a sound it was, like a musical echo.

"What is it?" I cried at length. "This is wonderful!"

"It is a musical beach—a singing beach!" he answered. "And I should say it was the finest in the world!" And then he said, for by strange chance he knew something about such a queer thing, "I believe there are only two or three 'singing beaches' known in the whole world; and this certainly must be the best."

You may be sure we lingered over that mellifluous swim. We pushed the boats ashore, and went in for the weird, sweet music of the stream. It was enough to make one howl with sheer sensuous enjoyment. As we pushed or scraped the pebbly bottom with our feet we felt or heard, I hardly know which, a rich resonance passing through us, clear and sweet as the soft note of distant cowbells. The slightest displacement of the gravel brought it up, as if it had just escaped from the earth.

When we had tried it a hundred and a thousand times, it occurred to us that neither could hear the note caused by the other—we only heard the sound of our own feet. Again the tenacious memory of my friend found an explanation. He remembered that divers can only talk under water by placing their heads on the bottom.

Another discovery here: You can't get your head to the bottom of a four-foot stream, unless you catch hold of a stone on the bottom and pull yourself down. You can dive, and get your hands or feet or knees down; but not your chin. We are both good swimmers, and we tried in vain. While under water, on the dive, or crawling along the bottom on hands and knees, the river was a drear and silent sluice. At last we got our chins on the bottom, each on a stone, and we heard it—oh! we heard such melodious discord, such a mixture of near and remote echo-like sweetness as can only be imagined in dreams. The river became as full of music as it was of water, and the inexpressible fusion of notes played through our senses like intoxication. Smith was twenty or thirty feet from me, and in deeper water; but every sweep he gave the pebbles sounded to me like a thousand cowbells melted into liquid harmony. Never, until we go to the same spot again, shall we hear such strange, suppressed, elfin music. . . .

It would be better, perhaps, if I could follow the river features *seriatim,* as we saw them; but then there are so many miles of every river that are only one uninteresting feature. No one cares for the names of little unheard-of villages, themselves quite featureless. Some whole days we did nothing but run insignificant rapids, until at last we came to despise them, so that we sometimes ran our canoes at them without searching for an opening, and for our pains always narrowly escaped upsetting, and always, too, had to get out and wade. The rapids of the Susquehanna teach as much patience and wariness as the logs of the Connecticut. You can manage both, like little children, when you take the trouble of finding the right way; otherwise they will crush your boat and you like the insensate brutes they are when opposed.

About ten miles above Towanda we entered on a memorable experience. The river was wide, about half a mile, and we heard an unusually loud rapid about a quarter of a mile ahead. It was noon, and we landed on a pretty shaded bank on the right, to eat our dinner. The day was hot, and the shade was luxurious. We gave plenty of time to cooking and eating and swimming and smoking, . . .

About two o'clock, a poor-looking fellow, in a poorer-looking old flat-bottomed boat, drifted past, going towards the rapid water. We asked him on which side the current ran.

"Don't know," he answered, sounding all his r's like a true native: "I was neverr hearr befoarr. I'm a strangerr!" And, looking anxiously ahead, he drifted towards the breakers. We were then dining, and we watched him for our own instruction as we ate. We saw the swift stream take him, changing his course a little, and carry him into the rapid. He went down a few boat lengths and struck. He jumped out, and saved the scow, hauling his boat back. Why he did not try to drag her down, instead of coming back, was a mystery. At last we forgot him; and an hour later we got afloat. The first thing we saw was the old boat, empty and aground, at the side of the rapid. The man was nowhere to be seen. What had become of him? He could hardly have been drowned in three or four feet of water, however rapid. And yet he had said he was a stranger.

We paddled to the other side of the river and shot down a rare piece of swift water without difficulty. We were in a hurry, for the sky behind us was "black as thunder" with an enormous cloud, and already the air was filled with dead leaves from the mountain, carried out on the river by the first gusts. A few heavy drops of rain struck our faces and arms, and made little towers on the river.

The river was running with extreme rapidity, and the increasing wind, right behind us, ruffled it into whitecaps in a few minutes, and drove us ahead at an exciting pace. We hardly knew what to do, being ignorant of the manner of storms in those parts; but as the gale was in our favor we simply steered straight, and held on. The stream ran "palpably down hill," deep and swift. On our left was a grand mountain, almost precipitous, but wooded to the top, and black with the coming gloom. The river almost ran under its brow.

As we plunged ahead we heard the sound of rapid water above the roar of the gale; we had no time to search for an opening; but fortunately the water was deeper than usual. We kept to the left, as the river fell toward the mountain and dashed for the rapid. Two fishermen in a boat were running before us, about a hundred yards ahead. Suddenly we saw them lurch forward, while the boat swung round and the water leaped into her. They had kept two yards too far to the left, but they had shown us the way. They were in the water up to their waists, holding their boat, as we shot past them without a word. They looked at us with grim faces, quite silent, as if dumbfounded. We were fairly lifted over the stones of that rapid by the wind and waves; and a few minutes later we knew what reason we had to be thankful, when the whole fury of the storm burst on us.

We had learned that an unbroken stretch of river lay before us, clear to Towanda, six miles away. We could see the spire of a church against the lurid sky far down the valley. The sky ahead was fast filling with heaps of dark clouds, racing faster than I have ever seen clouds move. Behind, from horizon to zenith, the air was like a slate-colored cavern, with masses and feathery sheets of dark-brown vapor, tumbling and rushing low down, so low as to strike the mountain. There was no rain—nothing but wind, and it was right astern, and held there by the towering mountain on our left. The waves combed out before us, higher than the boats. We could not have kept a quarter of a point off such a blast. We felt the gale on our backs like a physical pressure. It was a magnificent race. We had not even to steer. We sat still and were driven straight ahead, and, had there been a bend in the river, we should have had to run ashore. As quickly as the storm had risen, it subsided or passed. Far sooner than I would dare to write, we saw the tall bridge at Towanda half a mile ahead of us. We had run down five or six miles of river in as quick time, I think, as canoes could safely travel.

Before we reached Towanda the storm had crossed the mountain and the sun was out. We kept to the left of the river, ran under the bridge, round an island, and then dashed through a splendid little rapid, right in front of the city, and ran across to a boathouse. . . .

Of our nights on the banks of the river the details are too varied to be written. We enjoyed them intensely after the first three days, when the heat of the sunburn had abated. The only drawback was caused by our own persistent mistake; we did not pitch our camp early enough, and the darkness closed on us before we were quite ready for rest. We were tempted each day to go on paddling till the sun had reached the tops of the mountains; and we had not realized how the mountains hurry on the sunset.

The story of one night will do for all. We pulled our canoes ashore under a wooded bank twenty feet high, and pitched our camp in a lovely little meadow above. It was six o'clock when we left the boats. The river was exceedingly beautiful from our meadow, reminding me of the Connecticut in its superb reaches below Northampton. Across the river, against the distant hills, rose the spire of a church; but there was not a house in sight. The nearest village was Tioga Center, five miles away. The current in the river was almost still; the water under our bank was about ten feet deep. Though we had much to do before we lost the sun, we could not help giving a few minutes to drink in the extreme beauty of the evening scene.

Firewood was not to be had for the picking up, as usual; but we found a dead tree, partly fallen, supported by its fellows fringing the river. We cut it down in quick time with our axe, chopped off some punky lengths of the trunk, tied one of our painters to the remainder, and snaked it out of the underbrush. The dry branches broke and burned like tinder, and the larger ones, with the trunk, made us a roaring fire till morning. That night for supper we broiled some bacon and boiled some tinned beef, putting in a lot of Liebig's extract. Then coffee, eked out with our precious but ill-fated butter and marmalade.

Then—let us tell the truth, so that the price may be paid—we went to a stack of coarse hay in the meadow, and took two great armfuls, which we spread in our tent, and which was softer that night than down-of-eider. About the hour of this dark deed, the full moon rose over the hills and sailed into a sky black-blue, starlit, and absolutely clear from mist or cloud. The only vapor to be seen was a slight smoke that clung in a thin, wavy line to the middle of the river. The only sound, except our own voices, was the screech of an owl on the hills and the leap of the bass in the water.

The night was breathless; but we raised the bottom of the tent, and made a pleasant draft. Before ten o'clock we were asleep. How long that sleep lasted I cannot tell—perhaps three hours; but it was ended in a most awful uproar. In my sleep I had heard for hours, so it seemed, the thunder of rapids and falls greater than Niagara, into which the canoe was slipping against all my power to steer or stop her. Nearer and nearer the horror came; there were people on the shore shouting, and one of them blew a whistle that would wake the dead, and I sprang up in the tent at the same moment that Smith jumped to his feet. Without moving farther we saw the cause of the disturbance. Within forty yards of us ran a railroad, along which was thundering one of these interminable coal trains, that are longer, I am sure, than any other trains in the world. The noise had affected us both in almost the same way; and we were so completely awakened that to sleep again seemed out of the question.

So we piled up our firewood till the flames illuminated the somber hills. Then we mixed with sugar and water a stiff dose of our remedy for the malaria; but before enjoying this, the night was so warm and lightsome and the river so tempting, I plunged into the deep water for a short swim. When I came in, Smith was singing; and we sat by the fire and sang on and on, and the screech owl stopped to listen; and the fire and the tobacco burned as if they enjoyed it; and it was well for the malaria that it did not come around that night.

Say what you will, there is no other form of outing that makes possible, within sight of conventional life and labor, such days and nights of utter freedom, health, natural beauty, . . .

. . . There is no sport or exercise so complete as canoeing a river, for it embraces all sports—the excitement of rapid water, the delicious plunge, the long swim downstream, the fishing and shooting, the free camping out at night, and the endless beauty of the panoramic scene. Canoe clubs may meet and vote and compete and sail regatta races on the lakes. But the true canoeist knows not sail nor prize, but searches with the paddle all the bends and rapids and shadowed reaches of our peerless American rivers.

DOWN THE DELAWARE RIVER IN A CANOE

"You can run everything on the river but the Big Foul," said the teamster at Port Jervis, as he helped us launch the canoes from a gravel bank.

"Where is the Big Foul?"

"Below Belvidere: you'll strike it in a few days. No boat can run that rift at this stage of the water."

"Oh, it's a rift," said Moseley, standing knee-deep in the river, and packing his canoe. "I thought it was a bird. Why is it called the Big Fowl?"

"It is the foulest rapid on the Delaware," answered the teamster. "I know the river to Trenton; went down last May on a fresh. You can run all the rest; but you'll have to carry round the Big Foul Rift."

We had before heard about this rapid with the ominous name. . . .

I had with me also the notes of one of the best canoemen in the country, who had run the Delaware in the spring of last year, to which I referred, and found these words:

Great Foul Rift, short distance below Belvidere. Ran down on rafting fresh in May. Length almost a mile and a half from head of Little Foul to foot of Great Foul. Rapidity of water and danger much exaggerated.

"That's all right for a spring fresh," said the teamster, who had heard this note read. "But the river is ten feet lower now; and it's the bottom of a river that's dangerous, not the top."

Guiteras was the first in his canoe. "Here goes for Philadelphia!" he cried, as he pushed off. "Are there any rapids near us, down the river?"

"Listen!" and the teamster smiled.

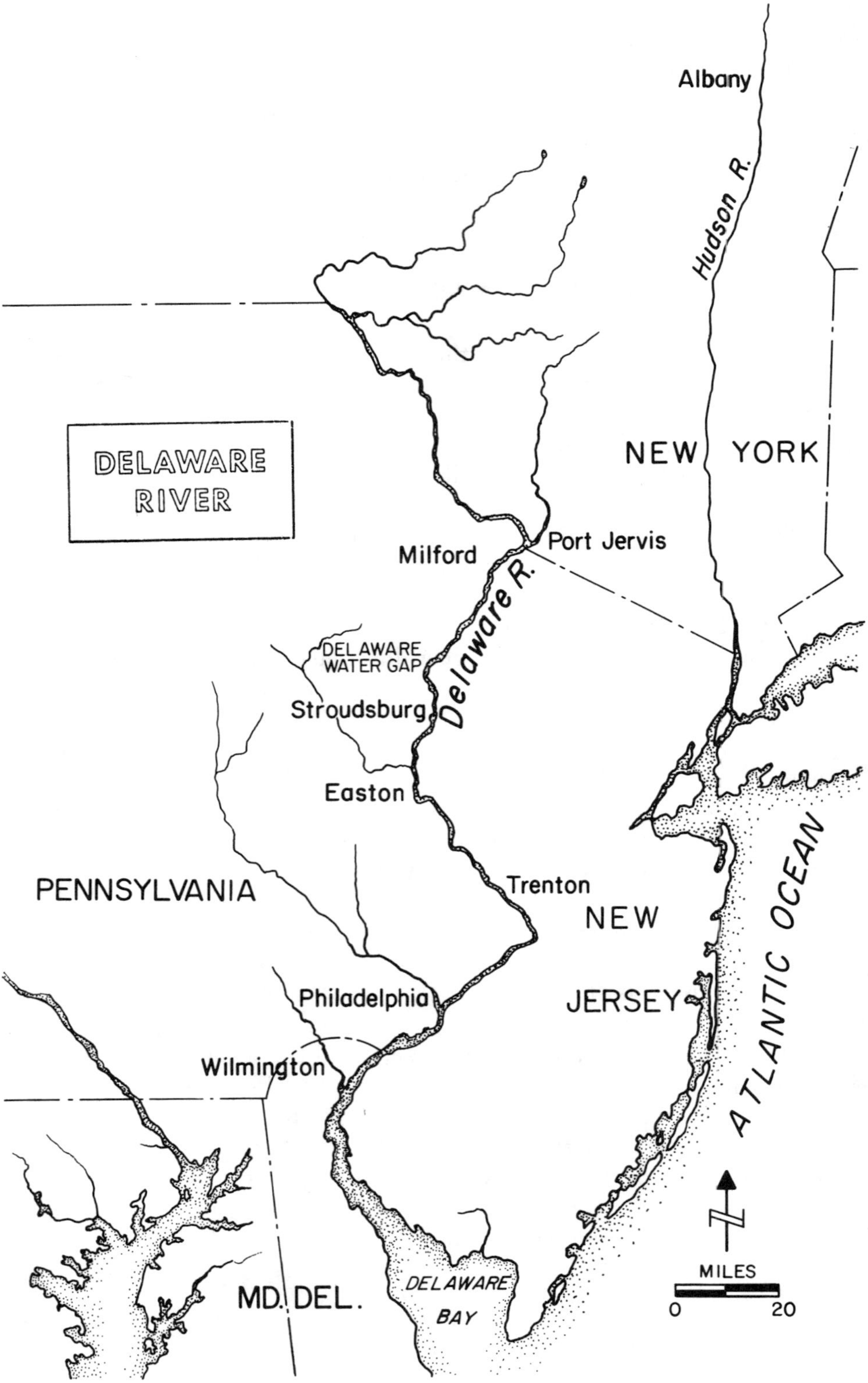
DELAWARE RIVER
Albany
Hudson R.
NEW YORK
Port Jervis
Milford
Delaware R.
DELAWARE WATER GAP
Stroudsburg
Easton
Trenton
PENNSYLVANIA
NEW JERSEY
Philadelphia
Wilmington
ATLANTIC OCEAN
MD. DEL.
DELAWARE BAY
MILES
0
20

We listened and heard one, the sound coming from the bend of the river half a mile below.

"It's only a little one," shouted the teamster, as we started. "Keep well to the left, and you'll find a channel. It is a smooth rift."

We were three, in three canoes—Mr. Edward A. Moseley in a stout boat built by Partelow, of the Charles River; Dr. Ramon Guiteras, in a strong Racine; while mine was a keelless, decked canoe, by the best builder in the world, Rushton, of Canton, N.Y.

It was two in the afternoon of a glorious day when we started from Port Jervis. After a long, dusty railroad ride, it is impossible to convey the exhilarating sense of freedom and enjoyment which one feels during the first moments in his canoe. To plunge the bare arms to the elbow into the river as you go, and let the cool water curl up to the biceps; to feel the soft breeze on bare head and neck; to be far from the busy crowds in the cities, with all the senses awake to new and fascinating objects—the swirl of rapid water, the brown and yellow stones on the bottom of the river, the large, free movements of clouds, the strange flowers on the bank; to grip the paddle with an agreeable sense of power in shoulder and hand; to brace the feet strongly against the footrest and feel the canoe spring with the elastic force of the stroke; to shout unrestrainedly to your companions, and hear them shout in return like hearty, natural men; to laugh consumedly with slight cause; and in the midst of all this joyous wakefulness, to be aware of the nearing rapid ahead—to hear its low, steady roar, as if the sound clung to the water; and to be aware also of a new preparation of nerve, sight, and muscle—a purely animal and instinctive alertness—for the moment of rushing excitement into which you are sweeping—all this we experienced within ten minutes of leaving the gravel bed at Port Jervis, and while the teamster still shouted to us from the shore.

We were silent at first, and surprised. It took us some moments to realize that the surprise was delight. The river was not deep—three or four feet at most; but it ran downhill like a hunted hare. There was something quite new in it, too, which I concluded to be the long, wavy green weeds near the bottom, that floated straight with the current like a yacht's pennant in a gale, and by their swaying and glistening in the depths indicated the course and the extraordinary rapidity of the water.

"This is superb!" said one. The others echoed the word.

Almost before we knew, we were in the rush of the first rapid. We had not carefully followed the teamster's instructions to keep to the extreme left; and we had passed the narrow mouth of the channel. Before us ran an oblique bar of heavy stones, over which the river poured like a curtain. It ran clear across the river, and we found ourselves far into the closed angle. The water on the curtain to the left roared like a heavy surf, and we knew that we could not get over or through. There was no opening between the stones more than two feet wide, and beyond or below was a hundred yards of chaotic rock and roar.

We turned and paddled upstream—I might have said uphill. Inch by inch we gained, working with feverish speed, the paddle slipping back in the glancing stream as if it were in air, holding hardly any force.

But we climbed the first descent, and steered across to where the channel hugged the right bank. Guiteras went in first; he had not gone up far enough by a boat's length, and as he shot across into the narrow channel, his canoe lurched upon one side, stood a moment and swung athwart stream. He had struck; but before a thought of danger could follow, the paddle was buried, and with a lifting push, his boat slipped over the stone and rushed down the rapid like a leaf.

The other canoes followed, avoiding the buried stone. It was a vigorous little rush—about two hundred yards in length, and not fifteen feet in width. The water was deep, but its speed made it rise in a leap over every stone on the bottom, and hurl itself in all kinds of ridges and furrows and springing whitecaps.

At the bottom of the rift we plunged into a heap of boiling breakers, still running like mad. Next moment we floated into smooth water, and turned and looked back at our first rapid with much laughing and congratulation.

The rapid, or rift (on the Upper Delaware all rapids are *rifts;* on the Lower Delaware all rifts are *falls;* the change beginning, I think, about Easton, as, for instance, Sawmill Rift, Death's Eddy Rift, Big Foul Rift, and below, Welles's Falls, Trenton Falls, etc.) —the rapid we had passed on, looking back, seemed insignificant in descent and roughness; but we were fairly astonished at the speed of the water, and I think we had a vague consciousness that it would have been no child's play to steer through that channel had it been of any considerable length, and broken by rocks. The teamster had called it "a little one," and "a smooth rift"; what, then, were the big ones? There was no mention at all of this rift in the notes of the canoeman which I had with me. What was the ominous Great Foul Rift in comparison?

As we gazed back at the rapid, it receded from us swiftly. We were on the quiet surface of deep water, but going down at the rate of several miles an hour.

The current still kept to the left bank, and an odd bank it was—worth describing, because it continued intermittently quite down to Trenton, where the last rapid on the Delaware pitches the canoeman into tidal water. The bank resembled molten metal that had hardened. It was almost black, a clean, smooth stone, with round puffholes in it, no vegetation whatever on the steep slope of, say, twenty feet from the water's edge, above which rose a wooded hill, almost a mountain. The metallic bank ended abruptly in the stream, and the deep current alongside ran with astonishing swiftness.

I realized in brief time that up to that day I had not known rapid water, continued in a long stream. The Susquehanna rapids are short and sharp descents, followed by slow and gentle reaches, some of which are miles in length. The Connecticut, in a memory of six years' distance, spreads out like a lake, with here and there a log moving alongshore, showing that there actually *is* a current. The Merrimack was remembered as a very millpond, except on the short descent of Miller's Falls, near Haverhill, and in the powerful tidal rush under Deer Island Chainbridge at Newburyport; while many lesser streams were quite forgotten in presence of this grand artery which carried us onward almost as fast as we could paddle on slower rivers.

I have given too much space to our first rapid on the Delaware, which, we soon found, was only one of scores before us, and a small one—even a "smooth one." But it will save other descriptions; and it gives our first impression of the river. Having run the Delaware from Port Jervis to Philadelphia, we found that this first rapid was singularly characteristic. All the considerable rapids are of a somewhat similar formation—except the Great Foul Rift, which is unique.

The rapids of the Delaware are formed in the main by an oblique line of rocks crossing the river, leaving a narrow channel on one side, or sometimes the opening is almost one third of the way across, with reefs on both sides.

With deep water, say in May or June, when the river is from eight to ten feet higher than it was in the last week of August, a canoeman may run two hundred miles of this incomparable river without striking a stone. But every foot of fall in the stream makes a totally new river; and he who goes down on a freshet in early summer cannot imagine what the river is like at low water in late autumn.

The Delaware is a river of extraordinary pitch, the fall from Port Jervis to Philadelphia being nearly 1,200 feet.

On that first afternoon we intended to run down to Milford, twelve miles distant, where, we had been told, there was a famous hotel. But we lingered on the way. In the sweltering heat we pulled the canoes ashore and plunged into the delicious water, drinking it as we swam—a sensation for epicures. We lay prone in the rapid stream, our arms outspread, and our faces under water, floating quickly down, and looking at the yellow and white pebbles on the bottom.

At last we came to a lovely spot, a soft white sandbank on the left, the Jersey side, formed by the junction of a bright little river with the Delaware. Every paddle was laid down. Half a mile below we heard the dull roar of a rapid. Here the river was very deep and swift, and not more than eighty yards wide. On the right, a wooded but precipitous mountain rose almost straight from the water to a height of at least eight hundred feet. From his eyrie far up we had disturbed a white-headed eagle which floated and tipped its great wings above us as it moved slowly downriver.

The sandbank was in the angle where the little river fell over a short rapid of twenty yards into the Delaware. The bank was hemmed in by a dense wood.

We camped on the sandbank for the night. One man erected the tent; another cooked dinner; the third went in search of a farmhouse for milk, eggs, melons and peaches—the staple of our food for the next fortnight.

While the dinner simmered we had a trial of strength with the Delaware itself, breast to breast. Swiftly we struck across and down the river for a hundred yards, and then turned and faced the stream. Three strong swimmers—two of the three extraordinary. Moseley, with the overhand stroke, which sends him about eight feet a stroke in still water, made progress at the rate of about one foot a stroke. Guiteras barely held his own, swimming as if he were anchored; and, watching the bank, I saw that I was actually going downstream. Under such circumstances you can do a great deal of swimming in a quarter of an hour.

The sun went down on the left, above the low trees, without cloud or haze. For a long time after its disappearance the upward rays flamed on the face of the great cliff across the river, the red gleam moving higher and higher, and the darkness creeping up the wooded wall like a vast tide. When the line of light had cleared the brow of the cliff the trees above, diminished to a fingerlength, blazed in gold and crimson; and then, almost suddenly, the light left them—rose over them, and was lost in space, and they, too, were swallowed up in the night.

"The light that shoots over the heads of trees or people," said Moseley, "might as well not exist."

With which philosophic reflection, we spread our rubber blankets on the sand of the tent, over these our woollen blankets; and then, with a big fire blazing a few feet from the tent's mouth, we lay or sat for our coffee and cigars.

Throughout our trip this quiet smoking hour, each evening with a strange scene before us, was a most enjoyable part of the day.

We slept as if the night were an hour long, and we woke to plunge into the sweet unchilled water. We started without breakfast, hoping to reach Milford and the "famous cook" at an early hour.

The miles were long, and the river unendingly broken. It was downhill all the time, rift succeeding rift. Do what we could with careful steering, we struck again and again, and we were in constant danger of smashing boats or paddles. So common became the striking that we coined a word for it—"hung up." And we could not help laughing, when one struck, as we swept past and saw him grimly poling his canoe over a rock, or raising his feet over the gunwale, as he got out to haul her over. For this we had to be always ready; trousers tucked up, and canvas shoes on.

It came to be a jesting habit, that when one led into a rapid he would do so with a boastful shout. This was my part, at one time on this second day. I had gone into a rift with much flourish, and, a third of the way through, had been "hung up." Down rushed the others with loud derision, avoiding the bad place. Imagine my feeling of disgust at their selfishness, as I saw their backs, leaving me there. Next moment, in the worst part of the rapid, I saw one of them strike and hold his boat with his paddle against a rock; and a second or two later the other struck just beside him. Who could help smiling? And that moment, by a fortunate lurch, my canoe floated and rushed down toward the two, who were now struggling knee-deep in the stream. They held on to let me pass, and scowled as if my laugh were in bad taste.

At ten o'clock we reached Milford, Penn., and climbed the hundred feet of steep bank on which the little town stands. Over the town, all around, rose still many hundred feet of grandly wooded mountains. The hotel, they told us, was over twelve hundred feet above sea level. The hotel we found to be even better than its report.

Ever since starting at Port Jervis, Moseley had kept referring to the beauty of the scenery at Walpack Bend, some fifteen or twenty miles below Milford. He had a camera with him, and his desire to get out and take a view grew on him like a disease. No impatience, or protest, or prayer affected him. "When we get home," he would unselfishly say, "these pictures will be the best part of the trip." And he was right.

The banks on both sides now rose into mountains, wooded to the top. The river was a series of deep and swift reaches, and then a leaping rift, with a steep descent.

In the very center of one of these rapids, an unusually deep one, my canoe struck on a covered rock and I knew in a flash that she must either get instantly over or be rolled downstream. Thought and act united. I lifted her by a vigorous push, and was whirled down, stern foremost, with my paddle broken.

Fortunately, the channel below was deep, though rough and very rapid. To meet the emergency I knelt up, instead of sitting as heretofore, and used the broken end of the paddle as a pole, fending off rocks, and steering occasionally with the blade end.

Before I had cleared the rapid I knew that my loss was a gain. The best way to steer a canoe down a rapid is to kneel and use *a long paddle with one blade, the other end to be used as a pole.*

I had a spare paddle in the canoe, a delicate spoon paddle, only fit for deep water. As soon as the rift was past, I jointed this and used it; but when the next rift was heard, laid it aside and took up the broken paddle.

The memory of that day is wholly confused with the noise of rapid water. We were no sooner through one rift than we heard another. The names of the rapids were quaint and suggestive: such as Death's Eddy, Fiddler's Elbow, Milliner's Shoe, Sambo and Mary, Vancamp's Nose, and Shoemaker's Eddy.

One must use colors, not words, to paint the beauty of the scene that opened before us on our third day, when we ran the upper rapid at Walpack Bend, and floated into a reach of river that can hardly be surpassed in the world. On our right and left the banks were low and richly timbered; and straight ahead, barring our way, about half a mile off, a high mountain, wooded from the water to the crest.

The river runs straight to the mountain foot, and there turns directly to the left. It is not a curve or a sweep, but distinctly a right angle; and then, for one mile with the hill to the right and the low farms on the left, and for two miles with the mountain to the left and the farms to the right, the grand stream paces slowly, like a proud horse in the eye of a multitude.

Here we had a striking illustration of the power of color. The wooded height before us rose at least twelve hundred feet. The river below was green with the immense reflection. But on the very line of union, where the leaves met and kissed in air and water, was a little flame of crimson, which held the eye and centered all the immensity.

It was one small cardinal flower, a plant that grows all the way along the Delaware. The intensity of its color is indescribable. After this superb exhibition of its power, one little red flower against a mile of green and silver, I gathered every day a handful of the lovely blossoms and set them on the bow of the canoe.

When one thinks of the marvels of this river, the regret becomes painful that they are unknown to the outer world, that they are only seen by the natives of the scenes and the accidental canoe voyager.

The rivers are the veins and arteries of a country, the railroads and roads the nerves and sinews. . . .

But one is tempted to linger too long on such a scene as this at Walpack Bend. Here, for the first time since we left Port Jervis, the water ran slowly. It is hard to leave a spot so beautiful, where so few strangers are led. Here was Nature at first hand. To impress it deeper on my mind, I retrace our course, on the bank, to where, a hundred yards above the bend, a little singing river flows into the Delaware. Only a few inches deep, babbling over brown pebbles, bright as the sun itself in its flashes, coming down under a dim arch of trees and fringing underwood—a very dream of a little singing brook, that "Knows the way to the sea." Here, sitting on a stone, enjoying the soft susurrus in my ears and in the leaves and in the ripples, comes along a country boy, fishing—down the dim arch, walking in the little river, barefooted.

"Bushmill Creek is its name," he says; and he knows no more about it—not how long it is, nor whence it comes. But yet a commentator and critic, this barefooted fisher.

"How far have you fellows come?" he asked, examining the canoes.

"From Port Jervis."

"And how far are you going?"

"To Philadelphia."

"Well"—a long pause—"you fellows must want something to do!". . . .

But we were approaching one of the glories of the Delaware—the most famous and certainly the most sublime—the Water Gap. We reached it unexpectedly. We knew when it was only a few miles away, but we could see nothing ahead but the unbroken mountain range on each side. One mile away, and the range had closed around us in a bight, leaving no perceptible opening for the river.

"Where is the Water Gap?" we asked a boatful of fishers, anchored under a bridge.

"You'll see it in half a minute," they answered. "And look out! for just round the turn there, you will be in the rapid."

We did not need the warning; we were in the quick water already. Looking into the stream, we saw the yellow stones on the bottom fly sternward at an extraordinary pace. The roar of a powerful rapid reached us as we came to a sharp turn in the river; and below us we saw a memorable scene.

I do not know the descending angle of that rapid, nor the measure of its fall; but it seemed as if we were on the top of a hill of rushing water, at the bottom of which, less than a mile away, was a vast wooded basin, its green slope broken by two white hotels set on the hillside, but still seeming far below us.

There was no time for admiration, or for anything but steering. We ran down the Jersey shore, close to the rocky mountain foot, in the fastest rush so far. The river plunged from ledge to ledge fiercely; but the channel was deep. At the foot of the fall, we were shot into a whirlpool of yellow breakers that curled up and washed clean over the canoes, drenching all, and almost swamping one of them.

We stopped at the Water Gap that night, and sat long on the wide veranda of the hotel, looking at the wonderful scene. The river passes between two mountains, as through a tremendous gateway; and one feels, without knowing, that beyond that imperial portal, the scene must change into something quite new and strange.

This we found to be true. The Delaware may be said to have left the mountains when it pours through the Water Gap. Henceforth, its banks are bold, or even precipitous, as the right bank surely is in a wonderful cliff some miles below Reigelsville; but it is a mountain river no longer.

In the morning, before starting, we climbed the mountain and looked down on the wild beauty of the Water Gap. From that height the fall in the river was imperceptible; and the rapid that had astonished us the day before looked like a mere shallow brawl.

Few people are aware of the force and danger of rapid broken water. To the person who drives or walks along a river, the rapid seems the safest spot, because it is obviously the shallowest. But, as the teamster said at Port Jervis, it is "the bottom that is to be feared, not the top."

"It is just the same with humanity," says Guiteras, when this thought is spoken, "it is the superficial and hasty people who make all the trouble. Depth of mind is as safe as depth of water."

The last word to us from the boatkeeper at the Water Gap was, of course, a warning about the Great Foul Rift. We ran two or three rapids that day that tested nerves and boats, and were exasperated to hear that they were "smooth rifts," and "nothing at all to the Big Foul."

In the high heat of the afternoon, we came to a place where a little waterfall leaped down a bank almost twenty feet into the river. The falling water was white as snow. We went under it and enjoyed a glorious shower bath, but found that in the center the water fell in lumps almost as heavy and hurtful as clay.

That day, too, we had another novel and delightful experience. We came to an unbroken reach of river on which the descent was so great that a stretch of two miles before us resembled a coasting hill of ice. The river was about five feet deep, with a gravel bottom. We let the canoes float, and we followed, with outspread arms and faces in the water, fairly coasting down that wonderful liquid slope.

Late in the evening, not finding a pleasant camping place, we settled at last on a tolerable spot, on an island. We were tired, and we soon fell asleep—to be awakened by a shout of horror from Guiteras, over whose hand a snake had crawled! He had flung the reptile from him, out of the tent.

After such a start, sleep was out of the question. We lay, however, and tried to rest. But every rustle of the leaves outside, every insect that stirred in the grass, brought a chill and creepy feeling.

"I am going to sleep in the canoe," at last said one; and at the word we gathered our blankets and abandoned the tent.

If it were not for the danger of straining the boat if pulled ashore, or of catching malaria if it be left afloat, the canoe is the pleasantest and easiest sleeping place.

In the morning a swim, a solid breakfast, and an extra careful packing of the canoes. No one spoke of it; but that morning we were each conscious of a particular attention paid to the trim of the boats and the stowing of dunnage. At about eleven o'clock in the forenoon we would reach Belvidere; and the Great Foul Rift was only a mile farther.

There was a camp of bass fishers near us, and they came to see us start. They learned our intention of going down without portage, rift or no rift. They did not dissuade us. One of them said he knew the Big Foul Rift, and he gave us precise, too precise, instructions. All I could recall half an hour later was, "Keep to the right when you come to the big white stone—if there's water enough to float your boats."

It was noon when we came to the town of Belvidere, and paddled into deep water under a mill. We needed some necessaries for our dinner, and we could buy them here. The schoolboys flocked to the bank to see the canoes, and the mill workers (it was the dinner hour) came down to have a chat.

"You are not going to run the rift?" asked one.

"Yes, we are."

"They can do it: they don't draw more than two inches," said another.

We knew that at least one of the canoes, heavily laden with baggage, and with a heavy man in her, drew more than six inches. We could get no information worth having, except a repetition of the fisherman's word: "Keep to the right of the big rock, two-thirds of the way down—if you can."

"Nobody has gone down the rift for five weeks," said the man who had first spoken.

Guiteras was going ashore for the necessaries; and as he stood in his canoe, about to step on a log that edged the bank, he slipped, and pitched headfirst into the deep water. We were so used to going into the water anyway, that the other two sat quite still in the canoes, as if not heeding, while Guiteras climbed out and shook himself, in a matter-of-course kind of way. This nonchalance created an impression on the crowd; and shortly after, when we started, the general prediction was audibly in our favor.

"Keep to the right of the big white rock, and you will strike the channel," shouted a man as we started.

Half a mile or so below Belvidere, we felt the water quicken and sweep to the right—the Pennsylvania bank. We knew we were in the first reach of the rapid that had been roaring for us since we started.

There are two distinct rapids—the Little Foul and the Great

Foul—divided by a reach of safe but swift water of half a mile.

From the moment we struck the Little Foul Rift, we knew we were in the grip of a giant. We were as much astonished as if we had never run a rapid before. We shot down the river—each one finding his own channel—like chips; and, with all our careful steering, we grazed several dangerous stones.

There was no stopping at the foot of the Little Foul Rift; but we ran with the stream without paddling, and examined the entrance to the Great Rapid ahead.

There was no bar or ledge formation here, as in the minor rifts behind us. The rocks stood up like the broken teeth of a sperm whale, irregularly across the river, and as far ahead as we could see from the canoes. Some of the stones were twelve feet out of the water, others of lesser height, and of all shapes; some were level with the surface, and some covered with a few inches of water. These last were the dangers: to strike and get "hung up" on one of these meant certain upsetting; for no boat could stand the rush, and there was no footing for the canoeman if he tried to get out to push her over.

But more threatening than the tall rocks, that looked like a disorganized Stonehenge, was the terrible nature of the bedrock, and the broken stones on the bottom. We could steer between the teeth we saw, but we suddenly became conscious of unseen teeth that lay in wait to lacerate the boats under the waterline.

The whole bed of the river is formed of a rock that is worn and wasted in a strangely horrible way, as if it were pitted with a hideous smallpox. Round and oval holes are seen everywhere in the rock, some of them as much as two feet deep and three feet across, and the upper edges of these bowls are as sharp as scythes.

We saw the process of this singular pitting. Heavy stones are caught on an angle of the bottom and rolled over and over without proceeding, till they wear out these cup-like holes, and are buried deeper and deeper in their ceaseless industry. As the bowl increases in size, it catches two workers instead of one, and these grind each other and grind the matrix till the very heart of Nature must admit their toil, and pity their restlessness.

Some of these great stone cups were high out of water, empty and dry; and their round tormentors lay in peace on the bottom.

Some were above the surface, but still half full of water that had dashed into them from the rapid.

But there was a keener evil than the circular knife tops of these vessels; and it was their broken edges.

When the torrents of winter and spring thunder through the Great Foul Rift, whirling and dragging trunks of trees and massive stones down the surcharged channels, the pitted ledges of bottom and bank are smashed like potsherds, the imprisoned stones are released and shoot down the river, and the fractured rock remains to cut the water with irregular edges as sharp as a shattered punchbowl.

We were going into the Great Foul Rift all this time, at the rate of—but who can tell the rate of rapid water? The best canoeman I know says there is no canoeing water in America over twelve miles an hour—I think he places this on the Susquehanna, below Columbia—and that eight miles is very rapid indeed. He may be right; but, were I asked how fast we went into the Great Foul Rift, I should say, at least, at the rate of twelve miles an hour, and, in parts of the descent, much faster.

Guiteras went first, but was caught on a covered flat stone in the quick, smooth water; and Moseley led into the rapid, Guiteras, who had floated off, following. I came about fifty yards behind.

From the first break of the water, the sensation was somewhat similar to that of falling through the branches of a tree. The river was twisting downhill in convulsions. We rushed through narrow slopes of ten or twenty feet as if we were falling, and then shot round a rock, flinging the whole weight of our bodies on the steering paddle. The tall stones ahead seemed to be rushing at us with the velocity of an ocean steamer.

All the time we were painfully conscious of the presence of the incisive edges under water, as one might feel the nearness of burglars' knives in the night. If we struck one of these stones on a downward shoot, it would rip the canoe from bow to stern.

Moseley steered skilfully, and we cleared two-thirds of the tortuous descent without a shock. A quarter of a mile ahead we saw the smooth water at the foot of the rift. We had crossed the river, and were running down on the Pennsylvania shore. Suddenly, the channel we were in divided at a great white stone, the wider water going to the left, toward the center of the river, and a narrow black streak keeping straight down to the right.

A memory of the warning came to me, "Keep to the right of the big rock—if you can." But it was too late. A man could not hear his own shout in such an uproar. The white rock rushed past us. The canoes ahead had turned with the main stream, and were in the center of the river in a flash. Suddenly both canoes ahead were shot out of the channel, their bows in the air resting on a hidden rock; and the current, just then turning a sharp curve, swept by their sterns with a rush. Fortunately they were out of the stream, driven into an eddy, or that had been the end of them.

I had time to profit by their mishap. Kneeling in the canoe, using the long-handled paddle, I rounded the curve within a foot of the grounded canoes, and fairly leaped downhill on a rounded muscle of water. In the rush, a thrill swept my nerves—and another—as if twice I had touched cold steel. I found later that my canoe had twice been pierced by the knife-like edges under water.

Before I realized it, the end had come, and the canoe shot across the river in a sweeping eddy. The Great Foul Rift was behind me.

A fisherman on the bank had been watching our passage. "You ought to have kept to the right of that stone," he shouted. "See, there's the channel!" And, looking up, I saw it, straight as a furrow from the big white stone, keeping swift, close to the Pennsylvania shore, unbroken, and safe. Had we kept in this straight way the Great Foul Rift would to us have been no more than an exaggerated name.

The grounded canoemen pushed free, and were down in a minute; and then we went ashore, and while Moseley photographed the Great Foul Rift, the others plunged into the delicious water, that seemed too peaceful and sweet ever to have been violent and brutal.

Half a mile below the Great Foul Rift, we came to the pastoral scene of the voyage, *par excellence*. It was ideal and idyllic—sunny and varied as a Watteau painting. It was not great or grand in any way, but simply peaceful, pastoral, lovely.

It was a sloping hillside, of two or three farms, rising from the river. There were low-roofed homesteads, smothered in soft domestic-looking foliage. A round-arched stone bridge spanned a stream in the foreground. Cows and horses stood in the shadow of the trees in the fields, and a drove of cows stood in the river, the reflection as distinct as the cow—like Herrick's swans, that "floated double—swan and shadow." Dark woods framed the scene on both sides and on top, children's voices at play filled the air, and a dog barked joyously, joining in some romping game.

We laid our paddles on the canoes in front of us, and floated a full mile through the lovely picture. It can never be forgotten. In its quiet way, nothing equaled it on the whole river.

"Photograph the place," I said to Moseley.

"No," he replied. "It is too good for anything but memory.". . .

CANOEING IN THE DISMAL SWAMP

The Dismal Swamp of Virginia and North Carolina is one of the celebrated features of the American continent. Its name is almost as familiar as Niagara or the Rocky Mountains. Its limits are not easily defined, no careful survey or good map of the region having ever been made. It lies in two States, on the Virginia side in the counties of Nasemond and Princess Anne, and on the North Carolina side in the counties of Gates, Pasquotank, Camden, and Currituck. Almost in the center lies Lake Drummond, or "the Lake of the Dismal Swamp," which is seven miles by five in extent, according to local records, but three miles by two and a half by our measurement. The area of the swamp is between eight hundred and one thousand square miles. Its reputation is that of a morass of forbidden and appalling gloom, a region impenetrable to the search of student or hunter; the fecund bed of fever and malaria, infested with deadly serpents and wild beasts; the old-time refuge of fugitive slaves, who preferred life in its lonely recesses to the life-in-death of the slave quarter and the man market. It is supposed by the outer world, and even by those who reside on its borders, to be a hopeless wilderness, an incurable ulcer on the earth's surface, a place that would have been long ago forgotten but for its shadowy romance—for its depths were once enlightened, though it is over fourscore years ago, by the undying song of a famous poet. Some of this evil character is true, but most of it is untrue, and much of the slander has not been accidental, but deliberate.

It is true that the hunted slave often heard the baying of the bloodhounds as he crouched in the canebrake of the Dismal Swamp, or plunged into its central lake to break the trail, and true also that its hundreds of miles of waterlogged forest is infested with repulsive and deadly creatures, reptile and beast, bear, panther, wildcat and snake; but it is not true that the Dismal Swamp is an irreclaimable wilderness, the pestilent source of miasma and malaria.

The Dismal Swamp is an agony of perverted nature. . . .

The Lake of the Dismal Swamp is the very eye of material anguish. Its circle of silvery beach is flooded and hidden, and still the pent-up water, vainly beseeching an outlet, is raised and driven in unnatural enmity to the roots of the tall juniper, cypress, and gum trees, that completely surround its shore. The waves that should murmur and break on a strand of incomparable brilliancy, are pushed beyond their proper limits, and compelled to soften and sap the productive earth, to wash bare and white the sinews of the friendly trees, and inundate a wide region of extraordinary fertility. The bleached roots of the doomed trees seem to shudder and shrink from the weltering death. There is an evident bending upward of the overtaken roots to escape suffocation. The shores of the lake are like a scene from the *Inferno*. Matted, twisted, and broken, the roots, like living things in danger, arch themselves out of the dark flood, pitifully striving to hold aloft their noble stems and branches. The water of the lake, dark almost as blood, from the surface flow of juniper sap and other vegetable matter, is forced from six to ten feet above its natural level, and driven by winds hither to this bank today and thither tomorrow, washing every vestige of earth from the helpless lifegivers, till its whole circumference is a woful network of gnarled trunks and intertwined fibres, bleached and dry as the bones of a skeleton, and sheltering no life, but that of the blue lizard and red-throated moccasin. . . .

The Lake of the Dismal Swamp is a victim waiting for deliverance. . . .

The Lake of the Dismal Swamp is the well of the swamp's desolation. The swamp is not from itself, but from the well. . . .

Its original undoing was probably some accident or cataclysm of

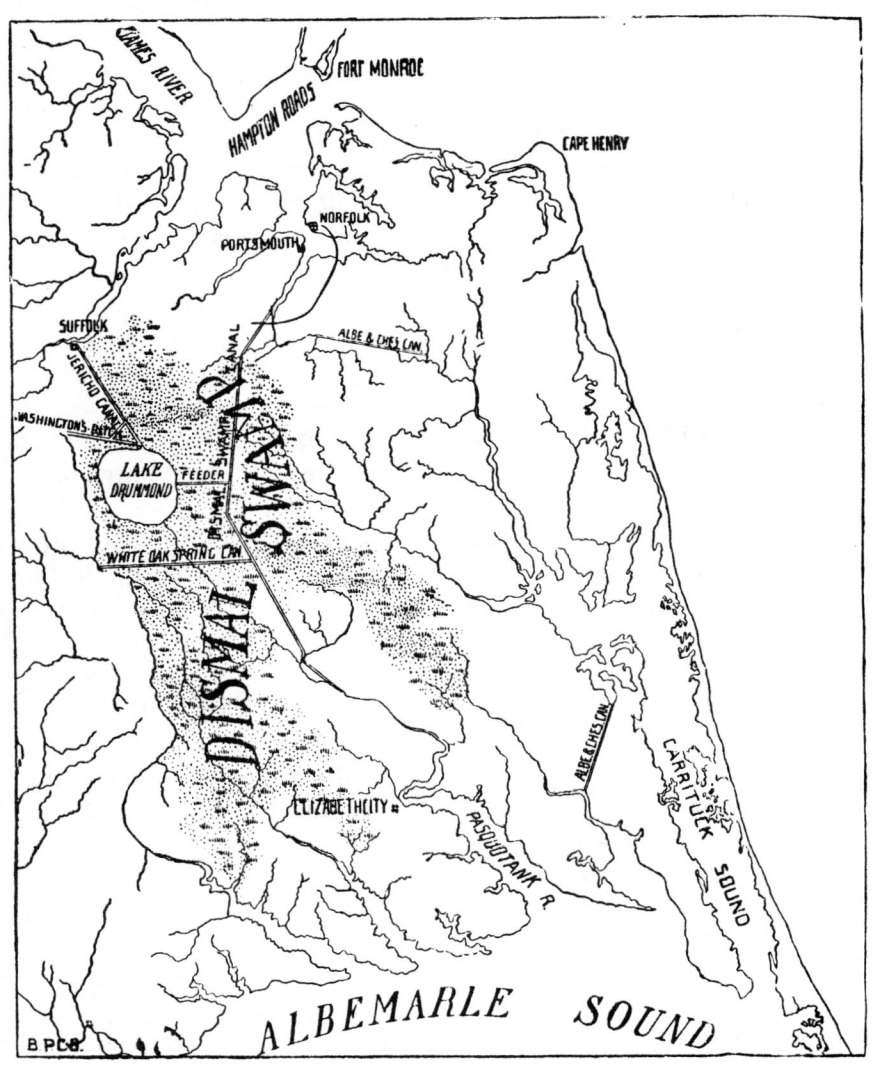

"General Outline of the Dismal Swamp," from *Athletics and Manly Sport*

nature, changing a watercourse or opening a crater-like spring or number of springs.

But the remedy from the first was as easy and as open to intelligence as the tapping of a vein to prevent plethora. The lake, it is probable, was the center and the cause of the swamp, as is proved by the streams flowing out of, instead of into, it. Its overflowing waters, when swelled by rains or springs, finding no natural channel of escape, rose foot by foot to the very lip of the cup, covering the beach and reaching the densely wooded shore.

In this way has been brought about the singular condition of the lake, which, instead of being the lowest, is the highest portion of the Dismal Swamp. It could be pierced and drained at any point, and reduced to natural and beautiful proportions. Its overflow, instead of constantly deluging the surrounding land, could be guided in ten thousand sparkling channels to enrich and adorn its wonderful environment.

The Lake of the Dismal Swamp is, by survey, about twenty-three feet higher than the sea, and it is not fifteen miles from tidewater, the intervening land being a level slope, and, except for the trees, exceedingly easy to channel.

And, stranger still, the channels have been dug for over one hundred years; but they are locked up at the outer ends with wooden gates.

Ponder on this marvelous fact: the Lake of the Dismal Swamp, three miles by two and one half in extent, and from seven to fifteen feet in depth, is situated on the side, and almost on the top, of a hill, beside a tidal river, and yet it creates by overflow all around it for about one thousand square miles, one of the densest and darkest morasses on the surface of the earth.

In 1763, George Washington surveyed the Dismal Swamp, and discovered that the western side was much higher than the eastern, and that rivers ran out of the swamp, and not into it. He then wrote that the swamp was "neither a plain nor a hollow, but a hillside.". . .

If the Dismal Swamp lies on the side of a hill, as science proves, and the flow of the water demonstrates, why does not its superfluous water run off into the sea?

If the whole extent of the Dismal Swamp, land and lake together, is from twelve to twenty-five feet higher than the sea level, while actually adjoining the sea, why, in the name of reason, is it not drained and reclaimed?

These are the vital questions relating to the Dismal Swamp. I shall answer them one by one, and the answer in each case shall not be an opinion, but a demonstration.

In the month of May, 1888, two sunburned white men in cedar canoes turned at right angles from the broad water of the Dismal Swamp Canal, and entered the dark and narrow channel, called the Feeder, that pierces the very heart of the swamp, and supplies the great canal with water from Lake Drummond, or the "Lake of the Dismal Swamp." The men in the canoes were Mr. Edward A. Moseley and the writer of this article.

These were almost the first canoes, except the "white canoe" of the poet, that ever paddled on the breast of the dusky lake since the disappearance of the Indian hunters a century ago. The only boats known to the lake are the long, rude "dugouts," of the Negroes, and the flat-bottomed dories or punts of the farmers along the east side of the canal.

While we were in the main canal we found the banks high, especially on the western side, where the diggings and dredgings of the channel have been heaped for a century. On this side, behind the bank, lay the unbroken leagues of swamp, crowded with dense timber and canebrake jungle, the surface of the land or mire being considerably lower than the surface of the canal. On the east side ran the road, and beyond this long stretches of level country, formerly part of the Dismal Swamp, but now more or less cleared, with here and there a farm of astonishing superiority, and at long intervals a straggling village, usually connected with a sawmill for juniper and cypress. Originally the canal ran right through the swamp, which it now borders on the eastern side.

The land east of the canal has been cleared, because it has been drained into the sea. The fall is to the east. But all the land west of the canal is still unrelieved and "dismal" swamp.

How is this? Does not the land on the west side drain into the canal, as the land eastward has drained into the sea? No! the canal has completely stopped drainage; it is higher than all the western swamp.

Then came the startling suggestion, striking us both at the same time. This canal is a cruel ligature on the vitals of the swamp, shutting it in on itself and suffocating it. The canal is higher than the swamp, and instead of draining it, drowns it. The canal is a straggler, and here before our eyes was a deliberate process of land murder!

But I have outstripped the canoes. Let me begin at the beginning, and tell this story of a delightful summer outing, and stop this "damnable iteration" of the sufferings and wrongs of the Dismal Swamp. The swamp cannot grieve at whatever infamy may be put upon it. What does it care, or who does care whether the wonderful lake be ringed with silver sand or hedged with bleached roots and twisting serpents? . . .

Go back again to Norfolk with me, and try to forget that you have been inside the gates of this brown-water canal of the Dismal Swamp. It was not fair to begin my tale in the middle. Surely I have made a mistake and told the story of the swamp too soon. But I have only told the story; it remains for me yet to prove it.

It is seven o'clock in the morning, and we two are in the market of Norfolk buying bacon, salt pork, hard bread, cheese, a ham, an alcohol stove, and all the necessaries for a few weeks' sojourn in the wilderness.

At eight o'clock, breakfast over, we are getting into rough suits. . . .

At ten o'clock we are on board a tug, kindly placed at our disposal . . . to take us to the first lock on the Dismal Swamp Canal, which runs into the Elizabeth River about seven miles from Norfolk. Just think of it! the entrance to the Dismal Swamp only seven miles from the busiest city in the South, . . .

At one o'clock the tug started with us for the lock. There was a queer nervousness about us as we neared the place, caused by our complete ignorance of what the swamp was like. . . .

Presently one of the hands on the tug pointed to the water; the river had grown dark like the stream from a dyeworks. "See," he said, "that is the juniper water of the Dismal Swamp."

It was singular that neither the captain nor his men could tell anything about the swamp. Their knowledge ended at the lock. This is characteristic of the whole neighboring population. Richmond knows as little about the swamp as Boston; even Norfolk and Suffolk know little more.

"All I know," said the captain, "is that there are lots of snakes in there."

"And bears," says another.

"And panthers," says a third, and so on, and so on, while each one gave a friendly hand to launch the canoes as we closed to a wharf near the lock. . . .

"If I were going in there, I'd keep my Smith-and-Wesson handy," said the second hand on the tug, as we touched the shore. Before we could ask the meaning of the unpleasant hint (which we found to be a libel on the swamp), the sturdy little steamer had backed out, and was whistling "Good-by.". . .

The lockkeeper, a gaunt, badly dressed white man, sauntered down from his lock to take a look at the strange boats. He was very obviously chewing tobacco, and he spoke slowly and nasally.

Before the loading was half done, our first and almost our last misfortune occurred. Mr. Moseley's canoe, with timbers warped from a winter's storage, was leaking like a sieve. Out must come the packages again—pork, blankets, camera, ammunition, etc.

"What shall we do now?"

"Hire a mule to tow us, and keep bailing the canoe till the wood swells and stops the leak."

"Mr. Lockman," we asked, "can you let us have a mule?"

"Yes," very slowly, and looking at the boats, not at us, "I have a mule; but them boats won't tow."

"But we know better. They will tow. Can we have the mule?"

"Them boats won't tow," still more slowly.

"Can we have the mule?" impatiently.

"Not to tow them boats. They won't tow, I tell ye."

Argument and entreaty were in vain. It was none of his business we held, and we knew better than he, anyway; but the man was stubborn, though not at all sullen.

It was getting late in the afternoon, and we had intended reaching, that evening, the house of Capt. Wallace, who had a large farm in the swamp, about twelve or fifteen miles up the canal, and to whom a friend of Moseley's had written about our trip.

At last we compromised with the lockman, who let us have the mule and a cart, with a one-legged colored driver, to carry our baggage to the village of Deep Creek, a few miles up the canal.

Then we entered the first lock of the Dismal Swamp Canal, directly from the tidewater of the Elizabeth River, and were raised probably eight feet to the lowest level of the canal. This means that if this lower lock were opened, the whole Dismal Swamp could be drained to the depth of eight feet.

We parted from the unreasonable lockman with no kindly feelings; but we learned before night that his intentions had not only been kind, but exceptionally honest, and his knowledge quite correct of the towing qualities of an eighty-pound canoe.

A word about the history of the canal. A company for the cutting of the Dismal Swamp Canal was chartered by the States of Virginia and North Carolina in 1787, and both states subscribed generously to the stock. The United States Congress also became a large stockholder. The names of George Washington and Patrick Henry were among the first subscribers for the stock; though this canal for commerce must not be confounded with an earlier system of canals or ditches, devised by Washington himself for the purpose of reclaiming the swamp by lightering the timber to the frontier. These canals still exist; but the charter of the commercial canal gave it absolute rights over the waters of the lake and all other canals in the swamp. It was not opened till 1822, in which year the first vessel passed through to Norfolk from the Albemarle Sound. It was completed in 1828. . . .

The Dismal Swamp Canal runs nearly north and South, joining the Elizabeth River to the Pasquotank, above Elizabeth City, N.C., the distance between those points being about forty miles. The canal is forty feet wide, chartered to be eight feet deep, fresh water, the color of dark brandy or strong breakfast tea (the color caused by the juniper sap and other vegetable qualities), but clear and palatable, and singularly wholesome. The banks, where we could see the cutting under the foliage, were composed of fine yellow sand mixed with broken shells. A profusion of wild rosebushes, myrtle, sweet bay, flowering laurel, white blackberry blossoms, and honeysuckle leaned over the water and made a most lovely border.

The afternoon was pleasant, with a cool wind in our favor, and, though Mr. Moseley had bailing enough to do, we reached Roper's enormous sawmill and factory at Deep Creek in about an hour.... The violent rising scream of the saws sounded everywhere, something like "p-sh-sh-sh-sh—hai-ai-AI-AI!" the last note an ear-splitting squeal, like a pig in direful pain.

Mr. John L. Roper, the owner of this sawmill, leases the timberland of almost the entire swamp to supply his mill. He keeps in the swamp probably one hundred men or more, in different gangs, cutting juniper and cypress, which they drag by mules over the "gum roads" to the lake, whence it is lightered through the Feeder to the Dismal Swamp Canal, and by this means carried to the sawmill at Deep Creek. The colored workers in the juniper groves of the swamp are its only inhabitants; they are called "swampers." Let me here explain that Lake Drummond is the center of the swamp's organism, acting precisely like a heart. Except the Dismal Swamp Canal, which runs along the border, all the roads, canals, and ditches that pierce the swamp radiate from the lake like spokes from a hub.

The swamp has only one natural feature—the lake. All the rest is simply swamp. The canals and roads are accidents.

Whoever would know the Dismal Swamp must study it from the lake, not from the exterior. This is the reason that even those living in its neighborhood know so little about it. Their knowledge is local, not constitutional. . . .

There was no one at Roper's sawmill who could give us any information, so we paddled on to the village of Deep Creek, before reaching which we passed through another lock. Here the Dismal Swamp proper may be said to begin. At this lock we were again raised several feet, so that we were now, although only a few miles from tidal water, probably sixteen feet above the sea level.

"Shall we pay toll here?" we asked the lockman.

"Not till you come out," he answered, making it clear that there was only one entrance and exit on this side of the Dismal Swamp.

"Does the swamp begin here?"

"Yes," said the lockman, leaning at an angle of forty degrees, and slowly pushing the great beam with his back. "It begins here, and it runs all the way to Florida."

This was true, in a way. The whole southern coast is margined by swamplands; but the Dismal Swamp is not of them. It is high land instead of low land; its water is fresh, instead of salt or brackish. Among swamps it is an abnormality. It leans over the sea, and yet contains its own moisture, like a bowl. Indeed, the Dismal Swamp is a great bowl, forty miles long, and ten to twenty miles wide, and, strange to say, with its highest water in the center. The sides of the bowl are miles of fallen and undecaying trees, fixed in a mortar of melted leaves and mold. Deep in the soft bosom of the swamp are countless millions of feet of precious timber that has lain there, the immense trunks crossing each other like tumbled matches, "since the beginning of the world," as a juniper cutter said.

At the village of Deep Creek, the lockman, evidently the leading person of the place, was a handsome and intelligent man, referred to by every one as "Mr. Geary.". . . We found later on that he was widely known as a famous hunter, who probably knew the Dismal Swamp as well as any man living. He had shot over it all his life. He told us that the fishing at the lake was "wonderful."

Moseley's canoe still leaking, we hired a team . . . to carry the baggage to Capt. Wallace's house, and we started to paddle up the canal.

It was a lovely evening, and the surroundings were so novel and so unexpectedly attractive, that we can never forget the impression. Far before us as the eye could reach, ran the canal, narrowing in perspective, till it closed to a fine point. On the right, there rose from the water a dense forest of cypress and juniper, flowering poplar, black gum, yellow pine, maple, and swamp oak, with a marvelous underwood of laurel in ravishing flower, the very air heavy with the rich perfume, which resembles that of a tuberose, honeysuckle heaped in delicious blossom, yellow jessamine, bay, myrtle, purple trumpet flowers of the poison-oak vine, with the ever-present roses, and white-flowering blackberry hanging into the water.

As the evening darkened, with a clear sky overhead, and a red glow from the west reaching over the trees, the effect was almost oppressively beautiful. No other tree darkens in evening silhouette so impressively as the two queen trees of the Dismal Swamp, the juniper and cypress. With the low sun behind them, the clear-cut delicacy of their foliage reminds one of the exquisite fineness of dried sea mosses on a tinted page. But when the sun has gone down, and the sky is still flushed with its glory, the cypress takes on a mystery of dark and refined beauty that is all its own. It rises still blacker than the dark underwood, the tallest among the trees, lonely, like a plume. It is not heavy or hearse-like, but thin, fibrous, the twilight showing through its delicate branches, and tracing every exquisite needle of its leafage on the air. It seems to be blacker than the coming night; blacker far in its fine filaments than the clustered laurel at its feet. The darkness and delicacy of the cypress are its genius. It does not oppress, it thrills. In the twilight it is the very plume of death, but of a death uncommon. A yew or a willow is a sign of mourning; but a cypress in the evening is a symbol of woe.

But with the decline of the lovely day came such a jubilant chorus of sweet voices! Never have we heard, except in the air of dreamland, such a concert of delicious bird music. In number and variety the singers were multiplied beyond conception. Far as we could see along the canal we knew that the air was vibrant with this harmony. The thought of such unbroken melody following the eye into the remote distance was a more delightful music in itself than that which was ravishing the senses. Here the mockingbird ceased to mock, and poured out its own ecstatic soul. The catbird, discordant no longer, shot its clear joy through the great harmony, and the wren and swamp canary twined their notes like threads of gossamer through the warp and woof of this marvelous tapestry of sound.

I shall have to speak by and by of the noxious and horrible denizens of the swamp. Let me dwell lovingly and gratefully on the pleasure derived from those that were innocent and delightful.

We let the evening fall on us unresistingly, to drink in the sweet thing that was around us. We were miles from our destination, but we could not settle to mere traveling till this incredible vesper song was done. We sat silent, absorbed, . . .

The charm was broken by the happy hailing of . . . two colored boys on the towpath, who were driving . . . with our baggage, and who had now overtaken us. Then came the thorn of our rose. Moseley's canoe was still leaking, and while he had been floating off with the divine mockingbird, the water had gained on him like a temptation. In an instant the concert had vanished. The curtain of the commonplace fell over that finer tympanum that almost hears spiritual voices, and the canoe man was bailing his boat with a tin dipper, while he grumbled at fate.

The dusky drivers waited on the towpath, and we soon started again, keeping up a lively conversation from boat to wagon. But the leak grew, the night was closing, and we were in a very strange land.

"Let us tie a rope to the cart and tow the boats," we cried, and the picture of riding indolently up the canal was like a charm.

We fastened the canoes bow and stern and tied the longest painter, thirty or more feet in length, to the tailboard of the cart, and away we went. But before we had proceeded twenty feet the light rope, slackened by the rapidity of the light and low boats, caught on a stump by the waterside. The leading canoe felt the pull, and darted headlong to the bank, and had not the boys at once stopped the horse the canoes would have been pulled to pieces, or dragged clean up on the towpath.

We tried again and again, with the same result, and then we felt ashamed of our superior knowledge of a few hours before, and interiorly begged the nasal lockkeeper's pardon. . . .

Soon after, through the gathering gloom, we saw the outline of a large house to the left of the canal, with outbuildings and white fences, and other large buildings on the right side of the canal. This was Wallaceton, where, at Captain Wallace's house, we received a most hospitable welcome. In a few minutes the canoes were cared for, many willing hands helping, and we were enjoying an excellent supper. . . .

We were awakened in the morning by a chorus of bird song rivaling that of the evening before. On looking from our window we saw a field like a dream—1,100 level acres without a fence—in which it appeared that not one inch was left neglected or unproductive. The splendid area of fertility was marked in squares of varying color like a map; here the rich dark brown of ploughed loam; there the green ridges of early potatoes and corn; yonder a long stretch of clover, and so on until every foot of the fine field was filled with natural wealth.

This field, called the Dover Farm, lies on the west side of the canal; that is, it reaches into the very depths of the swamp for nearly a mile and a half. Its position is between the lake and the canal.

How, then, if Lake Drummond and the canal be higher than the swamp, could this 1,100 acres of land be drained? The answer has in it the demonstration of the iniquity and stupidity of the canal system. Captain Wallace ran a deep drain around this Dover Farm, bringing the end of it to the canal; there he stopped, and waited until the canal was emptied some years ago, for the purpose of being cleansed from stumps and sand. The indefatigable farmer took advantage of the dry watercourse and dug his culvert under the bed of the canal, bridging it securely. His drain was then several miles long, and he continued it until it emptied into the Northwest River, which runs out of the swamp. Last year, the lake being swelled by heavy rains, the canal company did not, of course, open their locks and let the water escape; instead, they adopted a lazier, easier, and more ruinous plan; they raised the banks of the canal, one consequence of which was that the confined water percolated through the surrounding land, forced itself under Mr. Wallace's drain, and inundated and destroyed several hundred acres of his cleared land. Of course, from such an injury he had no protection. . . .

After an early breakfast we started up the canal, intending to reach the Feeder early in the forenoon, and, if possible, arrive at the lake about noon. Still the leaky canoe bothered us; but while we were considering how to make her carry her load, a handsome young farmer, . . . courteously offered us his boat and man to take our baggage to the Feeder lock near the lake. In a few minutes the boat started ahead of us.

The canal above Wallaceton resembled the stretch from Deep Creek to that place, the only change being that the trees in the swamp become thicker and taller. The majority of the trees here appeared to be black gum, with an outer border of poplar, maple, and swamp oak.

The Feeder is a deep cutting, about eighteen feet in width, running at right angles from the canal to the lake. It is four miles in length, with a lock about a quarter of a mile from the lake.

The current in the Feeder runs strongly from the lake to the canal. The banks of the Feeder are thickly covered with canebrake, the bamboos of great height. On the right, going toward the lake however, the swamp is more open and has large timber.

The condition of the Feeder was a shocking revelation. There was no raised bank here, as in the main canal. For miles of its length the water flowed freely over the banks into the swamp, creating a morass of dreadful appearance. No living thing could there find footing. Even birds were rarely seen, although we saw a few of beautiful plumage, one of which is known . . . as the redbird. It resembled a flame in the brilliance of its coloring, as it passed through the shaded light of the swamp.

In the Feeder we met several lighters, heavily piled with juniper logs, on their way from the lake to the sawmill. These lighters had each two men, colored, who poled them from the banks. At times, when the sides of the Feeder will permit, they walk on a line of logs laid along the mud bank, pushing the lighter with their poles resting against the breast.

Our passage up the Feeder was against a strong current. It was a steady and monotonous paddle through dim light, the canebrake and the boughs reaching over our heads. The air had a dense warmth as though we were in a closed room. Outside on the canal there was a strong breeze with a decided chill in it; here, we were stifled as if in an oven. And yet, up to this time we had not seen a mosquito in the swamp; and as for snakes and other wild creatures, we had almost made up our minds that they were a tradition or a popular romance. . . .

Like scales from our eyes began to fall the impressions of "Dred," and all the other dismal stories we had read and heard about the Dismal Swamp. Every day of our stay on the lake this conviction grew upon us; the slaves who escaped to the Dismal Swamp in the old time must have lived happily in their absolute freedom. The Negro in the swamp is at home. He has helped to spread and exaggerate the terrors of the place to keep it more securely for himself. If I were a slave, in slave time, and could get to the Dismal Swamp, I should ask no pity from any one.

But all this time we kept laboriously paddling against the strong current, for the lock ahead, only a quarter of a mile from the lake, was this day letting pass an unusual volume of water. Every stroke of the paddle now sent us deeper and deeper into the heart of the swamp. Suddenly, Moseley, who was ahead, stopped paddling and peered through the matted underbrush.

"What is it?" I asked.

"A cow and a calf! What can they be doing here in the middle of the swamp?"

There they were, sure enough; a red and white pair. They heard our voices, stopped chewing, stared a moment, then turned and picked their way into the jungle.

A few minutes later the lock came in sight, and we saw two men waving their hats. One was the man . . . with our traps, and the other was "Abeham" (not Abraham), who was to be our guide, philosopher, and friend on the lake. Abeham had been sent from Suffolk to meet us by Mr. Rudolph A. King of Washington, a gentleman deeply interested in the Dismal Swamp. . . .

"What are that cow and calf doing in the swamp?" was our first question.

"Wild cattle, sah," said Abeham.

"Are there wild cattle in the swamp?"

"Yes, hund'eds and hund'eds of wild cattle; I saw lots of 'em dis mawnin'. Yo' ought to have shot dat calf; we'll want him tomorrow."

This lock at the very lip of the lake keeps the water back to another height of several feet, so that lock after lock, from first to last, had backed up the lake to the height of almost twenty-three feet above tidewater.

Never can we forget the view that met our eyes as we were raised to that last level, and looked along the canal to the lake.

The lockhouse and the whole Feeder were completely overhung with tall trees. So close was their interlacing over the canal that the view to the lake was like looking through the barrel of a gun. The air along the dark and narrow sheet was actually green from the light sifting through the foliage. We were in the shadow; it was all shadow to the end, but the end of the view glittered like an immense diamond.

A ball of glorious and unshaded brilliancy lay at the end of the Feeder. A "talisman's glory" it was, set on the low water and framed in the dense cypress.

"What is that?" we asked after a long look of bewildered pleasure.

"Dat's de openin' to de lake," said Abeham.

We sat there for an hour. We ate our dinner and smoked a cigar;

and the wonder lessened as the strange glory grew. The radiance of the diamond became subdued till it had taken the form of a perfect arch, with its perfect reflection in the water.

We were looking along a dark, straight stream, shaded over like the low arch of a bridge, until the gun barrel simile was the most likely, and, at the end or muzzle, the vision was carried across three miles of open and smooth water flashing to the sun. . . .

Then we started down the gun barrel toward the lovely bridge, the perfection of which remained unbroken to the last. Here was no effort of landscape art, but the living hand of nature completing its own picture and putting all art as gently out of question as the mountain does the mole.

A weirdly beautiful view opened on us as our canoes shot under the outer leaves of the Feeder's bridge, and we floated at last within the marvelous ring of the lake of the Dismal Swamp. . . .

Our camp lay on the northwest corner of the lake, three miles from the Feeder's mouth. At the start we struck out to the middle of the lake before turning north, so that we took in at first glance the whole wonderful view. For myself, I longed to lay down my paddle and sit there motionless until the sun sank and the moon rose, for a dream and fascination that had drawn me from childhood was now fulfilled and completed. Only the lake of my fancy was much smaller and gloomier than the true lake.

There is no other sheet of water like this anywhere. No other so far removed from the turbulence of life, so defamed, while so beautiful. It fills one with pity and wonder—the utter silence and loneliness of it. It is a dead sea, but neither bitter nor barren.

I could not help the feeling, that increased as time passed, that this pure eye of water, ringed by one distinct line of dark trees, no farther horizon visible, was not on a plain, but on a high mountain. Later on, as we sailed around the borders of the lake, another delusive thought persisted in coming. It always seemed that the wooded shore rose abruptly thirty yards or so back from the water, and that I verily could see the uplifting of the trees and underbrush. Probably because it was unnatural that the shore should be just as low or lower than the water surface, the senses refused to accept it as true.

The first deep impression made on me by the lake was its size. I had expected to see a sheet not a tenth part as large, and gloomy with the shadows of its tall, overhanging trees. Instead, from the center the trees were a low, dark border on the far horizon.

From the center, the lake is the very ideal of loneliness and stillness, strangely emphasized by the solitary wide-winged hawk, tipping on his high circle. No smaller bird can be seen at this distance

"On the Lake," from *Athletics and Manly Sport*

in the trees on the shore—though birds are there, and in rich variety.

Here, for instance, are some of the birds we noted in a few days, many of them in great numbers: the catbird, robin, swamp canary, wren, sparrow, mockingbird, whip-poor-will, redbird (a blaze of plumage), thrush (with a crown), yellowhammer, woodpecker, owl (immense fellows), hawk, eagle, kingfisher, jay, heron, quail, wild turkey, woodcock, buzzard, crow, and numerous brilliant little birds of many species, whose names we did not know. In the winter the lake is fairly covered with geese, swans, and all kinds of duck. The bat, which I believe is not a bird, is at home here.

But crossing the lake that first day we saw only one bird, a hawk of great size. The water of the lake was deliciously cool in the center, where the average depth is about fifteen feet. Again and again we drank the sweet draught. Looking into it, no mirror could be more perfect in reflection. The flash of the paddles was brown, not crystal. On a day when the water broke (and we crossed the lake one day before the rush of a gale), the brown-brandy light through the lifting waves and the warm ruddiness of the breakers were singularly beautiful.

The lake is full of fish of many and excellent kinds, though it has never been fished in the deeper water. The "swampers," who live on the borders, never fish beyond the line of stumps, which are at farthest a hundred yards from the shore, so that the fish of the lake are not at all completely known. The garfish, because he jumps, has been seen sometimes eight feet long, but no other fish is seen in the deep water. You cannot see one inch into the lake; it is like looking into a bowl of ink. This makes it dangerous for light boating, for the snags are numerous, and though they may not be a nail's breadth under water, they are quite invisible.

The fish in the lake, great quantities of which we caught, and on which, indeed, we chiefly lived, are the speckled perch or "Frenchman," a delicious fish, the raccoon perch, chub (a black bass), yellow perch (small), flyer, garfish, catfish (very numerous), gaper, blackfish (thirty inches long), roach and eel. There are plenty of pike in the canals. . . .

I paddled up both these canals from the lake, and more oppressive surroundings it is hard to conceive. The Jericho Canal is ten miles long and eighteen feet wide, but the encroaching bamboo jungle reduces this width by over two feet on each side. The dense canes rise at least fifteen feet high on both banks, so that it is like canoeing in an unroofed sewer. To enliven the passage, the moccasins, on sunny days, climb to the tops of the bamboo canes, and are seen constantly dropping into the water. It is a common thing to have them drop into the open dugout of the "swamper," out of which they wriggle without delay. But the thought of a five-foot venomous snake dropping into a fourteen-foot canoe, with decks forward and aft, under which he would be sure to dart, and out of which there was no escape except by returning to the center of the boat, was a dismal imagining. To make sure of no such visitor, I kept firing now and then into the canes ahead.

The water in the Jericho Canal runs into the lake; but at one-third its length the stream turns and runs the other way, emptying into the Nansemond River.

This line where the watershed divides is unquestionably the highest portion of the swamp. It has not been surveyed; but calculating

"In the Canals," from *Athletics and Manly Sport*

the rise from the Feeder to the northwest corner of the lake to be two feet, and three feet for the old lock at the opening of the Jericho Canal, I predict that the extreme height of the swamp will be from twenty-eight to thirty feet above tide water.

The condition of the wholly abandoned "Washington's Ditch" is even more forbidding than that of the Jericho Canal. The heavy trees are crowding its banks and leaning into it; the bamboos meet across it for long distances. It is, I think, the most sombre and evil-looking waterway on the earth, and yet no foot of it but is beautiful. The water moves slowly toward the lake (any movement is a relief in the gloom and silence, for even the birds have deserted the place), but after a short distance, as in the Jericho Canal, the flow changes and goes outward. . . .

Scientists have accounted for the water in the Dismal Swamp, from cursory observations, by the rainfall, even denying the existence of springs in the lake. I venture, with much hesitation, to disagree with this conclusion, believing it to be impossible that the rainfall can account for the enormous supply of water, not only contained within the swamp, but which is, and always has been, flowing out of it.

First, it is granted that no more rain falls on the Dismal Swamp than on any other piece of Virginia forty by thirty miles square. Second, it is certain that it does not draw from surrounding country, for it is higher than all its environment.

Yet, out of the Dismal Swamp run no less than nine rivers, some of them very considerable, and still the lake continues to overflow, and the whole vast extent of the swamp remains inundated.

These are the rivers that, if traced to their source, will be found to take their rise in the Dismal Swamp: the south branch of the Elizabeth, the west branch of the Elizabeth, south branch of the Nansemond, the Deep Creek, the North River, the Northwest River, the Little River, the Perquimans, and the Pasquotank.

Granting that the dense foliage of the Dismal Swamp lessens evaporation, there is still nothing like a proportion between the rainfall and the water that remains in and flows out of this district. . . .

Booted to the thigh, armed with knife and gun, is the only safe way to enter the canebrake, or, indeed, to depart in any way from the open spaces of the swamp. During our exploring we did not see bear or panther or wildcat; but whoever leaves the beaten ways of the swamp must be prepared to meet these inhabitants.

For three days, with a cool wind and nightly rain, with the exception of one large king snake which we killed on a "gum road," we had seen nothing more noxious than a blue lizard with a red head, a harmless and friendly little fellow who seems to have no fear of man, for he will go on eating his invisible food and glancing up in your face in a most amusing and taking way. But the shape of the creature is against it, and the color of his head, which is exactly the hue of the moccasin's belly. When Moseley woke up from a doze one wet afternoon, and found one of these lizards (the Negroes call them scorpions) on his pillow, still eating invisible food and smacking his lips with a friendly glance, it was well the reptile didn't understand American, or he might have been offended.

Our first snake was killed in this way: On our second day, while passing up a "gum road," we came upon a large dark-skinned snake lazily coiled on a sunny log. Having killed him by striking him with a heavy cane, we were afterward told by Abeham that it was a harmless king snake, and that, moreover, it spent its time destroying the poisonous snakes in the swamp, which it does by crushing them.

On the morning of the fourth day—and what a day that was, with a copper cover on it, and a crater underneath—sweltering, we woke up, and both had the same thought—a swim. . . .

We did not jump in; we contented ourselves with a bath in the boat . . . and sat down to breakfast in the open air.

"What is that swimming out there?" asked Moseley, pointing to a slight dark streak about twenty yards out in the lake.

"A moccasin!" cried Abeham, getting on his feet excitedly. Abeham was used to snakes, but terribly afraid of them. "Shoot him!"

We shot him; slight and short as he looked swimming, he was four feet seven inches in length. In a minute another—his mate probably—swam past and was killed, and was exactly the same length.

The moccasin swims with its head and about fourteen inches of its back over the water. The head is very small for the thickness and length of the snake. It swims rapidly with a wavy motion. It is dark on the back, with a violently red belly, like inflamed scales, from the loose skin of the under jaw to the tail. Most of those we saw (and after that day we ceased to count them) were of an average length of about four and a half to five feet, thick as a man's arm, and repulsively fat. The prevailing suggestion of the creatures when you kill them is fatness.

All the snakes of the Dismal Swamp are shy and timid. Very rarely do they bite, and then only when driven by fear. The largest snake in the swamp is the king snake, which grows to be ten feet in length. The rattlesnake is fortunately rare in the swamp. It is mostly seen near the Feeder, and is the diamond or water rattlesnake, the largest and most sullenly ferocious of its dread family. It has a brown back, and a dirty yellowish belly. A "swamper" said he had seen one this year that was eight feet long.

The most dangerous snake in the swamp is one of the smallest, called the poplar snake. He is about twelve inches in length, green in color, like that of the poplar tree in which he lives. We escaped him most fortunately, for before we heard of him we had deflowered many poplars of their beautiful blossoms. This snake is a direful pest; from his size and color he is not easily seen; and his poison is said to resemble the rattlesnake's.

The water moccasin is a venomous snake, and it is surprising, considering his countless presence in the swamp, that so few people are bitten. This reptile literally infests all quarters of the swamp. Other snakes, more or less numerous, are the black snake (sometimes nine feet long), the horned snake, and the jointed snake. . . .

Strange as it may appear, the chief drawbacks of the Dismal Swamp are not its serpents, or bears, or other formidable wild creatures, but its flies, most pestilent of which are the yellow fly, before which for six weeks in July and August even the colored "swampers" are forced to abandon the "gum roads." The yellow fly raises a burning blister with every bite; and, helped by the "red-horse mosquito," gnats and gallinippers, they can, it is said, kill a mule.

The largest wild animal (except cattle) found in the Dismal Swamp is the black bear. . . . There are also hog bear (from the size), Seneca bear (white breast), panther, wildcat (numerous and large, about three times the size of the ordinary cat), deer (quite numerous, and some with noble antlers), coon, opossum, rabbit, fox, squirrel, otter, weasel, and muskrat. . . .

One day Moseley was out on the lake fishing, and I was paddling quietly under the trees on the bank, hoping to shoot a redbird or a crowned thrush for specimens. I heard Moseley hail me, and answered, but then he went on in a very queer way talking with some one in the swamp beyond me. At last I went out to him and found that he had discovered an echo of wonderful clearness, and which was otherwise interesting. Near the shore I had not heard it, but a quarter of a mile out it was startlingly distinct.

The sound was quite unlike the hard resonance thrown back from cliff, mountain, or cave. It smacked of the swamp in a manner hard to describe. The repetition was largely magnified, though it seemed to be thrown to a distance, and to come from a great height, as if it had bounded up from the wide field of the swamp. The sound had an elastic click about it, like the remote stroke of a woodman's axe. It was the echo from a wood, unmistakably, and not from a wall.

Strange to say, the best word to throw to an echo is its own name. It loves to fling it back unclipped and sudden. Divide the syllables, stopping at the "ech," and it seems to wait impatiently for the

"'Abeham' and the Canoes," from *Athletics and Manly Sport*

"o." We had a long conversation with it, and wondered whether it resided in the dense canebrake and higher foliage that lined the waterfront, or rebounded upward like a boy's ball that had fallen on the vast concavity of the treetops.

Abeham said he had never heard of the echo before, and he listened with all his ears, laughing consumedly when the echo shouted defiance; but he would not try it, from shyness as we thought.

We spent the days exploring lake and swamp, returning to camp tired at night, but repaid by our experience. We were seeing the lake and swamp as no one can ever see them without such boats as ours. A heavy boat, with oars, cannot pass through the ditches and canals, nor even coast the lake inside the line of stumps. . . . The birchbark canoe would get snagged at every length. The only safe and pleasant boat for the swamp is the cedar canoe, and an open one is better than a decked one, to let the moccasins wriggle out if they happen to fall in while you are passing through the narrow canals. . . .

"There are two things I should like to know," said Moseley, during our last day on the lake, "and one is what that fellow in the Nor-

"The Last View of the Lake," from *Athletics and Manly Sport*

folk tug meant by advising us to keep our pistols handy? Surely there could be no men more good-natured and lawful than these poor fellows who work in the swamp."

This was emphatically true. . . .

"What is the other thing you are in doubt about?" I asked Moseley.

"The wild cattle. We have seen only that red and white cow and calf, though they say they are numerous. I can't believe that that tame-looking cow was wild."

"But what business would a tame cow have in the depths of the swamp, and how could she get home if she had a home to go to?"

He admitted that it was hard to find a domestic reason for the cow being in the swamp, but still he doubted. We were passing at the time through a narrow and dark waterway, where the sheets of deep water under the trees lay like black glass. We came to a dry bank in the morass, and, standing there, quietly and proudly looking at us as we approached, was a red bull about three years old. We stopped paddling and returned the stare. He stood beside our only passage, a narrow one. Abeham was behind, and he shouted, "Look out, dere; dat wild bull dang'ous!"

We shouted at him, but he paid no heed. He was a superb creature, dark red all over, roundheaded and very small. We broke branches and waved them and shouted, at a distance from him of about twenty yards. Not an eye winked, but his tail gave one or two quiet waves from side to side. Abeham wanted us to load a rifle, and kill him; but this would be wanton, as we were to leave the swamp the next day. Still we must pass, and he would not move. He paid no attention to a gun pointed at him. The poor fellow was only half wild, one could not help thinking; the hereditary taint of human association was in his blood. Probably his grandfather had fed in a fenced field, . . .

At last a shot fired into the canebrake close to him gave him a shock. He looked at the canes where the small shot rushed, and then turned and trotted into the swamp.

That night we decided to leave the lake next day, . . .

It rained in torrents in the early part of the night, and then cleared up, and the full moon shone on the lake. It was a scene of marvelous beauty, which color alone, not words, could reproduce. The lake was smooth, and incredibly black, the water retaining absolutely no light, and only appearing to be liquid by surface shining. The moon's reflection, on the contrary, was whiter than it would be on common water, . . .

It was five o'clock in the morning, and the eastern sky was paling the moon, when . . . we broke camp.

As our canoes shot out on the lake and we looked back on the camp, we knew that the days and nights spent there could never be forgotten. . . .

Edward L. Chichester

I would guess that Chichester and his friend Simpson were fairly typical of the last wave of preautomotive age artists pitching their white umbrellas along the scenic and picturesque streams of the north and east. Jaunts like theirs provided materials for painting, sketching, and writing, sometimes (as here) sold and published in magazines. Chichester's gentle account of a leisurely trip is full of praise—thanks, one might say—for canoeing and life in the open.

THE CRUISE OF THE *SYBARIS* AND *SHAW SHAW* *

THE CHENANGO AND THE WEST BRANCH

Simpson and I were on our way to Norwich, not the famous city sought after by that lunatic of nursery note, but a beautiful village lying in the Chenango Valley in New York State. On the morning in question we had paddled three miles in a pouring rain to ship ourselves, canoes and duffle to this town, and now occupied a seat in a railway carriage filled with respectably dressed people.

We were much annoyed by the critical inspection of an individual with an eyeglass, for, although our personal appearance was quite satisfactory to ourselves when contemplated in still water, it must be owned that the dudish young man opposite had some excuse for staring.

Simpson's hat, a shapeless thatch of gray felt some fellow canoeist had left him in exchange for a new one, had done duty as fire fan and filled other offices known only to a cruiser for at least three years, and was retained by him only through a kind of natural perversity.

We both wore short breeches and sneaks—those low cloth shoes with rubber soles that are just the things to wear in a boat and excellent to protect the feet when one is obliged to jump overboard in a rift and pull his craft over sharp stones—but they are not beautiful. Indeed we had felt all the morning like marmots whose hibernation had been rudely interrupted, for we had spent the past ten days in the woods, with the sound of tinkling waterfalls and rustling leaves to soothe our slumbers, and no more objectionable inspector than a sedate cow, with an eye to our meal chest.

* *Outing*, May–June, 1889.

I have always found that a canoe, though a most delightful adjunct in its proper element, is a decided care when stowed in a baggage car. One can never tell how many iron-bound chests may be dumped on those light decks or jammed against the delicate sides, and every jolt of the train brings to mind direful pictures of catastrophe. But on reaching Norwich we had the pleasure of see-

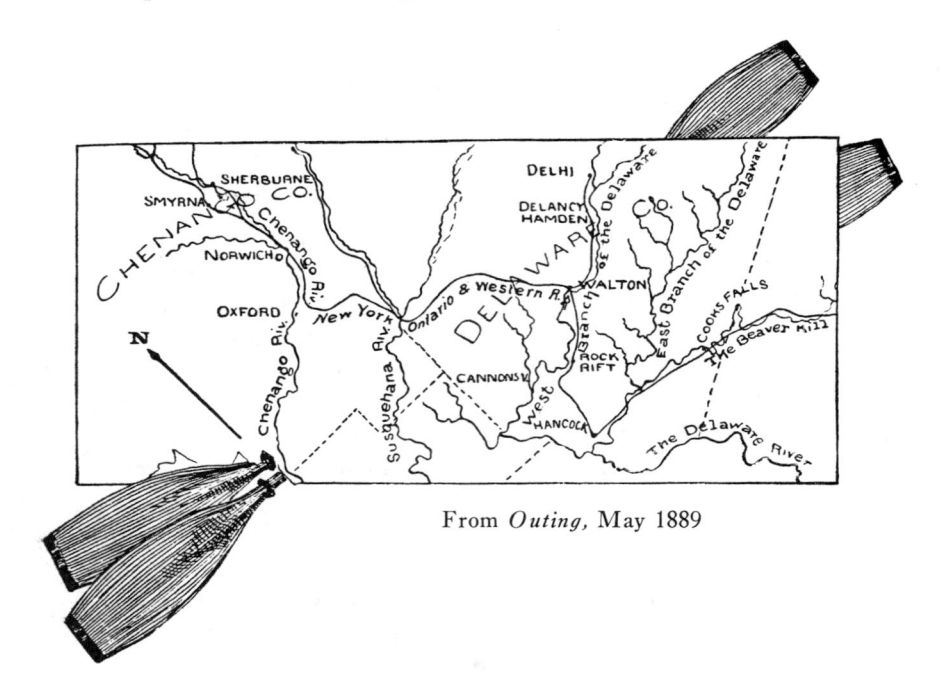

From *Outing,* May 1889

ing the *Sybaris* handled like an eggshell by the careful express agent.

She was safe and sound. So was the *Shaw Shaw,* a long Canadian boat I had secured for this cruise, high fore and aft, with a bottom like a toboggan for toughness, and a capacity that was simply marvelous. . . .

A railroad passing through Norwich takes a direct southeasterly course to New York, crossing and following on its route the northern branches of the Delaware River. . . . We shipped the canoes on this line and started for Delhi. . . .

It was nearly dark when we reached Delhi. The village is some distance from the station, but fortunately the river, or creek, for it is little more than a creek here, is close at hand. The stream, rising in the Catskill ranges, flows south, but comes into the Delaware from the westward, giving it the name of the West Branch. We were not long in getting into the boats, and, leaving a knot of curious loungers at the depot, floated off with the current. Only those who have learned to love nature's solitudes know the relief experienced by such a transition—the puff of steam, the rush of feet, the clanging and crowding, followed by the soft ripple of water sweeping one along under thick foliage, cool and silent. The people of Delhi appreciate the possibilities of their stream, and have built a small wooden dam near the station, which keeps the water back enough to form a very respectable pond. A few jaunty pleasure boats are housed along this basin and much used by the city people who pass the summer months in the village.

After we were over this dam the stream splashed along through a succession of bends and rifts that required the utmost watchfulness to prevent grounding. Often our available channel was little more than two feet wide, and as the shadows lengthened progress became more and more difficult.

It was dark when we put up our tent in a meadow and made preparations for supper. Bacon, that staple for campers, was to form the *pièce de résistance,* and I rashly undertook to prepare it while Simpson went for milk. Just how it happened I never knew, but, having gone to the stream to wash a tin plate, I was startled by a lurid blaze which lighted up the whole region, and, turning round, saw a sheet of flame rising from the frying pan. The bacon had caught fire, and that night we had cold mush and coffee.

The region we were in was high, and, though it was August, the mornings were decidedly cool. At about seven o'clock the fog was so dense that objects were scarcely distinguishable twenty feet away. A little later the rich bottomlands began to show below the heavy curtain of vapor, then the sunlight burst through in places, and herds of cream-and-white Alderneys could be seen here and there, browsing on the wet grass. It was an English landscape, till the clouds rose still higher and disclosed the partially cleared hillsides and thickly wooded peaks, which, however, refused to throw off their torn veils till the sun came out and melted the last vestige into clear blue.

A mile or so from Delhi is the old Sherwood House, standing back from the road and screened by a high picket fence. An arched gateway opens on a grassy path that cuts straight through lines of box to the front door, whose plain, white surface is relieved by a brass knocker. Behind the house is a garden, resplendent with hollyhocks, peonies, and other old-fashioned flowers. We wandered about this place till Simpson remarked that he felt like a tramp and should not like to see the owner drive up.

"I don't wonder," I said, fixing my eye on the hat; but Simpson was past shame on this point. He simply said something about a tramp's brother, and started across lots toward the smoke of the campfire that rose a thin thread above the trees.

Though the flatlands in the valley were thoroughly cleared, there was plenty of small wood fringing the stream, such as willows, patches of witch hazel, alder and sumac. In addition to these we met with the water beech, whose branches, almost black in color and shaped like bare bones, would occasionally obstruct the progress of the boats. This, however, was a slight annoyance compared to the barbed-wire fences which occasionally crossed the stream at the swiftest places, and proved a serious inconvenience in rift running. Scarcely visible until we were close upon them, they kept us constantly on the lookout. Simpson had a way of clutching quickly with his hand between the barbs and throwing the wire over his head, for they usually hung low enough to barely clear the deck, but, being of a more conservative nature, I would lie down, with the paddle held in such a way as to shed the obstruction over the edge of the blade and cherish a hope that no specially savage point would reach me. As we wriggled through these obstructions we came upon trout fishermen, whipping the rifts and angling in the tiny basins at the mouths of occasional rivulets that brought icy water from the hills.

The trout haunt these last-named places when they can be found nowhere else in the stream. Rounding a bend, I found Simpson had landed and was picking blackberries. He offered me some rather red ones and said he was sorry there were no more growing there. I was sorry too, and advised him to wash the stain from his face and hands before we reached the next village, whose chimneys were just visible among the trees farther down the stream.

The place proved to be Delancy, a spot in the valley where rich pasturage and a plentiful water supply offered every facility for dairy farming.

We were kept in this vicinity for some time by what the farmers called "a spell o' weather," and roamed about the country, making studies here and there, when it was not actually pouring.

Only those who have led an outdoor life in all weathers know the zest of such an existence. After a few weeks of nature's rugged hospitality one begins to feel some of that exuberance of life which we see in the lower animals. If he is Nature's child he can live as her children do.

The mink and muskrat splash in cold streams contentedly, the creatures of the wood prowl about in the night winds and frolic fearlessly under the stars, and if we share the earth with the wild things about us we but draw closer to Mother Nature, and the thrilling experience of being alive in every nerve, and actually sharing existence with creatures whose freedom we envy, will prove a delight to the most highly cultivated organism. A civilization that bars the tracks leading back to the sources of its own life is certainly an unhealthy growth, and he is not truly developed who sneers at all the race enjoyed in barbarism. "Better the song of the lark than the squeak of the mouse," quotes Dr. John Brown, referring to an outdoor existence, and Simpson and I used to echo this sentiment when we were wakened by the call of birds to take a morning plunge in the river, the coldest water we ever swam in.

Speaking of birds reminds me of the numerous hawks that haunted this region about Delancy. We used to watch them through the field glass, and could study every move as they quivered and floated in the clear air overhead.

There was the large chicken hawk, whose shadow swept along the meadows like a passing cloud; the tiny sparrow hawk, darting viciously among the bushes that bordered the stream, and the sleek fish hawk, with his speckled breast and long, powerful legs hanging threateningly down over the water. His cry can never be forgotten, a kind of shrill but plaintive squeak, suggesting anything but a bird of prey.

One day some men came up from the village and presented us with a supply of green corn, which they deposited in the canoes drawn up each side of the tent. While we were being plied with the regular questions as to where we were from, the cost of the boats, etc., and were endeavoring to answer them satisfactorily, we noticed a young fellow coming across the meadows in a peculiar way. He was constantly turning this way and that, and on inquiring the cause we were told that the way was "full o' binnacles." "Binnacles?" we asked in perplexity. "Ya-as," said the men, "that's what we call 'em here, the medder's full of 'em." "Do you mean the old riverbeds with standing water?" I asked. They nodded, but could give no information as to the origin of the name.

Farther on we struck some that were decidedly picturesque, being shaded with overhanging trees and filled with lily pads. One would suppose such places to be excellent breeding places for mosquitoes, but we were singularly free from them throughout the cruise. Perhaps the fact that the binnacles were often fed with springs and stocked with small fish would explain this.

We were so absorbed here in our efforts to take away some lasting impression of the region that we begrudged the time spent in preparing meals, and soon our menu dwindled down to bread and milk. We did vary it, however, with chubs fried in bacon, for we could catch them when it rained, and eels, we discovered, could be taken at night with that most unsportsmanlike contrivance, a set line.

At Hamden, lying a little farther down the stream, we were attracted by two or three singular mounds rising from the flats, and suggesting an artificial origin. The most careful study failed to reveal a clue to their history. The people we questioned assured us they were perfectly natural, but the principal ground for this assertion lay in the fact that the mounds had been there ever since they could remember. The village was divided by one long thoroughfare, shared by the railroad, and from the point where we landed only the small station was visible, peeping from behind a mound.

One warm day, when our tent was pitched in a little hollow at the foot of a steep bank, we spread our effects on the grass in every direction, and rambled off. On returning in a couple of hours and lifting Simpson's red blanket we discovered that it was full of holes. A coat I had thrown nearby was perforated in like manner, and all our wearing apparel left exposed was more or less damaged. Every article looked as if it had been a target for bird shot.

At first we were puzzled to account for this singular misfortune, but at last discovered that the harm had been done by grasshoppers. We baited the set line with them that night, and had the additional ill luck to catch no eels.

Near this camp a highway wound along the hillside, perhaps fifty feet above the stream. Much of the distance it lay in the full glare of the sun, then plunged into a thick wood, whose cool shadows were broken only by stray spots of light that flickered through the foliage. Simpson called this spot Lover's Lane. It seemed to be a favorite promenade for berry pickers.

Before we reached Walton the stream slacked its course, rifts were less frequent, and the channel broadened and swept with stately flow between high walls of dark rock, and deep hillsides thickly covered with wood; schools of fish, chubs and suckers, with a sprinkling of black bass, swam close to the rocky bottom, and scattered as we glided over them. The rat-tat of the woodpecker resounded among the dead trunks overhead, and warblers chirped in the underbrush. As our eyes scanned the dark course of the stream an occasional *Lobelia cardinalis* shone out like a flash of red fire against a black wall.

Frequently a spring spilled its surplus down a crevice lined with snapdragon and the white candy-like blossoms of *eupatorium,* to fall into the dark waters below, that received it with the ringing echo of a cistern. We would glide up in passing such places and fill a cup with water, so cold one's fingers ached against the tin. It was not in the least brackish, but had a sweet, woody flavor, as if brewed among the roots of wintergreen.

When we came out into the sunshine the river showed a freakish tendency to fork in every direction, sometimes offering three courses at once from which to choose. There was no danger of losing one's way, however, for these different courses naturally united again farther down, but there was a decided choice between the routes, for some were full of shallow rifts, and consequently entailed wading, and only a practiced eye could decide at once which channel was the best. Simpson and I often disagreed on this point, and separated, to exchange experiences farther down.

I had a theory that his judgment was usually correct, but would not, of course, tell him so. However, on the occasion I have in mind he swerved at the last moment, and shot down an ugly-looking break on the left. I looked up in surprise, for the stream he had taken had the current of a millrace, disappeared under some ugly branches, and whitened itself with a roar against a mass of rock farther down.

As the *Sybaris* shot under the overhanging limbs his paddle caught, and his head and shoulders plunged into the foliage, while his weight, as he wriggled to free himself, forced the boat down till the water boiled over the decks and threatened to swamp her.

In fact, the high coamings of the cockpit were all that kept her from filling. I do not know how long he might have stayed there had I not landed the *Shaw Shaw* and gone to his assistance, wading in as far as I could and pulling the canoe back till he managed to free himself.

At Walton, a town of considerable importance, the river is spanned by a long iron bridge, and below it the stream widens into a shallow rift, down which we slid for a few rods and then stuck fast, making it necessary to get out and wade, an operation annoying to us, but interesting to the pedestrians collected on the bridge.

As we proceeded the formation of the country changed. Instead of broad and fertile valleys, wooded hills, towering into mountainous proportions, closed in the river on all sides, and huge boulders obstructed the current. The sun was sinking in a clear sky, and as the shadows lengthened the windings of the river revealed some remarkable effects. At one point a mountain, whose precipitous sides were partially cleared of timber, loomed up in the west, and as the sun disappeared behind it the clearings that scarred its face appeared like great chasms of purple haze, through which the treetops rose here and there. The roar of the water as it surged through the rocky passes was ominous and we craned our heads forward and held the paddles with a nervous grip, occasionally shouting a word of warning, or giving a cheer, as some unusually bad obstruction was passed without a scratch. The change from the quiet drifting through sunny pastures to this rapid darting among the darkening rifts made one's blood leap. It was an experience only a canoeist can have. We camped that night in a little grove of butternuts—Mallory's Grove, they called it. . . .

A distance below this point the river pursued a westerly course, and a wind from the same quarter, blowing almost a gale, made our progress slow and difficult. In the afternoon, when the sun shone in our faces, a rift would appear like a slope of burnished silver, against which every object stood out in silhouette, the dazzling light making it impossible to choose a course or detect hidden rocks till we were upon them. This gave us trying work till we reached Cannonsville, a most attractive country village. Landing here, just below a bridge, I climbed the bank to a pine grove, and stood spellbound, motioning to Simpson to approach with caution, for less than ten rods away hung a hammock, and, with her back toward us, one hand supporting her head and a small foot swinging back and forth, reclined a veritable Margery Daw.*

Neither of us moved for some seconds, then Simpson heaved a sigh, and I glanced around in time to see him trying to press some shape into his forlorn hat. It was of no use, however, and even had he had the most presentable headgear at command, our soiled knickerbockers and unshaven faces would have insured us the reception of tramps had we made ourselves known. Beyond the hammock, the white sides of a house were visible across a strip of lawn, and somewhere from behind a hedge the click of croquet balls and an occasional peal of laughter reached our ears.

We stood back there in the shade and furtively watched this picture of civilized life, then slid down the bank, stepped into the canoes, and floated silently away. . . . That night, after frying the bacon, Simpson washed his hands with great care and sat up very late writing a letter, a task he never essayed unless in the right mood.

THE BEAVER KILL AND THE EAST BRANCH

When Simpson and I had reached Hancock by way of the West Branch we again sought higher country and shipped our canoes for Cook's Falls, or Butternut Grove, as it is also called, a small village on that fresh and rapid stream so well known to sportsmen, the

* Hammock-swaying, novel-reading, lovely heroine of *Marjorie Daw*, a clever epistolary short story by Thomas Bailey Aldrich published in 1873. W. T.

Beaver Kill. . . . There was some question in our minds whether this water would prove navigable for the canoes. They drew little to be sure, but even the *Shaw Shaw,* which had no keel, could not float quite like an autumn leaf, and Simpson shook his head as we caught glimpses from the car windows of the white water surging among the black rocks down below. An individual whom he always referred to as the "chump" had advised us not to try the stream.

He had called at our camp while we were at the West Branch, and had expatiated at great length on its peculiarities, dwelling with force on the fact that bear and wildcat filled the woods on all sides and that rattlers were thick as blackberries, making it risky to sleep on the ground.

"Them boats go down the Beaver Kill! Mebbe so; most everything that gets in there's boun' to go down!" and he laughed heartily. We might have been discouraged by this picture had we not learned later that the youth had never seen the Beaver Kill.

Our first day on the stream will never be forgotten. The water was fairly high, as there had been recent rains, and scarcely a moment was permitted us in which to hunch forward with elbows on knees and contemplate the panorama unfolding before us as we floated down. This had been a favorite occupation along the quiet stretches of the West Branch, but here we were either in the midst of a roaring rift, throwing our whole weight on the paddle and twisting the boats rapidly around the rocks, or standing up, scanning some white line a few rods ahead, to choose the safest opening through which to pass—a choice that always had to be made with great promptness. This need for watchfulness, keeping one constantly on the alert, and the necessity for prompt action give to canoeing its peculiar zest. A noticeable feature of the region watered by the Beaver Kill is the ancient appearance of many of the houses scattered through the valley.

For so wild a country this strikes one as singular, but we learned that the spots of fertile lowland were early settled, and many of the oldest houses were built on the sites of still older. These were weather-stained buildings, with broad verandas shaded by climbing vines and having big, breezy kitchens with shining rows of milk pans by the door.

Usually the water brought from a spring in the hills bubbled near at hand and a tin cup hung ready for use. The hills here, as at Rock Rift, are being gradually cleared of hardwood for acid factories, and stump lots, covered with blackberry and second-growth oak, hickory and sassafras, are common.

In some parts these clearings afford a feeding ground for bear, who grub up the roots and feast on berries in their season, and the deer still linger in sections, though, as our course led us through the natural thoroughfare of the region, we started no large game. . . . I had an uncomfortable dream that night; a bear seemed to be standing over me, and would occasionally draw a cold nose across my hand or face. While having an impression that they would not touch a man lying motionless, I moved neither hand nor foot, but lay in a miserable nightmare trance till Simpson shook me awake and whispered, "What's that?" in a startled voice, close to my ear. "Wh-a-t?" I gasped. "Something crawled over me," he said. We both lay still and listened. Something cold touched my cheek; small wet feet skipped lightly over my face. Some leaves rustled; then it was still.

"Hark!" he said, hearing the leaves. "Do you suppose that could be a rattler?" "If it is it has feet," I muttered; "something walked on me, nothing crawled; it was probably a field mouse;" and throwing my arms about to frighten off the intruder, if he still remained, I turned over and went to sleep. Simpson did the same. Only the possibility of a visit from a rattlesnake could keep us awake after the day's exertion. A search among the blankets the next morning revealed a small frog.

On this cruise we learned many of the finer points of canoeing. A stream like the Beaver Kill affords a variety of conditions that more placid waters lack. Its surface, reflecting the bottom, shone a rich, transparent brown, the deep and shallow stretches presenting little variety in color.

The general rule in navigating shallow streams, to keep well on the outward sweep of a bend, often failed us here, and many times the channel followed the inner bank, or wound in and out in eccentric curves that were extremely puzzling.

Experienced cruisers know how to detect hidden obstructions at a glance, but it may not be out of place to say a word on this point to beginners.

Where a stone lies just beneath the surface of a rapid stream the water slides over it with an unruffled current, then breaks back on itself, making a white boiling spot. This spot serves as a warning, but as it occurs close under the obstruction it is often difficult to see it from above.

In close quarters the canoe can be pushed through these white spots without danger, provided the treacherous stillness just preceding them is avoided. Another appearance presented by rapid water is deceptive and at first very alarming. A broad stream suddenly narrows, and the water tumbled in on itself forms a white channel full of choppy waves, an angry-looking path, but seldom, except in case of a great volume of water, a dangerous one, for it is deeper than the quiet stream above it.

Sometimes the roar in these narrowings of the Beaver Kill could be heard a long distance and the waves gave us a thorough wetting.

I carried a light hazel fishing rod besides my sketch book, and would toss a grasshopper over the eddies that swirled at the foot of the rifts, seldom without result in the shape of a chub. The stream swarmed with these fish and they sometimes reached a full pound in weight. The trout were more numerous in the tributary creeks, where the water was colder, but in this high region it seldom grows very warm anywhere, while the mist, looking white as hoar frost and feeling quite as cold, makes the grass glisten in the early mornings, even in August. We often pitched our tent in spots where wintergreen and prince's pine dotted the turf, making a balmy bed to stretch out on. One night we slept on warm sand that lay along the shore in ridges like graves. It felt wonderfully comfortable at first, but when the rubber blanket was worked in till one's form was cast like iron in a mold, it might as well have been a bed of rock.

Some long bridges span the streams at the point where the Beaver Kill joins the East Branch, and a little village bearing the name of the latter nestles about the fork. The added volume of water below this point gives dignity to the stream that sweeps along with the steady movement of a river.

A small boy and girl, wading in the shallows, stared in astonishment as the canoes floated toward them; but the lad recovered himself sufficiently to ask for a ride before we had passed. By shifting our cargo forward a sort of nest was made for the reception of passengers, and the boats bobbed down the next rift with extra ballast.

A pair of fat steers standing in the river were nearly run down by the *Sybaris* and floundered snorting to the shore, closely followed by the boat. The young man whom I carried in the *Shaw Shaw* had a long string of fish, chub and dace, most of which, he took pains to tell me, he had caught himself, gently implying a slur on feminine prowess. Both children were delighted with the tiny crafts that floated where they could wade and bore them in safety over the deepest holes, and the dream of owning a canoe gave an additional gilding to that long-delayed heaven referred to by Simpson's passenber as "When we grow up." After we left them they stood with their brown legs in the water, like a pair of herons, and watched us out of sight. . . .

Along the deep, still stretches of the stream we would pass an occasional scow moored under the shadow of a rock or overhanging tree, and occupied by a fisherman. These crafts were built of pine or hemlock boards, and sometimes of plank two inches thick. One huge boat lying among some rushes bore the name of *Dauntless,* the title covering a whole side, in yellow letters on a red ground.

It was not a good day for fishing, our first on the East Branch; the sun was too hot and the air too still, but the conditions made it easy to inspect the ground, and we could lean over and count the black bass lying along the bottom, with heads upstream and making just enough movement of fin and tail to keep stationary against a gentle current. On a cloudy day we saw a basket filled with as fine a collection of these beauties as we have met with anywhere.

On rounding a bend at one point I found Simpson had landed and was trying to catch a mink he had cornered in a bunch of smart weed, but the game was too quick for him and ducked into the river under his very paddle. Later on, as we were floating close to the bank, some wood ducks darted from under the bows of the canoes and cunningly fled up the stream. They were young, and did not rise readily, but beat the water with their wings, progressing with a noise and splash that would have done credit to a steam tug.

We camped for some days near Read's Creek. A ford used by the farmers when the river was low crossed the stream close by, and back of us rose a thick wood fragrant with wild flowers. The rhododendron with its waxy leaves and clean stems grew close around the tent, and after the sun went down and the stillness seemed more profound than ever we could hear the splash of a

Illustration by Edward L. Chichester
from *Outing,* May and June 1889

rivulet that emptied into a binnacle close by. We would light the lantern and read or write letters or look over the day's sketches till we grew drowsy from a very excess of snugness and comfort, and then go to sleep. A large tent proved a decided improvement on the tiny shelter one could button over the gunwale of a boat.

It afforded more commodious quarters on rainy days and left the canoes free for fishing or short excursions. The advantages offered by the canoe to sportsmen are too well known to need further comment here, but a word as to its peculiar adaptability to an artist's requirements may not be out of place. First, any quantity of sketching material can be carried without inconvenience, an advantage readily appreciated by anyone who has tramped across the country loaded like a pack horse, with color box, camp stool, easel and umbrella.

Again, with a stream for thoroughfare one passes through the most picturesque section of a country. Every bend reveals something of interest, and facing in the direction one goes each point can be noted.

The forward deck serves as a desk under which a sketch book lies always at hand, and paddle can be readily exchanged for pencil. Our plan on this cruise was to move slowly down the stream until some point of special interest was reached and then camp, often remaining in the same place for days together.

A river of any length offers great variety in scenery, and the Beaver Kill and East Branch were no exception to this rule.

The upper waters, with their thickly wooded banks, gave way below to open meadows, and highways winding between stone walls succeeded the rough wood roads. . . .

Our only annoyance was an occasional watchdog who regarded us with suspicion, and I do not know that the animals could be blamed. A huge Newfoundland rushed at Simpson one morning as he was sketching by the roadside, but as the artist detected a muzzle strapped tightly to the dog's nose he paid no attention to the attack and affected not to know the creature was barking at him. The dog's look of perfect bewilderment as he slunk away was ludicrous. . . .

As the river neared Hancock it divided and wound in and out among a succession of small islands. These were covered with masses of brilliant color, goldenrod and a dull purple-red flower predominating, while here and there were the white blossoms of boneset. Rich color gleamed in everything.

On one of our rambles back in the country we discovered a cedar thicket, the stumpy trees standing so close that the lower limbs had died for want of air and light, while the tops were clothed with dense foliage. Creeping under we found the place had an atmosphere of its own—a kind of cave-like character—and the ground was perfectly dry after hours of rain. It formed a natural home for owls and bats.

I was really anxious to meet with a rattlesnake on this cruise, if only to secure a set of rattles as a trophy, but though we both searched every stretch of rocky ground from Cook's Falls to Hancock no specimen was secured or even sighted.

I had one adventure, however, that made me fear my wish had been granted in a startling manner.

I was walking along a highway, and, feeling my feet entangled in something, was horrified to see a large snake wriggling in the dust. It is needless to say that I sprang high in the air, and the serpent made a hasty retreat, turning a very ordinary tail as he disappeared down the bank toward the river.

He was only a water snake and not worth capture, but for a brief moment inspired all the respect due his more venomous brother.

About a week after we entered the East Branch the familiar aspect of the hills told us we were again approaching the mouth of the river. The Cadosia Creek was passed, and the bluestone quarries told of our near approach to the union of the stream with its western sister.

The canoes carried us past Hancock, around a bend and out into the meeting of the waters. At this point we made our last camp and lingered for some days, but the trees were already showing autumnal tints, and the river smoked in the early mornings. It was time to go. We packed everything into as small a compass as possible and carried the boats to the station, leaving a stuffed dummy of well-worn garments to startle the discoverer of our last camping place. . . .

Frederic Remington
1861-1909

Remington, famous delineator of the last western frontier, was born in Canton, New York, raised in Ogdensburg on the St. Lawrence, studied art and played football at Yale. Physically and creatively he drove hard and kept on the move ranging far and wide over North America. To get beyond what he called "civilized rivers" he went to Ontario, apparently to Rice Lake, thence to the head of a stream he left nameless.

Tall, blond, sporting a mustache, weighing over two hundred pounds, he was in his early thirties when he made this canoe trip. Action (the dominant theme of his life and unceasing toil) leavened with chivalrousness and compassion, springs from his good-humored pages.

BLACK WATER AND SHALLOWS *

The morning broke gray and lowering, and the clouds rolled in heavy masses across the sky. I was sitting out on a log washing a shirt, and not distinguishing myself as a laundryman either, for one shirt will become excessively dirty in a week, and no canoeist can have more than that, as will be seen when you consider that he has to carry everything which he owns on his back. My guide had packed up our little kit and deposited it skilfully in the *Necoochee* —a sixteen-foot canoe of the Rice Lake pattern.

We were about to start on a cruise down a river which the lumbermen said could not be "run," as it was shallow and rocky. We could find no one who had been down it, and so, not knowing anything about it, we regarded it as a pleasant prospect. Harrison, being a professional guide and hunter, had mostly come in contact with people—or "sports," as he called them—who had no sooner entered the woods than they were overcome with a desire to slay. No fatigue or exertion was too great when the grand purpose was to kill the deer and despoil the trout streams, but to go wandering aimlessly down a stream which by general consent was impracticable for boats, and then out into the clearings where the mountain spring was left behind, and where logs and milldams and agriculturists took the place of the deer and the trout, was a scheme which never quite got straightened out in his mind. With many misgivings, and a very clear impression that I was mentally deranged, "Has" allowed that "we're all aboard."

We pushed out into the big lake and paddled. As we skirted the shores the wind howled through the giant hemlocks, and the ripples ran away into whitecaps on the far shore. As I wielded my double-blade paddle and instinctively enjoyed the wildness of the day, I also indulged in a conscious calculation of how long it would take

* *Harper's New Monthly Magazine,* August, 1893.

my shirt to dry on my back. It is such a pity to mix a damp shirt up with the wild storm, as it hurries over the dark woods and the black water, that I felt misgivings; but, to be perfectly accurate, they divided my attention, and, after all, man is only noble by fits and starts.

We soon reached the head of the river, and a water-storage dam and a mile of impassable rapids made a "carry" or "portage" necessary. Slinging our packs and taking the seventy-pound canoe on our shoulders, we started down the trail. The torture of this sort of thing is as exquisitely perfect in its way as any ever devised. A trunk porter in a summer hotel simply does for a few seconds what we do by the hour, and as for reconciling this to an idea of physical enjoyment, it cannot be done. It's a subtle mental process altogether indefinable; but your enthusiast is a person who would lose all if he reasoned any, and to suffer like an anchorite is always a part of a sportsman's programme. The person who tilts back in a chair on the veranda of a summer hotel, while he smokes cigars and gazes vacantly into space, is your only true philosopher; but he is not a sportsman. The woods and the fields and the broad roll of the ocean do not beckon to him to come out among them. . . . A real sportsman, of the nature-loving type, must go tramping or paddling or riding about over the waste places of the earth, with his dinner in his pocket. He is alive to the terrible strain of the "carry," and to the quiet pipe when the day is done. The campfire contemplation, the beautiful quiet of the misty morning on the still water, enrapture him, and his eye dilates, his nerves tingle, and he is in a conflagration of ecstasy. When he is going—going—faster—faster into the boil of the waters, he hears the roar and boom ahead, and the black rocks crop up in thickening masses to dispute his way. He is fighting a game battle with the elements, and they are remorseless. He may break his leg or lose his life in the tipover which is imminent, but the fool is happy—let him die.

But we were left on the "carry," and it is with a little thrill of joy and the largest sigh of relief possible when we again settle the boat in the water. Now you should understand why it is better to have one shirt and wash it often. My "canoe kit" is the best arranged and the most perfect in the world, as no other canoeist will possibly admit, but which is nevertheless a fact. One blanket, a light shelter tent, a cooking outfit, which folds up in a sort of Japanese way, a light axe, two canvas packs, and tea, bacon, and flour. This does not make long reading, but it makes a load for a man when it's all packed up, and a canoeist's baggage must be cut to the strength of his back. It is a great piece of confidence in which I will indulge you when I caution you not to pick out invalids for canoe companions. If a burro would take kindly to backwoods navigation, I should enjoy the society of one, though it would not be in the nature of a burro to swing an axe, as indeed there are many fine gentlemen who cannot do a good job at that; and if one at least of the party cannot, the camp fires will go out early at nights, and it is more than probable that the companions will have less than twenty toes between them at the end of the cruise.

All these arrangements being perfected, you are ready to go ahead, and in the wilderness you have only one anxiety, and that is about the "grub." If the canoe turn over, the tea, the sugar, and the flour will mix up with the surrounding elements, and only the bacon will remain to nourish you until you strike the clearings, and there are few men this side 70° north latitude who will gormandize on that alone.

The long still water is the mental side of canoeing, as the rapid is the life and movement. The dark woods tower on either side, and the clear banks, full to their fat sides, fringed with trailing vines and drooping ferns, have not the impoverished look of civilized rivers. The dark water wells along, and the branches droop to kiss it. In front the gray sky is answered back by the water reflection, and the trees lie out as though hung in the air, forming a gateway, always receding. Here and there an old monarch of the forest has succumbed to the last blow and fallen across the stream. It reaches out ever so far with its giant stems, and the first branch had started sixty feet from the ground. You may have to chop a way through, or you may force your canoe through the limbs and gather a crowd of little broken branches to escort you along the stream. . . . The quietness of the woods, with all their solemnity, permitting no bright or overdressed plant to obtrude itself, is rudely shocked by the garish painted thing as the yellow polished *Necoochee* glides among them. The water rat dives with a tremendous splash as he sees the big monster glide by his sedge home. The kingfisher springs away

"Breaking a Jam," by Frederic Remington, from *Harper's New Monthly Magazine,* August 1893

from his perch on the dead top with loud chatterings when we glide into his notice. The crane takes off from his grassy "set back" in a deliberate manner, as though embarking on a tour to Japan, a thing not to be hurriedly done. The mink eyes you from his sunken log, and grinning in his most savage little manner, leaps away. These have all been disturbed in their wild homes as they were about to lunch off the handiest trout, and no doubt they hate us in their liveliest manner; but the poor trout under the boat compensate us with their thanks. The mud turtle is making his way upstream, as we can tell by the row of bubbles which arise in his wake; and the "skaters," as I call the little insects which go skipping about like a lawyer's point in an argument, part as we go by. The mosquitoes, those desperate little villains who dispute your happiness in the woods, are there, but they smell the tar and oil of our war paint, and can only hum in their anger. A stick cracks in the brush, and . . . a little spotted fawn walks out on a sedge bank from among the alders. He does not notice us, but in his stupid little way looks out the freshest watergrass, and the hunter in the stern of the boat cuts his paddle through the water, and the canoe glides silently up until right under his nose. We are still and silent. The little thing raises its head and looks us full in the eye, and then continues to feed as before. I talk to him quietly, and say, "Little man, do not come near the ponds or the rivers, for you will not live to have five prongs on your antlers if any one but such good people as we see you." He looks up, and seems to say, "You are noisy, but I do not care." "Now run; and if you ever see anything in the forest which resembles us, run for your life"; and with a bound the little innocent has regained the dark aisles of the woods. You loll back on your pack, your pipe going lazily; your hat is off; you moralize, and think thoughts which have dignity. You drink in the spell of the forest, and dream of the birch-barks and the red warriors who did this same thing a couple of centuries since. But as thoughts vary so much in individuals, and have but an indirect bearing on canoeing, I will proceed without them. The low swamp, with its soft timber, gives place to hills and beech ridges, and the old lord of the forest for these last hundred years towers up majestically. The smaller trees fight for the sunlight, and thus the ceaseless war of nature goes on quietly, silently, and alone. The miserable "witch-hoppel" leads its lusty plebeian life, satisfied to spring its half-dozen leaves, and not dreaming to some day become an oak. The gentle sigh of the forest, the hum of insects, and the chatter and peal of the birds have gone into harmony with a long, deep, swelling sound, becoming louder and louder, until finally it drowns all else.

The canoe now glides more rapidly. The pipe is laid one side. The paddle is grasped firmly, and with a firm eye I regard the "grub" pack which sits up in the bow, and resolve to die if necessary in order that it may not sink if we turn over. The river turns, and the ominous growl of the rapids is at hand.

"Hold her—hold her now—to the right of the big rock; then swing to the far shore: if we go to the right, we are gone."

"All right; let her stern come round," and we drop away.

No talking now, but with every nerve and muscle tense, and your eye on the boil of the water, you rush along. You back water and paddle, the stern swings, she hangs for an instant, she falls in the current, and with a mad rush you take it like a hunting man a six-bar gate. Now paddle, paddle, paddle. It looks bad—we cannot make it—yes—all right, and we are on the far shore, with the shallows on the other side. This little episode was successful, but, as you well know, it cannot last. The next rift, and with a bump she is hung upon a sunken rock, and—jump! jump!—we both flounder overboard in any way possible, so it is well and quickly done. One man loses his hold, the other swings the boat off, and kicking and splashing for a foothold, the demoralized outfit shoots along. At last one is found, and then at a favorable rock we embark again.

You are now wet, but the tea and sugar are safe, so it's a small matter. A jam of logs and tops is "hung up" on a particularly nasty place, and you have a time getting the boat around it. You walk on rotten tops while the knots stick up beneath you like sabres. "Has" floats calmly out to sea as it were on a detached log which he is cutting, and with a hopeless look of despair he totters, while I yell, "Save the axe—you—save the axe!" and over he goes, only to get wet and very disgusted, both of which will wear off in time. For a mile the water is so shallow that the boat will not run loaded, and we lead her along as we wade, now falling in over our heads, sliding on slippery stones, hurting our feet, wondering why we had come at all. The boat gets loose, and my heart stands still as the whole boatload of blankets and grub with our pipes and tobacco started off for the settlements. . . . There was a rather lively and enthusiastic pursuit instituted then, the details of which are forgotten, as my mind was focused on the grub pack, but we got her. About this time the soles let go on my tennis shoes, and my only pair of trousers gave way. These things, however, become such mere details as to be scarcely noticed when you have traveled since sunrise up to

"Hung Up," by Frederic Remington, from *Harper's New Monthly,* August 1893

your waist in water, and are tired, footsore, and hungry. It is time to go ashore and camp.

You scrape away a rod square of dirt, chunks, witch hoppel, and dead leaves, and make a fire. You dry your clothes while you wear the blanket and the guide the shelter tent, and to a casual observer it would look as though the savage had come again; but he would detect a difference, because a white man in a blanket is about as inspiring a sight as an Indian with a plug hat.

Finally the coffee boils, the tent is up, and the bough bed laid down. You lean against the dead log and swap lies with the guide; and the greatest hunters I have ever known have all been magnificent liars. The two go together. I should suspect a man who was deficient. Since no one ever believes hunters' yarns, it has come to be a pleasurable pastime, in which a man who has not hunted considerably can't lie properly without offending the intelligence of that part of his audience who have.

The morning comes too soon, and after you are packed up and the boat loaded, if you are in a bad part of the river you do this: You put away your pipe, and with a grimace and a shudder you step out into the river up to your neck and get wet. The morning is cold, and I, for one, would not allow a man who was perfectly dry to get into my boat, for fear he might have some trepidation about getting out promptly if the boat was "hung up" on a rock; . . .

Hour after hour we waded along. A few rods of still water and "Has" would cut off large chews of tobacco, and become wonderfully cynical as to the caprices of the river. The still water ends around the next point. You charge the thing nobly, but end up in the water up to your neck with the "grub" safe, and a mile or so more of wading in prospect.

Then the river narrows, and goes tumbling off down a dark canyon cut through the rocks. We go ashore and "scout the place," and then begin to let the boat down on a line. We hug the black sides like ants, while the water goes to soapsuds at our feet. The boat bobs and rocks, and is nearly upset in a place where we cannot follow it through. We must take it up a ledge about thirty feet high, and after puffing and blowing and feats of maniacal strength, we at last have it again in the water. After some days of this thing we found from a statistician we had dropped 1,100 feet in about fifty-one miles, and with the well-known propensity of water to flow down hill, it can be seen that difficulties were encountered. You cannot carry a boat in the forest, and you will discover enough reasons why in a five-minute trail to make their enumeration tiresome. The zest of the whole thing lies in not knowing the difficulties beforehand, and then, if properly equipped, a man who sits at a desk the year through can find no happier days than he will in his canoe when the still waters run through the dark forests and the rapid boils below.

George Elmer Browne
1871 - 1946

This trip was made in a Swampscott dory, a boat with high flaring sides, sharp bow, and deep V-shaped transom, indigenous to the New England coast—Browne was born in Gloucester, Massachusetts—and noted for seaworthiness. It turned out to be a well-nigh perfect vehicle for accommodating to a rushing river and for carrying all the gear needed by two artists on a working trip.

CANOEING DOWN THE ANDROSCOGGIN *

. . . I had long wished for an outing that would furnish me with abundant material for sketching. And how could I have been more fortunate than to meet a man who, like myself, was an artist, and a veteran camper-out of some twenty years' experience!

When I had proposed a summer in the Maine woods, he had consented to accompany me. He pooh-poohed the thought of our taking a canoe, especially as the cruise I had mapped out consisted in a trip the entire length of the roughest and wildest river in all New England. "No, a canoe would never do," he remarked; "the wear and tear on so frail a craft would be too great." But he had the very thing, a Swampscott dory, which would make the very best of boats for rough travel. And, besides, he had had the boat so altered and adapted that, if he wished, a tent could be raised at a moment's notice that would cover the whole deck. By so doing, the interior could be converted into a splendid shelter, where, at night, bunks could be constructed on the floor, and everything made as home-like as could be desired.

Besides this novel and useful equipment, we also carried with us a regulation letter "A" tent, which we would use whenever our stay at any one place was to be prolonged. This tent covered a floor space of about ten by twelve feet, and had a drop wall of about two feet in height. An extra protection from sun and rain was furnished by the use of a large fly, which was fastened to the two supports or tent poles, and was pinioned out to stakes down (in the ground) along the sides of the tent. The rest of our outfit consisted of the customary number of articles that are indispensable; namely, a good-sized oil stove for cooking, pans and dishes, lantern, gro-

* *Outing,* July, 1898.

ceries and provisions. Then we carried in a number of small wooden cases that could be easily handled and moved around. We each carried one rubber blanket, so made that in rainy weather it could be fastened around the shoulder and would answer as a very good cape. Each also had a pair of army blankets. Our coats, rolled up, answered as pillows. With these and the smooth ground for a mattress, we could pass a good night's sleep in comfort.

For wearing apparel I had made up for me, at very little cost, a full suit of tanned duck, with warm leggings of the same color. The coat was arranged with large pockets on the inside for carrying sketching materials and lunches, while the outside resembled the ordinary sportsman's coat. A blue flannel shirt, a broad-brimmed hat and rubber-soled shoes completed the costume, and for service and comfort no better rig could be conceived.

The morning gave every promise of a pleasant day, and as we dipped our oars and shot out toward the deep water, the effect of the early gray light upon the low, slowly rising cloud of mist that soon surrounded us was beautiful; and as the heavens became more brilliantly illuminated the opposite shores could be plainly seen.

It was not long before we reached . . . the source of the Androscoggin, and started on our trip down.

The river, immediately after leaving the lake, widens until it forms a good-sized pond, caused by the outlet of the principal tributary to the Androscoggin, the Megalloway River. . . .

The current, so far, had been rather dead, but as we drew away from the village it increased in swiftness until we were going along at a very fair rate. Now and then a slight "rip" (rapids) broke the smoothness of the water as we pushed on, but no rapid worthy of any notice obstructed our path during the forenoon. The scenery all along was picturesque. The shores on either side were fringed with tall trees that stretched back for miles from the river. At one place the river was divided and ran on either side of a thickly wooded island, the trees on the right side hanging over so that their branches interlocked with those on the left bank and formed a veritable arch of foliage. This little island was the first of the Seven Islands, and the beauty increased as we shot in and out among the verdure-grown islets.

Selecting a spot on a shelving bit of ground that sloped away

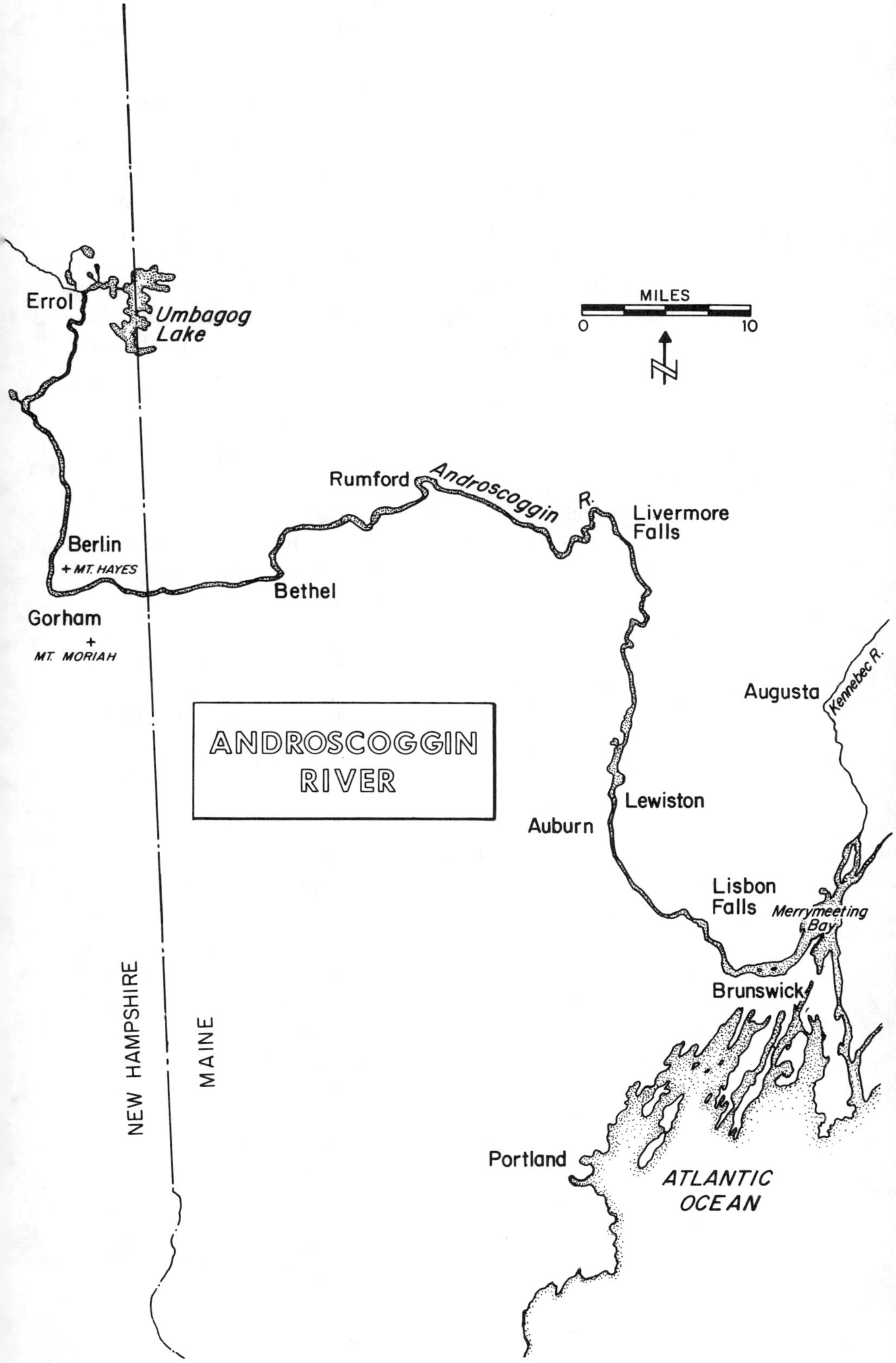
ANDROSCOGGIN RIVER
MILES
0
10
N
Errol
Umbagog Lake
Berlin
+ MT. HAYES
Gorham
+ MT. MORIAH
Bethel
Rumford
Androscoggin R.
Livermore Falls
Augusta
Kennebec R.
Lewiston
Auburn
Lisbon Falls
Merrymeeting Bay
Brunswick
Portland
ATLANTIC OCEAN
NEW HAMPSHIRE
MAINE

from the river, we ran our boat ashore and pulled it high and dry upon the beach. We then placed the two supports for the boat tent in position, together with the ridgepole, and in a few moments had the canvas spread and fastened tightly to the gunwale of the boat by means of a series of reef lines. We then opened our canvas shutters, and everything was ready. We found the bunks, which we constructed on the floor of the dory by spreading the A tent and fly out first to answer as a cushion over the uneven surface and cleats, to make remarkably good beds, and much better than our rubber blankets on the hard floor had been the night before.

All that day we had to work our passage as best we could down the log-choked river, and at six o'clock we found ourselves within sight of the steeple and housetops of Berlin Falls, having covered but a little over twelve miles since morning.

We ran ashore and started to look up a teamster, and were soon placing our tent and equipage aboard his team and making ready for a carry through the town and around the falls.

It was growing late ere we arrived at a spot about two miles below the town, where the view in both directions of the river was very fine, and where a sandy beach to the water's edge furnished an admirable opportunity for launching the boat. Here we staked out the A tent once more.

Directly across the river the long slope of Mt. Hazen, a well-known peak of the Presidential range, stretched far into the clouds, while the vista downstream in the direction of Gorham furnished us with a fine view of Mt. Maria and the adjacent mountains.

Above us, and within a few rods of our camp, the roar of falling waters attracted our attention to a series of beautiful cataracts known as Tinkers' Rips. Here the river was clogged and ruffled with numerous great boulders, which poked their jagged heads above the surface in all directions and caused the rapidly moving river to bound and splash over them in a shower of silver spray. Above these enchanting falls a small, primitive bridge, constructed on the suspension principle, swung from shore to shore and formed a picturesque addition to the surroundings.

After staying at this camp about a week, one sunny morning we reloaded our boat and pushed off.

We very soon, however, found ourselves caught in a long stretch of rapids, which, to our inexperienced eyes, appeared most dangerous to navigate. Indeed, in some places it was so rough that, in order to save our boat from being shattered on the rocks, I was obliged to leap into the water in my clothes, and, obtaining as firm a foothold as possible, lower the boat by means of a long rope attached to the bow, while White, standing in the stern, managed to keep clear of the rocks by the aid of a stout setting pole. In this

"Our Teamsters on a Haul Round," by George Elmer Browne, from *Outing*, July 1898

way we made slow progress, and at dusk had only traversed about three miles, a remarkably short distance in such swiftly moving water. However, we were inexperienced at the business of shooting rapids at this time.

It was beginning to sprinkle as we pulled our boat ashore that evening, and so, rather than run the risk of getting our traps drenched while pitching the shore tent, we ran the boat high up on the beach, and soon had the tent over her, lashed securely to the gunwale.

Hardly had we housed ourselves and hustled all our baggage under cover than the rain began to beat upon the canvas in a perfect fury. But, like all showers of this kind in the mountains, it was soon over. And, to give an additional charm to the picture, a beautiful rainbow gradually formed.

The next day, after a slow passage down the remainder of the rips, we reached the little town of Gorham, nestled at the very base of Mt. Maria.

At this place we stayed a week, sketching, tramping, or fishing in the river or in its many tributary brooks. . . .

On the Monday following our arrival we resumed our cruise.

"A Cosy Corner for a Camp," by George Elmer Browne, *Outing,* July 1898

Soon we had left the great mountains far behind us, and were gliding through the broad, green intervales of Shelborn. As we advanced, the scenery became grander.

Gilead was our next stop, which we reached about dusk. The day had been one of the finest, and our trip from Gorham a delightful one. Some rough and exciting rapids had been shot in safety, and we had gained much practice in guiding our boat through.

The next day brought us to Bethel, a beautiful little town on the right bank of the river. Here we stopped for a couple of days, sketching and rambling.

Next to Bethel came Newry, a limited collection of primitive dwellings that surround a rustic old sawmill. We shot some rather wild rips at this point, but, finding the run smooth for the rest of the way, enjoyed a pleasant trip as far as Hanover, where we went into camp.

The next morning we got an early start, and, passing the little hamlets of Rumford Point, North Rumford, Rumford Center and East Rumford, arrived about two o'clock at a place called Virginia Heights, close to the very brink of the great Rumford Falls, the highest and most wonderful fall in New England. All that night, as we lay around our campfire, we could hear the roar of falling water. . . .

The sky was thickly overcast with clouds as we set out the next morning; and at almost the same moment that the rain came, our boat grounded on a bar and there stuck fast, while White and I, hastily grabbing the rubber blankets and spreading them over the groceries and bedding that they might not get wet, and having no time to look after ourselves, were soon drenched.

In a short while the shower had passed over, and we had got out of the boat and were making exertions to shove her off the bar. At last we succeeded in getting free, and, having first dragged her into deep water, had soon left the shoal far behind us.

Our camp we made on the shore of a small island, and we there pitched the A tent. The ground was especially unsuited for camping, as it was covered with small white rocks which made staking out the tent a bothersome task. And, to add still more discomfort to our already tired-out bodies, the uneven surface of our ground floor made a most uncomfortable bed to lie upon.

It was about midnight, I should judge, when we were both aroused by hearing a great crash and feeling something crowd suddenly down upon us. I awoke with a start and shouted to White, who, like myself, was trying to tear himself loose from the weight upon him.

"What in time has happened?" he shouted back.

"The tent's blown over," I replied, as I emerged from the wreck and crawled out onto the ground.

"Light the lantern," I cried, "while I see if the boat is secure," and I made off, shivering in the cold wind, toward the water.

On reaching the edge of the river I found that the boat had worked off from the bank and was slowly dragging her anchor out into the water. Hastily pulling her once more upon the shore, I made her secure and hastened back to camp, where I found White still vainly searching for the lantern.

"Never mind that now," I cried, "but give a hand here to the tent." We soon had the thing raised up. The canvas at once filled with wind and floated out into the night like a great balloon, and it required our utmost strength to again get control of it and fasten out the guy lines. All the pegs had disappeared, and we were obliged to tie the ropes around some large rocks and then around some drift logs.

The morning found us early awake. The wind had somewhat abated, but was still strong enough to make us long to break camp, and so, at about eight o'clock, we were again on the river. . . .

We had now traversed a trifle over one half the length of the river, which had hitherto been remarkably free from bad rapids and the water quite deep.

The first intimation of what lay in store for us farther on was in a small rapid through which we shot just before going into camp that night. The river at this point was thickly choked with large boulders, and as we ran past these obstructions, often grazing as we swept by, the excitement for the moment was great.

The next day we encountered a long boom chain over which we worked some time before we could effect entrance through. At six o'clock we camped at the head of what is known as Capen's Rips. At an early hour the following morning we were ready to make our charge through the dangerous place. And, indeed, it was dangerous enough.

We entered the rapids near the right bank and swept through diagonally until we had reached about the center. Here a slight fall was encountered, and, as we dropped over and struck on the opposite side, the boat struck against a snag, and there was held fast, while the swift current rushed around us in a perfect fury. Seeing at once that we must work quickly if we were to keep from being torn to pieces, I sprang onto a great flat rock, and, grasping the gunwale, endeavored to lift the boat off.

After a few pulls she cleared, and at once swept round, but with so much violence that I was pulled off my feet headlong into the water. However, I managed to keep a firm hold of the unwieldy craft, and as she dashed between the rocks and over the drop I was dragged through the water.

White, in the meantime, was making frantic endeavors to hold back the boat, and at last succeeded in holding his oar against a rock and turning the boat about, so that for the moment I was given an opportunity to make a foothold. No sooner had I got control of myself, however, than I began scrambling in over the bow, and was about aboard when the boat once more slewed around and headed

"Shooting Huntoon Rips," by George Elmer Browne, from *Outing*, July 1898

straight for a rock, with me clinging to the bow, one leg over the gunwale. Had it not been for White again using his oar at the proper time in the right way, I should have probably been dashed against the boulder. But, pushing bravely against another rock, he managed again to clear the bow from colliding, and I was carried by without accident. The next moment we were out of the rapids and gliding through calm water.

A short rest, and we were entering other rapids much rougher to shoot. These were Peterson's Rips, and it was as we were making our way with great speed close to the end of the chain that we encountered a most startling adventure. As in the previous rapids, we were just dropping over a slight fall when the current, getting full possession of the boat, lifted it wholly out of the water and dashed it with a great thud directly on top of a large pointed rock. For a moment we thought a hole had been stove in the bottom of the dory. The next instant we were spinning around on the rock like a top, and then, with a sudden lurch, we slid off into deep water, and, with a plunge, we were clear from the rapids and pulling for the shore. With the exception of a slight bruise on the bow, we had come through unharmed. . . .

All that day the ever-changing scenery kept us busy with our camera and pencils, and the swift current sent us along at a brisk rate. . . .

We camped near a settlement bearing the rural name of Green Corner, and after a good night's sleep were fresh for another day on the river. As we passed the mouth of a small tributary stream at Keene's Mills the next morning, we found the water to contain many trout, which had undoubtedly come down from the brooks farther inland.

About ten o'clock we came to a large island where the river plunged over a rough bed on one side and made a great drop or fall on the other. We chose the rough side, and were soon dashing down a most treacherous rapid.

For some distance we shot straight ahead, and then, without warning, we were slewed around at a sharp bend in the channel, and the next moment were driven hard onto a great rock and nearly capsized. There we hung for a moment, and then we were swept off and once more were dashing onward. Another turn, and we were out of the Ledge Island Rips without damage.

The rest of that day we spent in sketching and fishing. We passed through a most beautiful section of the country, and found a slow cruise on the calm river a delightful one.

It was late in the day when we came to Clark Rapids, where we were forced to lower the boat over a great fall at the beginning. Before doing this, however, we ran the boat inshore, and, making it secure to a tree, pushed our way out over the rocks and ledges until we stood on a great shelving piece directly in the center of the river and on the brink of the fall.

Here we had a good chance to study the nature of the channel, and to ascertain the chance we would stand in case we decided to shoot the fall. We went ashore again, and, throwing a big log into the river, watched its progress over the fall and down the rapid.

This was enough to satisfy us that we had better not venture with the boat in such a place; and so, standing with his feet firmly braced against a rock, White carefully lowered the boat over the fall by means of the long painter, while I, having made my way onto the rocks, about a quarter of a mile below, stood ready to catch the boat as soon as he had cast her free. As luck would have it, she came through all right.

But we were by no means free from Clark Rapids, as we found on starting out the next day. For fully ten miles the river was a steady chain of rips, and to add to the trouble of navigation the wind was blowing hard in our faces, making our treacherous path through the water all the more dangerous.

At last we were once more in deep water, and hurrying on to Lewiston.

We camped at the foot of a great bluff directly at the head of a wild rapid, and about midnight we were awakened by hearing something come crashing against the side of the boat in which we were camped. Scarcely had we got our eyes well opened when another thump came, this time on the ridgepole of the tent. Scrambling out, I found the moon high in the heavens, and eveything clearly visible. Glancing quickly in the direction of the cliff, I thought I could see some figures dimly outlined on the top. Whispering to White to come out, I reached into the tent and got my revolver; and when White was beside me we hid in the shadow of a bush and waited. Presently a large rock struck the ground in front of us, and then another went bang! against the boat. The next moment I shouted to the hoodlums on the cliff and asked them what they were trying to do. They replied by raining down more missiles, and so I at once took aim well over their heads and blazed away. This seemed to satisfy them that we would not stand any more fun of the kind they wished to furnish, so they disappeared.

Next morning the air was quite chilly and we hovered over the campfire for some time before starting out. At last a good breakfast put us in the right spirits and we were ready for Crooked Rips, which place we shot in short order, making one of the quickest passages through any rapid on the river.

Shortly after, we came in sight of a tent pitched on the right-hand bank, and a little further on we saw two boys. They told us that they were on their way to Lewiston, and they would like to have us go back with them to their camp and they would push off and go along with us. We readily agreed, and were soon paddling back to where we had seen the tent. We were soon heading down river with our young friends.

Their canoe was some distance in our wake, and as the boys shouted to us to look out for the rapids we looked ahead, and there, directly in front of us, was a fall of about five feet. Before we had time to consider what to do we were almost on the brink, and White heading straight for the center of the fall. We shot out into the air and struck with a resounding shock on the other side, and with such force that a great wave came pouring over the bow, drenching me through and through. The boat at once shot ahead, and for a few moments we were busy dodging the boulders that in all directions protruded from the water.

This was too much for the boys, as they had watched us with much misgiving, and they decided that the best thing to do was to make a carry.

. . . we pushed away from . . . the last settlement of any kind on the great Androscoggin, and set out for Bath. The morning was a most delightful one. A refreshing breeze was rapidly clearing the valley of the mist as we headed downstream.

The nature of the country through which we now made our way was low and flat; and, strange to say, as we approached the mouth of the river the stream became very narrow, at one place not wider than thirty feet.

After possibly three hours' sail we came in sight of a long wooden bridge, which we presently reached; and as we passed between its supports and emerged on the other side, we knew, from the grand expanse of water that now confronted us, that our paddles had for the last time dipped in the waters of the good old Androscoggin, and we were drifting on Merrymeeting Bay. . . .

Seven weeks had flitted by since we left the forests of Umbagog; magnificent scenery had filled the leaves of our sketchbooks, and we had . . . cruised the entire length of the roughest and wildest of all New England rivers—the Androscoggin.

Gerrit Smith Stanton
1845 - 1927

Urban man in the woods. Stanton was almost sixty when he embarked on his canoeing safari, a comfortably outfitted banker's special guided and catered by Indians. A Long Island lawyer and real estate operator, he tells his story with commuter train wit and sophistication; in his company the city seldom seems far away. Born in Chelsea, Massachusetts, and a graduate of Columbia University, he was the youngest son of Henry Brewster Stanton, reformer and journalist and Elizabeth Cady Stanton, famous leader in the women's rights movement.

WHERE THE SPORTSMAN LOVES TO LINGER

NEW YORK TO MOOSEHEAD LAKE

As one of the officers of the "North Star," of the Maine Steamship Company, as she lay alongside of Pier 32, East River, in New York Harbor, on a hot afternoon in July, was calling, "All ashore! Who is going ashore?" there rapidly drove on to the pier a wagonette. The footman jumped from his seat and assisted a careworn gentleman to alight. The occupant of the wagonette was a member of the New York bar, and, being far from well, an old friend had recommended a canoe trip through the woods of Maine. . . .

An attractive city is Bangor, the town at the head of navigation on the Penobscot. To the north of it lies the great wooded wilderness. Here we were to lay aside the dress appropriate along Fifth Avenue and don the woodman's attire, buy our stock of provisions, select our canoes, purchase our wearing apparel, meet one of our guides, and, last but not least, greet the friend who was to accompany us on the trip—Dr. Hazelton. While we were at breakfast at the Bangor House we received the Doctor's card. With him was a noble specimen of the red man, an Old Town Indian, young, tall, athletic and unusually intelligent. To him was left all the arrangements for the trip, the hiring of an additional guide and the selection of the camping outfit. We spent the day shopping. One of the most enjoyable additions to our camping paraphernalia was a pillow. It may seem a little tenderfootish to take a pillow into the woods, but it will help you to many an hour's good sleep. . . .

Everything was at last in readiness for our departure. One morning bright and early we left on the Bangor and Aroostook Railroad for Moosehead Lake, arriving at Kineo that afternoon. There the second guide, another Indian, joined us. Before our departure from

Bangor we got the first glimpse of what was in store for us. A joyous lot of sportsmen were at the depot. Canoes were being loaded into baggage cars. The trucks were loaded with bundles of tents, bedding and the like—in fact, the camping outfit of many a sportsman was piled here and there. Guns and fishing rods were in evidence. Men, and ladies as well, in sporting costume, were making ready for the start. What a jolly ride it was from Bangor to Moosehead! The whole atmosphere of the car was a tonic. What a contrast between that trainload of merry passengers and the anxious commuter on his way to the busy city, with its "pace that kills.". . .

That night at Kineo was the last we were to spend for some time in a civilized abode. On the morrow we were to enter the vast wilderness, the haunt of wild beasts, nothing between us and the stars but a piece of canvas, and the ground for a bed. That night visions of Indians, bears, bull moose and the like were constantly before us. We could see ourselves wounded and no physicians within a hundred miles; our canoes smashed, provisions gone, and perchance ourselves lost in the woods. How did we know but that these Indian guides would scalp and rob us? . . .

Arriving at Northeast Carry, the canoes, camp equipage and all were carted across the Carry by a team belonging to the prettily situated hotel at that place. It was two miles across the Carry to the West Branch of the Penobscot. All our belongings, the guides and ourselves included, were deposited on the bank of the stream, the team returning across the Carry and leaving us alone in our glory. Everything in connection with our outfit seemed frail and small. The canoes that were to carry us and all our belongings over rocky rapids and across deep, boisterous lakes one of the guides could pick up with one hand and shoulder with little effort. The tent, our house, which was to shelter us from the wind and weather, was a little bundle not larger than a pillow, nor much heavier.

The guides soon had the canoes loaded, and with an Indian in the stern of each, paddle in hand, the trip down the Allagash to the St. John, up the West Branch and down the East Branch of the Penobscot, was on. . . .

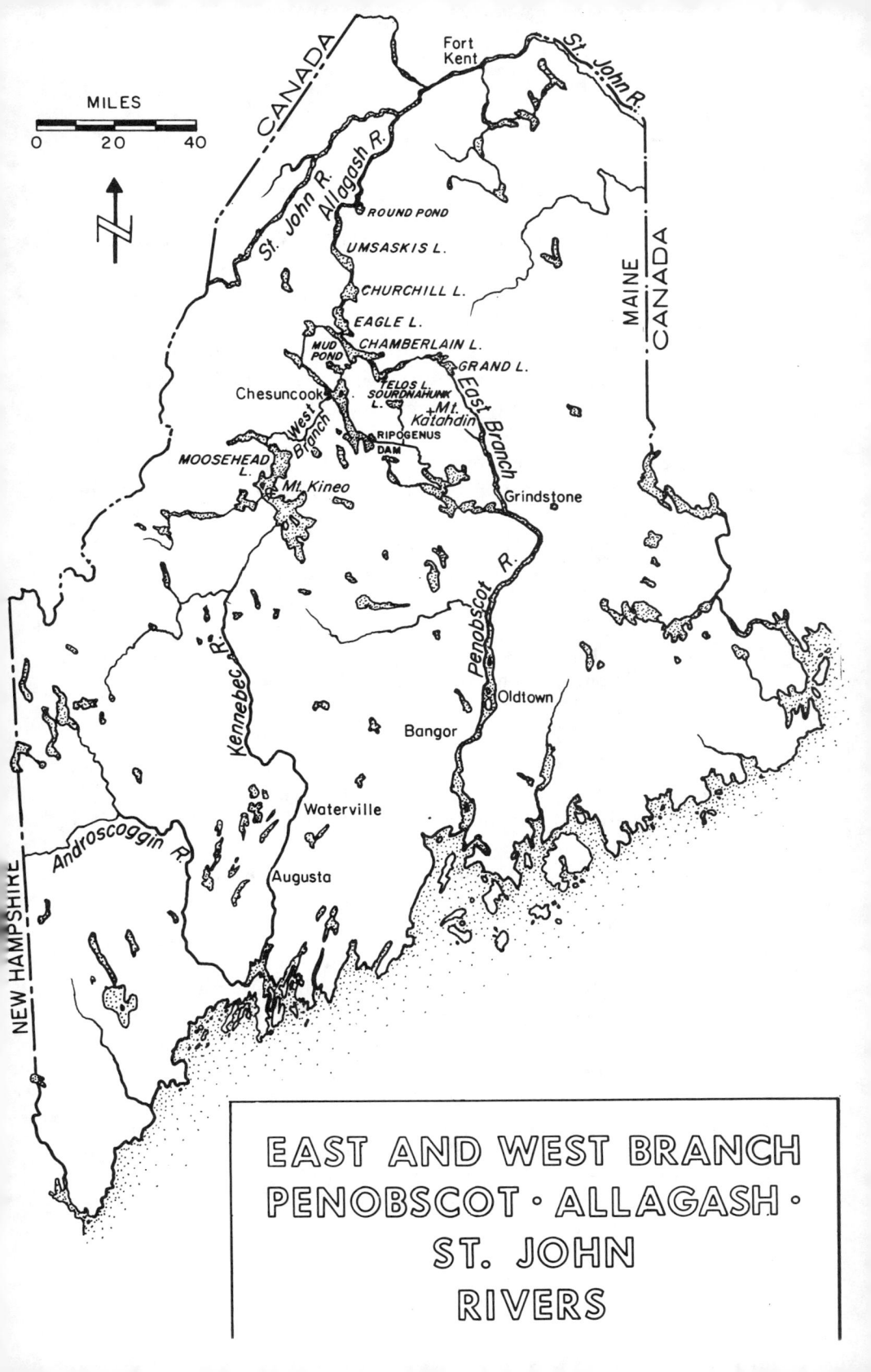

EAST AND WEST BRANCH PENOBSCOT · ALLAGASH · ST. JOHN RIVERS

FROM MOOSEHEAD TO CHESUNCOOK LAKE

One's first experience in a canoe is a feeling of uncertainty, expecting every moment to be upset and, on account of its frailty, to see it crushed like an eggshell; yet a canoe is as tough as a pugilist trained for a prize fight. It is surprising the rocks it can run into and on top of without any apparent damage, and the heavy loads it can carry.

We were surprised and amused at a load the owner of a hotel for lumbermen, ten miles below the carry, was putting into his canoe. The man himself weighed at least three hundred pounds, and he was loading the canoe with two barrels of kerosene. As he started away the canoe sank so deep in the water that it looked as if two kerosene barrels and a fat man were floating on the surface. The fellow was so fat his "habeas corpus" extended beyond the canoe and hung over the sides like the jowls of the prize porker at a county fair. About all you could see of the canoe was the points at each end, . . .

The canoe and bateau are the means of transportation over the rivers and smaller lakes of Maine. They correspond with the depot wagon and the heavy truck. The smooth, symmetrical canoe is to the rough, ill-shaped bateau as the sleek, handsomely formed deer is to the ungainly moose. . . .

The West Branch at Northeast Carry is a sluggish, deep stream, about two hundred feet in width. The water courses of Maine are either dead water, quick water, rapids or falls. What most strikes the tenderfoot as he embarks on one of these canoe trips is the utter silence of that vast region. The canoe cuts the water with hardly a ripple, and the paddling is as quiet as the grave. Though the dense jungle that lines the rivers and encompasses the lakes is inhabited every square mile by wild beasts, yet all is still. The young are taught that silence is golden. Even the breaking of a twig might lead to instant death. No bleating of the calf for its mother, nor vice versa. An old cow in a town barn makes more noise than all the game in the State of Maine.

We had gone down the stream about a couple of miles when, rounding a bend in the river, one of the guides called our attention to what appeared to be a red bush, but was in reality a deer. During what is known as the "closed season" the game is very tame. Standing on the bank of the stream with a little fawn, it watched us as we passed. What a shot it would have been! On account of the frequent canoes passing between Northeast Carry and Chesuncook Lake it is risky business to supply your larder with deer meat during the closed season, but the opportunities we had that day were very tantalizing. We were informed by the guides that when we reached Churchill Lake we would then be safe to toy with venison, so we anxiously looked forward to our arrival there. . . .

Just before we came to Moosehorn, a stream that empties into the West Branch from the south, we saw our first moose. He was feeding on his favorite food, the roots of the lily pad. He paid but little attention to us. He was standing in the water, belly deep, with head submerged half the time in search of his favorite dish. As there was a spring near the mouth of the Moosehorn, and as the noon hour had passed, lunch suggested itself. The canoes were headed for the bank, a fire soon started, and, with the Kineo Indian as head chef, the first meal on our long trip was soon before us.

From Northeast Carry to Moosehorn the West Branch flows sluggishly on its course. The guides informed us that in the next ten miles, from Moosehorn to Chesuncook Lake, we would get a taste of rough water, and, sure enough, the first bend in the river disclosed foam and rocks. The river became shallow and rapid, and rocks poked their heads through the stream in every direction. The guides stood up, substituting poles for paddles. It was wonderful with what skill they handled the canoes in the onrushing waters and among the great boulders. Time and again it looked as if we were going headlong into a rock, but a jab of the pole would turn the canoe into the channel again. Thus the dreaded Fox Hole, Rocky Rips and Pine Stream Falls were safely run.

Six o'clock found us on the headwaters of Chesuncook Lake. As the daylight that was left before the setting of the sun would be needed to prepare for camp, and as just below Pine Stream Falls was a beautiful camping ground, the canoes were headed for the shore, soon unloaded and their contents carried onto the high bank, the canoes themselves being turned upside down a short distance from the water. A dense jungle was on three sides of us. Poetry and prose have vied with each other in depicting the pleasures of camping out. Friends have gone into ecstasies over it, but we approached the moment more with dread than pleasure. The small heap that lay before us that was to protect our inner and outer man seemed entirely inadequate. With interest we watched the Indians convert our small belongings into an imposing array.

With axes they disappeared into the jungle, soon appearing with forks and poles. The forks were driven into the ground, the poles laid across, the tents unfolded, thrown over the poles and tightened down. We had four tents, one for each of us, one for the Indians, and a toilet tent. The balance of our belongings were carried into the respective tents. A fireplace was next selected, a fork on each side and a pole across, back and end logs secured, and hangers—a small forked stick with a nail in one end—were hung across the pole, a proper distance from the fire. On the hangers are hung the pots and kettles. One of the most important adjuncts of a camping outfit is a "baker," a peculiarly constructed piece of tinware. We enjoyed many a hot biscuit from our little baker.

The Indians again disappeared into the woods, this time to return with boughs for our beds; armful after armful they brought and entwined, until the softest, cleanest and most inviting bed was before us. Firewood was next procured. Along the shoreline of all the lakes of Maine dry wood abounds, cast there by the ravages of time. The winter and summer storms and high water play havoc with the timber along the shore of the lakes; consequently, no matter where you camp, dry wood is there—not a punky, rotten log, but wood as "sound as a dollar" and "dry as a bone," and of all sizes, ready to cook your daylight meal and for the campfire in the stilly night.

Of all the firewood for the camper, the most necessary is the bark of the birch; without that, many a cold meal would have been eaten and many a campfire never lighted. No matter what the weather conditions, the birch bark will burn. It is easily secured; with a "rip up the back" it readily peals from the tree, and is as inflammable as kerosene. The guides soon had ample firewood in stock, and then they attacked the boxes and bags of provisions. In making a canoe trip one is naturally exposed to all kinds of weather, so your provisions are packed with that contingency in view. Anything that water would injure is protected by waterproof material. Sugar, tea, coffee and the like are put up in little waterproof bags, which are then put in a larger bag. In our long trip bags of provender fell into the water without any apparent damage to their contents.

A well-cooked, bountiful meal was soon at our disposal, and as the sun sank amidst the dense forest the campfire was lighted. Around the campfires on our long trip the Indians interested and amused us with reminiscences of their lives. In the streams and woods the Great Spirit provided everything for them. The wild animals gave him rations and raiment. From the bark of the birch tree he made his canoe; with the bow, arrow and tomahawk he procured his game; from friction he obtained fire; from bark and poles he made his house; herbs were his medicine; and, with the money and servant question obliterated, a happy and contented life he led. We never heard our guides telling about their "old man" having to go to a sanitarium for nervous prostration, nor walking the floor nights on account of the note due at the bank on the morrow; nor did they have any recollections of hearing their mother discuss with other squaws about "my operation"; nor did they remember in their papoose days of having been introduced to Mrs. Winslow or Mr. Paregoric.

Upon our arrival at Chesuncook we already began to feel the delightful effects of the change. He who continually lives along the coastline knoweth not the benefit of the woods of Maine. The word humidity is not in the bright lexicon of the Pine Tree State. Poor appetite has no abode there. Indigestion is a stranger in the land. Stomachs that rebelled are forgiven and forgotten. Nervousness soon seeks other climes. Imaginary evils vanish into thin air. What seem mountains elsewhere to the tired brain become molehills. Morbid thoughts give way to pleasant reflections. The inward antipathy hidden by outward courtesy of man towards man resolves itself into the true Christian spirit. Woman's jealousy of woman has no abiding place in the woods of Maine. The struggle for worldly goods that is driving many business men to the asylum and penitentiary ceases for the time being. In fact, the surroundings there give one that quiet repose that enables you to see this life as it should be seen.

CHESUNCOOK TO UMSASKIS LAKE

Fragrance from hemlock boughs must be a panacea for insomnia, as the night passed mid pleasant dreams. For breakfast we had some delicious trout caught in the early morn by one of the Indians. The tented field of the night before, with all our belongings, was loaded into the canoes, and we started on a day's journey in which before nightfall we were to experience all the varieties of canoeing through the wilds of Maine.

An hour's paddling on the headwaters of Chesuncook Lake brought us to the lake proper. The lake lay to the south of us, and off to the southeast old Katahdin loomed skyward. At the little settlement at the head of the lake was a post office, the last until we arrived at Connors, on the St. John, one hundred and twenty-five miles further north. Our course lay across the head of the lake to the mouth of Umbazooksus stream. The canoeman gets lots of experience going up Umbazooksus stream to a lake of the same name. The first six miles is narrow, winding and muddy; the last three shallow and rocky, where one has to don rubber boots and lead the canoe.

Umbazooksus Lake is situated in a country wild with scenic beauty. Across the foot of it our course lay to some sporting camps near the famous Mud Pond Carry. Mud Pond Carry, which is two miles long, crosses the vertebrae of the State of Maine. It is on the watershed. It was raining when we crossed it, and stopping for a moment on its apex, we saw the raindrops choose their course, bidding each other good bye, some to follow the Allagash and the St. John, others the West Branch and the main Penobscot, to meet, perchance, again among the "sad sea waves."

On the shore of Mud Pond we ate our noonday meal. Mud Pond is an uninviting body of water—that is, to man, but not to the ungainly moose. It is shallow and abounds with lily pads, in consequence of which it is surrounded by a great moose country. From our noonday camp we counted nine moose, some far from the shore, with their heads half of the time under the water seeking the roots of the succulent lily pad. Our course lay across the pond to its outlet, which empties into the second largest lake in Maine—Chamberlain. We found the outlet of Mud Pond similar to the last half of Umbazooksus stream.

As we entered Chamberlain Lake its waters were calm, which fact the Indians said was somewhat unusual. Our course lay across the lake and up its eastern shore to Chamberlain dam, which we hoped to reach in time to camp for the night. Unfortunately for us, when halfway across the wind began to blow, and continued to increase until a high sea was running. Being anxious to get across as soon as possible, we took our first lesson in paddling, and were surprised how soon we caught on. Water continually swashed into the boats, giving everything a good wetting. We finally got under the protection of the eastern shore and slowly worked our way up the lake to Chamberlain dam. The clouds began to lift and Old Sol came out, showing that we had an hour before sundown to pitch our tents. . . .

The next day we passed down Chamberlain outlet to Eagle Lake, through the thoroughfare between Eagle and Churchill, and late in the afternoon we pitched our tents within hearing of the roar of Chase's Carry. We informed the guides that we would tarry a day or two on Churchill; so they set to work and arranged a camp with that idea in view, and a most comfortable one they staked out. The game at that time of the year is very tame, and, the Doctor being a good shot, we could already see a piece of juicy venison in the frying pan.

We were amused while in camp at Chamberlain dam, where there was a watchman stationed to see that no one disturbed the gates. He had the usual characteristics of night watchmen, for when nightfall came he retired to his tent and peacefully snored the night away.

While we were in camp on Chamberlain outlet we met two game wardens with a prisoner on the way to Foxcroft. Any one who shoots deer out of season and partakes thereof wants to be careful when strangers come around. It seems that this fellow was camping on Eagle Lake and living, as General Sherman did when marching through Georgia, on the fat of the land. The game wardens heard of the gentleman and made him a visit under the guise of sports. He invited them to dine, and had deer on the bill of fare, with the result that he contributed fifty dollars to the exchequer of the State, and in consideration of his kindness the State insisted on his being its guest for thirty days in order that he might study the beauties of the eleventh commandment. . . .

The dread of Chase's Carry began to keep us awake, so we broke camp and started down the long lagoon that leads to the commencement of the Allagash.

If anyone wants to get his mind off his business, we will guarantee, when he is going down the Allagash from Churchill, no matter what his occupation, he will be thinking of nothing but rocks. We doubt if that eleven miles has its equal for wildness in the State of Maine. Towering banks, with dense jungle, are on both sides; immense trees lean over the stream as if to grab you. The current runs like a mill race; great boulders are everywhere, alongside of you, under you, and you are lucky if some do not get on top of you. The channel, if there is one, is narrow and constantly circling around and among huge boulders, first on one side of the river and then on the other; in the middle and then where the onrushing waters take you. Canoes are constantly being swamped. Along the bottom of the river one catches glimpses of bakers, tin cans, kettles, bags of provisions—in fact, all kinds of camp equipage lost by unfortunate canoemen. Some day Chase's Carry will be worked to good advantage, as there is lots of pay dirt deposited there and more being constantly added.

The day we made the run was dark and lowering. We had worked our way downstream not more than a mile, when the elements concluded they would take a hand in the game and opened with one of the worst thunder showers we ever passed through. The rain came in torrents and the lightning was a hair-raiser. Through it all the faithful guides stood their ground, pole in hand, guiding us safely through the treacherous channels. As the darkness passed away and the sun shone forth we dropped into Umsaskis dead water, completing the wildest ride on the entire trip. We were drenched to the skin and were half scared to death along the whole eleven miles. Chase's Carry and the headwaters of Umsaskis Lake are simply a repetition of this life; do not falter when the tug comes, as come it will, but brace against it, as there are always quiet waters beyond.

UMSASKIS LAKE TO FORT KENT

... The sportsman who enters the woods of Maine should leave cotton goods at home. Every article of clothing should be wool. Strong, common-sense shoes and moccasins should be the footwear; a pair of rubber boots would not come amiss. More than once, after a good drenching, our woolen clothes saved us from catching cold. Many times we have taken off our moccasins, emptied out the water, wrung out our woolen socks, and put the same socks and moccasins on again, with no bad results.

On the second day of our stop on Umsaskis we saw a battle royal between two bull moose. Coming from opposite directions, they met at the lakeside, not far from our camp. They locked horns, shoving each other up and down the beach, paying no attention whatever to us. After smashing all the dry-ki and overturning every stone within a radius of a hundred feet, one, evidently having enough, plunged into the lake and swam for the opposite shore. . . .

On the afternoon of the same day we saw the most laughable incident that occurred on our trip. Our tents were pitched on high ground, a short distance from the lake. The woods had been cleared away in front. There was a small island a short distance off shore. We noticed several moose here and there in the water. One was well out in the lake and gradually working his way to our camp, his head being under water half of the time after the roots of the lily pad. He kept on coming nearer and nearer, evidently not seeing us. He no doubt had traveled the same route before. He finally caught sight of the camp, stood for a moment looking at those white objects with the dark woods as a background, became frightened, whirled and started for the island, disappearing therein, but in a few moments reappeared and plunged into the water, with two more moose with him, all striking out for the opposite shore. One could imagine that as soon as he struck the island the other moose had asked what was up, and he no doubt replied, "Don't ask me any questions, but run for your life." Two other moose, who had been feeding well out in the lake, saw the rush coming, and they, too, were stampeded, and the whole bunch were still on the lope as they disappeared in the timber. . . .

All day long we glided down the rapid, rocky waters of the winding Allagash, seeing deer and moose at every turn, eating our lunch as we floated over the only dead water on the river, and as twilight was casting its shadows across the stream Allagash Falls was reached, near which we pitched our tents.

The only sleepless night on the whole trip we passed at Allagash Falls. It seems the Allagash log drive failed to get through, and logs were scattered along the river from Round Pond to the St. John. Below Allagash Falls the river was full of them, except a narrow channel for canoes. About midnight we awoke, hearing a sound like that of a crying baby; whenever the wind blew the sound of the falls away we could hear the cry. Sometimes it would sound like a child and then like a calf. At the break of day we dressed, still hearing the same little wail. It sounded among the logs. The Indians were already up and we called their attention to it. Together we investigated, and there in the water, between some logs, was a little fawn. One of the Indians said at dusk the night before he had seen a doe crossing the logs, followed by a fawn. The little fellow had evidently fallen in and was nearly chilled to death. The mother was nowhere in sight. We carried the poor thing up to the camp, rubbed it dry and fed it some condensed milk and hot water. It became a passenger on our trip as far as Connors, where we gave it away. We stopped at a farmhouse a few miles below the falls, obtained some cow's milk, and fortunately a rubber nipple, and our little charge had its rations early and often and seemed to enjoy our society. . . .

Among the trophies we gathered on our trip, a bear pelt we obtained at Allagash Falls we prize above all others. While the Kineo Indian was getting the noonday meal the Bangor guide went in search of raspberries. He had been gone about half an hour, when we heard a shot, the growl of an animal and the Indian crying for help. We all started in the direction of the noise, but neglected to take our guns. The cook, who was cleaning fish at the time, had a knife in his hand, and fortunately took it with him. The

Kineo Indian told us as we ran, tumbling over logs and limbs, that it was undoubtedly a bear. It seems a large-sized she bear was also hunting berries, and the guide, getting sight of her, sneaked up to close range and fired. Unfortunately he had but one cartridge; the

"The Kineo Indian and the Author," from *"Where the Sportsman Loves to Linger"*

shot only wounded and infuriated the animal, who made for the Indian. He had no means of defense except a club, and when we arrived the Indian and bear were having a rough-and-tumble fight among the brush, first the bear on top and then the Indian. The Kineo Indian, knife in hand, jumped into the fray, and soon poor bruin was dead. The Bangor Indian's arms were fearfully lacerated, putting him out of commission. He was unable to paddle, and we found ourselves the next day going down the Allagash with the stern paddle in hand. If it were not that the Kineo Indian knew every foot of the river and took the lead, we would have been in the water more times than in the canoe. While running Twin Brook rapids our heart and Adam's apple were holding close communion. . . .

[Stanton and Hazelton continue the journey from Fort Kent to the West Branch and Mount Katahdin and on to Sourdnahunk Dead Water—two chapters.]

SOURDNAHUNK DEAD WATER TO CHESUNCOOK

Our next camping place was on Sourdnahunk Dead Water, at the foot of the Horserace, and was the ideal camping ground of the entire trip. Here the river broadens into a miniature lake, calm and placid, the banks easy of access and timbered, not with the Maine jungle, but similar to the woods of the Central States, into which one can see long distances. Spring water and birch abound, the scenery is picturesque beyond description, deer and moose are plentiful, and the waters of the nearby brooks are alive with delicious trout. There the weary toiler from the hot city will find his haven of rest. He will indeed believe that "God made the country and man made the town."

The next two miles before us was the dreaded Horserace, a second Chase's Carry, and the toughest proposition for the canoeist along the whole West Branch trip. It is difficult and dangerous to go down, but going down is not a bagatelle to going up. The way the waters run no doubt gave it its name. Along the river banks of Maine there are paths made by lumbermen and game on which one can easily walk. The day we went up the Horserace we were to meet our first misfortune of any consequence, losing practically all our provisions. The Horserace going down can be run on the paddle, but going up canoes have to be led all the way. From the high cliffs along the river bank we could see the Indians in the valley below battling with the rushing waters among the rocks.

The Kineo Indian got reckless, and in endeavoring to pole his canoe upset it, and, with the exception of some salt pork and prunes that were in the other canoe, our stock of provisions mingled with the waters of the Horserace, to be seen no more. Yet with all his faults we loved him still. He was the cook, and a good one. . . .

Big Eddy was our next camping place, and there we spent the most miserable time of all our trip. Fighting black flies and "nosee-em's" on a diet of salt pork and prunes is not a very enjoyable occupation. If it were not for a smudge, campers-out would pass many sleepless nights.

The next three miles was over the roughest carry and alongside of the grandest gorge in the state. Big Eddy is at the foot of Ripogenus Gorge, the dread of the lumbermen of the West Branch. The water rolls and tumbles over and among great precipices, and when the drive is on log jams are of frequent occurrence. In the settlement of the early West there was a common expression that "life there was death to women and oxen." The Ripogenus Carry and gorge is death to horses and logs.

On all the other carries the guides either did the carrying or our outfit was transported by wagon; but a two-horse sleigh, or, in other words, a "jumper," was the means of conveyance over that carry. With the canoes and dunnage securely tied on the jumper, we started on foot over the three miles that ended at Ripogenus Lake. . . . Over stumps, logs and boulders the horses picked their way and the jumper jumped. We expected any moment the jumper to upset or climb a tree. Some of the gulleys were so steep they had to snub the jumper with a rope to keep it from jumping clear over the horses. If ever a person earned six dollars, the old man who jumped us across that carry was the individual.

We paddled across Ripogenus Lake, another short carry, and were again on the waters of Chesuncook. We took lunch with the owner of the jumper at his log hut at the foot of the lake. . . .

By energetic paddling, in which we all took a hand, the seventeen miles to the little town of Chesuncook, at the head of the lake, was covered as dusky twilight stole upon us. With our arrival at the head of Chesuncook Lake we had looped the loop, so to speak. We had surrounded all the country lying between what is known as the Allagash trip, on the north; the Bangor and Aroostook Railroad from Fort Kent to Norcross, on the east; the West Branch, on the south, and Chesuncook, on the west, embracing one-third of the state, and we were now to go through the center by way of the East Branch.

What a game preserve that would make! One hundred and

seventy-five miles in length by seventy-five miles in width, inhabited by thousands of wild animals, fish and feathered fowl. On the borders of the preserve are the postoffices from which the dwellers of that vast wilderness obtain their mail. You who find fault with only one mail a day, and kick if your morning newspaper is not in the vestibule before daylight, should have a dose the inhabitant of that portion of the Union gets.

Chesuncook, or, as it is pronounced by the natives, "Suncook," is the ideal frontier town. As a general rule the names of the lakes and streams of Maine can stand cropping off a syllable or two with a certainty that there will be plenty left. . . .

"SUNCOOK" TO GRAND LAKE

We laid in sufficient provender at Chesuncook for the trip to Grindstone, and the morning after our arrival at the hotel saw our canoes again crossing the head of the lake for Umbazookus stream. Again we were toted across Mud Pond Carry; again cut the waters of Mud Pond, with its lily pads and moose, and down the outlet again to Chamberlain Lake. Our course lay down the lake instead of up it. As we reached Telos Lake the afternoon was fast passing away, and on its shore we pitched our tents for the first night by the waters that flow to the East Branch. The devout angler camping at Telos Lake should take the mile tramp over to Coffeelos; there he will find as good fishing as in the ponds of the Sourdnahunk region.

While passing down the outlet from Mud Pond we met coming up the narrow, rocky channel a canoe, or, more properly speaking, an improvised ambulance. A poor fellow had had his leg crushed at the tramway between Eagle and Chamberlain Lakes, and his companions were hurrying him to Kineo, sixty miles distant, it being the nearest place where he could receive medical treatment. You who live in the city, with a doctor on every block, think of what this man had to endure.

When the accident happened he was seventy miles from a physician and nearly a hundred miles from a railroad. He was placed in a bateau, rowed ten miles down Chamberlain, transferred into a canoe, taken up Mud Pond outlet and across Mud Pond, transferred to a wagon and transported over the rough and rocky Mud Pond Carry, placed in a canoe, passed over Umbazookus Lake down the nine miles of Umbazookus stream, across Chesuncook Lake, and then poled and paddled twenty miles up the West Branch to Northeast Carry, placed again on a wagon, transported over the carry to Moosehead Lake and then twenty miles by steamer down the lake to Kineo, reaching a physician thirty-six hours after the accident. How would that strike the impatient invalid who growls at the nurse if his wants are not satisfied as soon as the button is pressed? . . .

The day after our arrival on Telos we had a seance with some feathered fowl, and we are not likely to repeat the experience. Leaving the guides at home, we went on an unsuccessful expedition for another supply of venison. Not a deer or a moose did we see. On the rivers and lakes of Maine one often sees flocks of young ducks skipping along, too young to fly; they are always led by the old ones. As we were coming out of a small tributary of Telos, just as we entered the lake, not less than forty ducks came out of the grass, slid into the water, and started swimming up the lake. We fired our rifle and expected them to rise and fly; as they did not, we, of course, thought they were too young, and so an easy task to run down.

Away went the ducks, churning the water, and we after them. Soon they strung out in line, one seeming to be the leader, which kept up a peculiar noise—a call, we inferred. We paddled with all our strength, the ducks kicking up the water in great shape, making a noise like a cataract. Occasionally they would rest for a moment; we thought they were winded and that we were gaining on them, but the gaining was merely a delusion. For several miles we kept up the chase, but finally, through exhaustion, were compelled to call a halt and started home.

We did not mention the occurrence to our guides, as we were not very anxious for them to know that we had been making fools of ourselves. . . .

The next day we were more successful in supplying our "meat market." But the meat we threw away; we could not bear to eat it. It was a doe we killed, and she was giving milk. We imagined we could see the helpless little fawn in that lonely wilderness waiting and starving for the mother that never returned. We decided then and there to lay aside our firearms for the rest of the trip, and we kept our resolution. The thought of what we had done saddened in a measure the balance of the trip. We derived some consolation from the fact that if we were the means of the death of a fawn at Telos, we saved one on the Allagash. . . .

FROM GRAND LAKE HOME

The East Branch from Grand Lake to Bowlin Pitch is about as rough a piece of water as the average canoeman cares to tackle, and when, in addition, you have a lot of logs sailing on all sides, it is enough to give you a good start for a sanitarium. There was no alternative for us but to go on with the logs, for if we waited for the drive to get through to Grindstone the business of a certain New York law office would come to a stop and the patients of a Bangor dentist would be howling with pain.

The telephone is a godsend to the river driver. Prior to its use, whenever there was a jam there was no way of stopping the oncoming logs or securing help except by the slow information conveyed by men on foot. We found the telephone all along the East Branch. At all the falls, rapids and sharp bends in the river were telephone boxes nailed to trees, with men nearby ready to notify those above of any jam below.

The day we selected to start from Grand Lake, on account of a jam further down, they stopped sluicing, leaving the river free of logs and affording us smooth sailing to Stair Falls. At that point there is a carry. As we neared Haskell Rock we could see logs and trouble ahead. They were holding back the logs on account of the jam below. The banks of the river where we struck the logs was low, the water backing far into the interior. There was a quarter of a mile of logs between us and Haskell Rock; the afternoon was waning away; there was no place to camp there, and we were simply being devoured by that affectionate litle creature, the mosquito, which seems to be ever in evidence, whether you are in the tropics, under the bamboo tree, or in the Arctic Circle seeking gold along the Yukon. After two hours of punching logs and dragging the canoes over them we struck solid ground that led to Haskell Rock.

There are always pitched at convenient distances along the river during a log drive two tents—one a large lean-to, for the men to sleep in, and the other a place to eat. In the latter, called a wangan, are the cook's quarters, where all the cooking is done. There are no more hospitable set of men on earth than the cooks in the woods of Maine. As a stranger enters a wangan almost the first word spoken is an invitation from the cook: "Will you have a dish of beans and a cup of tea?" No one knows when a stranger enters a wangan where he comes from. Possibly he has been lost in the woods and is in a starving condition. . . .

It was a beautiful moonlight night; one could see the passing logs rolling and plunging over the falls into the whirlpool below. Occasionally a jam would form below the falls, and men with dynamite would break it, throwing pieces of logs from the river valley far back into the woods. Between the plunging logs, roar of the waters and discharges of dynamite there was an awful noise the whole night through. All the next day, down to Whetstone, we had many narrow escapes from being crushed, and it required the best kind of a canoeman to save us from being sucked under while rounding log wings.

From Whetstone to Grindstone, the end of our canoe trip, was ten miles. From what they told us up river about the log jam at Grindstone, we considered ourselves fortunate in getting to Whetstone. At every turn of the river we expected to see our further progress blocked. As luck would have it, we struck the solid jam opposite some sporting camps, where we hired a team to take us overland to Grindstone, there catching the evening train for Bangor. . . .

At Bangor we parted with our faithful guides, changed buckskin for broadcloth, bough beds for microbe mattresses, the plain cooking of the guides for the dyspeptic combination of the average chef, eight hours of refreshing sleep for more or less tossing, three square meals for no appetite, pure air for sewer gas, the rod and the rifle for the pen and the rolltop desk, health and happiness for work and worry—in fact, turned our backs on what they tell us is a barbaric life for what we are taught to believe is civilization. . . .

Isobel Knowles

She was one of the few to shoot rapids while wearing long skirts, one of a very small band so encumbered since the days of the black-robed missionary explorers. The Gatineau River, named for Nicholas Gatineau, a fur trader said to have drowned in its waters in the late seventeenth century, flows out of lakes in the Province of Quebec, trends southward more than two hundred miles and joins the Ottawa River opposite the city of Ottawa.

TWO GIRLS IN A CANOE *

I am an experienced canoeist, but those rapids on the upper Gatineau caught me unawares. We had been paddling for mile after mile through comparatively sluggish water, when a sudden narrowing of the channel brought us to the head of a gorge down which the river tossed and roared angrily like a living thing.

We were two in the canoe, and we had passed the rapids on our way up the week before, but did not recognize them now that we approached from the opposite direction. Then we had portaged around them, carrying the canoe on our shoulders, over trunks of fallen trees and through the matted branches of the brushwood. Since that time we had seen much of river scenery, seen hills rising beyond hills till lost in the distant haze, great silent forests of spruce and pine, and placid sheets of crystal lake, and now, toward the close of our two weeks' outing, we were two days' travel from the nearest outpost of civilization.

So stealthily had the swiftening water above the turn carried us on, that we were going at a ten-mile-an-hour gait before I realized our position. Then the sudden leap of the canoe, the roll and pitch of the water under us, warned that the time to land had passed. There was no turning back against a ten-mile current, no making for either side, where the broken ripples on the surface showed jagged rocks only a few inches below. Down the middle of the channel lay our only course—and the path of the wave was narrow and the rocks harder than birch bark.

Quickly I changed places with my companion, crawling cautiously over the camping outfit stowed in the bottom, while she crept as carefully backward. In a rapids the bowsman guides the canoe, and I was the more expert. But this maneuver nearly brought disaster. A treacherous eddy just before the first pitch whirled our canoe

* *Cosmopolitan Magazine,* October 1905.

around and we struck broadside on a boulder, where we hung, held fast by the rush of the current at the bow and stern. The edge of the canoe upstream began to settle, the water grew quickly up the side, and we avoided a spill by jumping overboard, almost up to our waists.

This, however, was only a beginning. Pulling the canoe to one

From *Cosmopolitan Magazine*, October 1905

side and holding it headed downstream, we stood on the rock for a breathing space while we surveyed the river, above so gentle in the sunlight, around and below so wild with the new spirit which had possessed it. Making a quick entry, with difficulty, from the rock, we again started down, steering our way where the comparatively smooth water showed the rocks well covered, working our arms till they seemed pulling from their sockets. Below us, the dashing spray, the circling eddies, the increasing clamor of the torrent, seemed to lure us as the call of a Lorelei to destruction.

The excitement of the course filled us with an ecstasy of abandon; but a sudden dash of water over the bow into our faces brought us quickly back to a sense of the danger which a moment's relaxed vigilance would bring. With every nerve alert, and guided by my previous experiences with Canadian rapids, I picked the way down the channel, my companion in the stern keeping the canoe straight with the current.

Thirty yards of fairly smooth water intervened between the upper and lower pitches, and here, somewhat awed by the spectacle of the leaping whitecaps farther down, we attempted a landing. Swinging the canoe across the current and heading for the shore which promised best, we applied our whole force to the paddles. But we had no more than half covered the distance when the futility of the effort became apparent, and we quickly turned and made in the opposite direction, where, we now discovered, the main channel lay.

Even the excitement of the adventure did not blind me to the peril which now faced us. On the lower side, as we bent our paddles to reach the channel, a row of partially submerged rocks grew ever nearer as the current drew our canoe toward them. Should we fail to reach the channel before striking, nothing human could prevent an upset, and, so far as I could see, nothing human could prevent a drowning. Although a good swimmer, I could not hope to breast such waves and, escaping them, avoid the whirlpool at the foot.

With all our strength in our paddles, we lifted the light bark canoe over the water, and just as the farthest rock grated our side we swung into the channel and boiled down between the boulders, the current sweeping us on at a rate of fully fifteen miles an hour. But as we swung, my maple paddle had snapped from my hands, caught in a fissure of the rock where I had jabbed it to keep from striking.

In impotent despair I looked around at my companion. Until the present trip she never had been in a canoe, and her only knowledge in its management had been gained by my coaching and by less than two weeks of practice. But plainly the river and the forest now were in her veins, and the craft of the paddle had come by inspiration. The hesitation of the city-born was dispelled, and with skillful stroke, scarce noting my discomfiture, with eyes fixed on the winding channel ahead of us, she steered safe through the boiling waters of the second pitch. With a whirl of spray at the finish—for the rapids keeps its greatest waves for the foot, as an orator his fiercest invectives for his peroration—we brought up in the eddy below, gasping from our effort yet thrilling with the joy of it.

That was the incident of our canoeing trip which I am likely longest to remember. There were three inches of water in the canoe when we reached the foot of the rapids, which had come in over the sides as we bowled through the last big pitch. We went ashore and bailed it out, and had a view of what we had come through from a safer point than the rock in midstream.

"No more rapids for me today," said the helmswoman who had steered us so safely. Now that the excitement was over, all her bravado was gone, and but for the remembrance of the flashing eye, flushed cheek and rigid muscles which had confronted me when I turned to look back after losing my paddle, I could have fancied her again the city girl who stood hesitatingly with a bunch of skirts in one hand when I first invited her to step into a canoe. . . .

Anthony Weston Dimock
1842 - 1918

Wall Street and the Wilds, *Dimock called his autobiography. Born in a "little village of Massachusetts," he went to New York where after years without achieving success on the financial exchanges, he packed up and began a new life in a field that had fascinated him since boyhood and where he probably had belonged in the first place —natural history and life outdoors.*

He was in his middle sixties, in the prime of his second career, when he and his son Julian (the Cameraman of his narrative) zigzagged along the west coast of Florida from Peace River, Charlotte Harbor, and Gasparilla Sound to Harney River and Seminole Point well down the Everglades—canoeing hundreds of miles on what turned out to be (among other good things) a zesty gastronomical trip. An alert, experienced, amiable realist, an escapee from the "disenchantment of a too material civilization," he wrote a suitably sensible, straightforward story wherein he announced not how much everything cost, but rather how little—one of the joys and satisfactions of a month, in his words, of camp and canoe.

YACHTING IN A CANOE *

The hurricane month had come. We had laid up our cruising boat and were footloose—with four weeks to spare.

"Why not go down the coast in the canoe?" suggested the Cameraman.

"Without a guide?" I asked.

"Sure!" he replied. "What do we want of a trained nurse?"

"Supplies?" I inquired.

"Ellis's equipment—'matches, gun, and a handful of salt,'" said he.

Three hours later we were paddling down the Peace River, with Punta Gorda low on the horizon behind us. We had outfitted with the aid of a stereotyped schedule of a hundred cruising essentials, using it as a list of the things which we didn't require. A blanket, mosquito bar, and the usual toilet things for each of us were rolled in a piece of waterproofed canvas on which we knelt or sat as we paddled the canoe. The one essential of every cruise was met by a fifty-pound lard can filled with water; the needs of the commissary were assured by a cheap shotgun, fly rod, hooks and trolling lines; a tin plate, cup, fork and spoon for each of us with a saucepan, cornmeal and coffee made for comfort; while a lunch basket of bread, cheese and fruit added luxury to our send-off. Our provisions would have been accounted inadequate for an afternoon picnic, but it served us for a month of camp and canoe in the wilderness of South Florida. The money cost of the entire outfit within the canoe, excepting camera fixings but including the clothing we wore, was well within twenty-five dollars, and the expenses of the month that followed added barely 20 percent to this sum.

Two hours of paddling had carried us well within the mouth of the Miakka River, when black clouds, rising from nowhere in par-

* *Outing,* September 1908.

SOUTHWEST FLORIDA

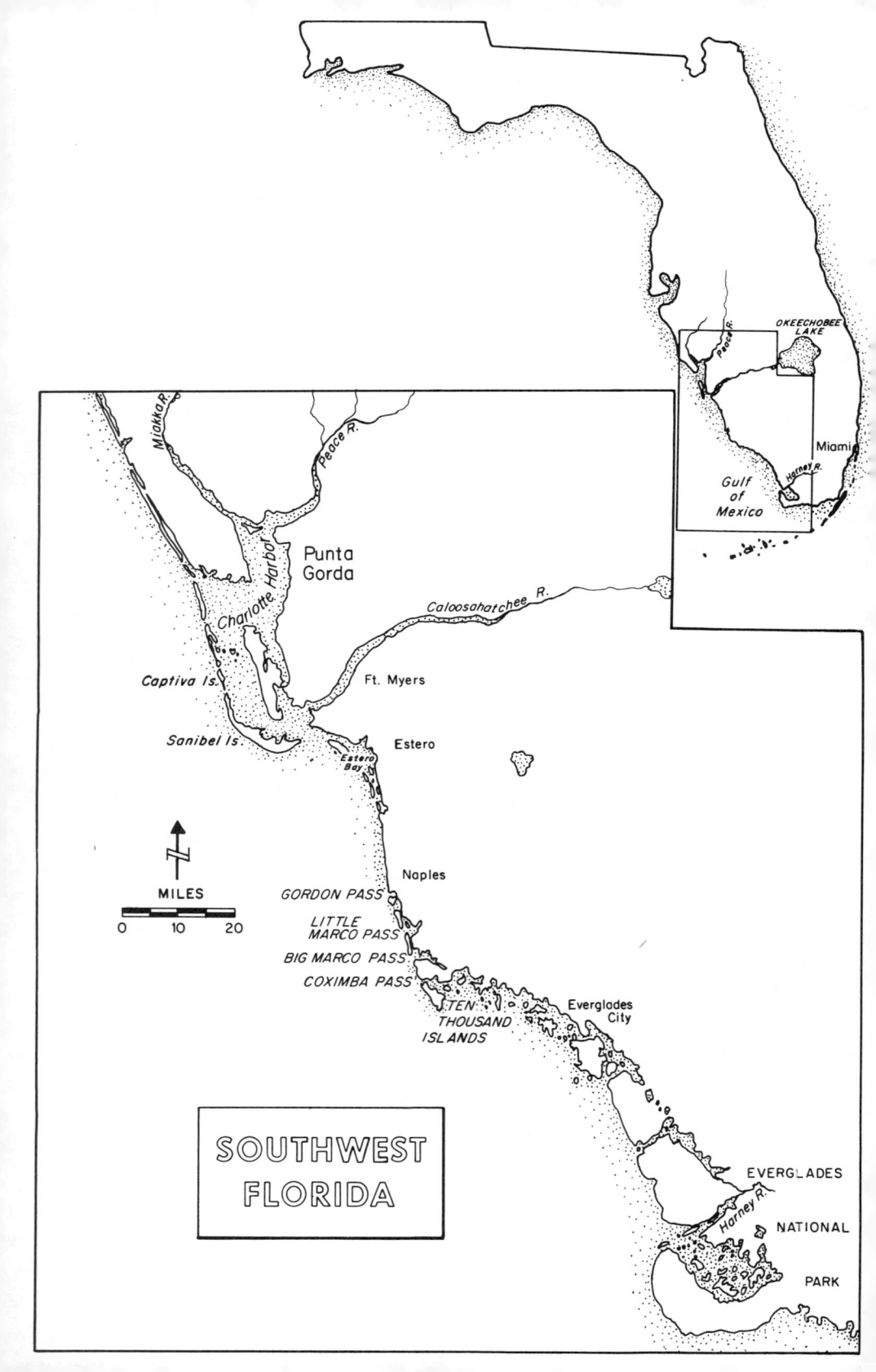

ticular, sent down upon us a squall of wind and rain. We kept under the lee of the river bank, but quite ignored the pluvial portion of the performance. Darkness overtook us where the meadows meet the pine woods, and we slept the sleep of the just on a grassy bed beneath the stars. Our supper was hurried and cold, of bread and cheese, but the coffee of breakfast, although made in a saucepan, was delicious to us as the finished product of the civilized chef to the epicure of the yacht.

For nine hours we paddled easily against the current of the river, resting five minutes during each half hour. In avoiding the swift, midstream current we paddled among rushes and tall ferns; past broad meadows; around the borders of palmetto-dotted islands; beside banks of myrtle and scrub palmetto; and beneath the shade of great live oaks covered with orchids and streaming with Spanish moss. From every bend in the river birds flew up, and I secured four ducks at a cost of half a dozen cartridges.

In the middle of the afternoon we camped on a high bank of sand where our dinner, consisting of a brace of ducks broiled on a bed of coals and an ash cake baked in a jacket of leaves, would have seduced an anchorite. It was the fear of mosquitoes and not their presence that persuaded us to stretch our bars for the night, but I was glad of it later, when in the darkness I heard the soft step of a panther not far from my cheese-cloth barricade. These creatures, which are plentiful in South Florida, are as cowardly as they are powerful, and I have often known them to prowl around a camp at night, but never heard of one attacking a camper. I was awakened in the morning by a redbird's reveille, sounded joyously from the top of a nearby tree, and putting aside my bar watched the birth of a new day, until the tops of the palmettos were blazing in the light of the rising sun. For an hour the Cameraman and I reveled in a sense of freedom never before realized during the cruise of a year. Always had been the inharmonious presence of an alien spirit. The irritating conventions of civilized life have their analogues in the wilderness and the ideas of guides, boatmen and cooks are bounded by phantom walls of precedent. The creatures of the wild were all about us and unafraid. A little brown rabbit nibbled at a husk of pineapple that I had thrown aside; a tree rat showed himself among the leaves of the branches above us; while a grave old 'gator floated on the stream that flowed past. Fat grasshoppers, four inches long, garbed in garments of many colors, climbed stalks of wild cane; birds, singly and in flocks, flew over and around us; from every side glad cries of creatures of forest and field came to our ears. We dawdled for another hour, ate the cheese that was left and some wild grapes that we gathered; and lastly, built a fire and made coffee, finishing our breakfast later with a duck that we broiled over the fire.

It was about the middle of the forenoon—we carried no watches—when the spirit moved us to embark and we began an exploration of the upper Miakka which made strenuous the working hours of the rest of the day. Sometimes our course lay between banks ten feet high, canopied by branches of great trees tangled with ropes of vine and long festoons of gray moss, where the current was so swift that to make a mile an hour demanded desperate paddling. Birds were plentiful and alligators abounded. Soon after starting I shot the four birds that our commissary called for, and when later a wild turkey flew across the stream a hundred feet ahead of the canoe, I remembered that the game laws protected him and also that my gun was empty.

The spirit of exploration continued in possession of us and we devoted another day of much toil to getting nearer the source of the stream. After a night of oblivion, on a bed of Spanish moss, we paddled, rested and floated with the current to the mouth of the Miakka in a single day.

The next morning the tide helped and a wind from the east sped us on, so that we reached Charlotte Harbor early in the day. As we were passing a supply boat that lay beside a fish ranch near Mondongo Key, I was hailed by name and recognized an old acquaintance in the captain of the craft. When I asked for a cool drink he filled our water can with fifty pounds of ice. We tied a thick layer of moss around the can and for three days we reveled in a luxury quite unknown to dwellers within the pale of civilization. As we took up our paddles the captain tossed four fat pompano into the canoe, and when I asked if I could pay him, replied:

"If you're lookin' for trouble, you can." I seldom passed Mondongo without stopping, and on this occasion we bought of its occupant a peck of sweet potatoes, a small bunch of bananas and received

"I stared in wonderment at the close lacing of undergrowth," from *Outing*, September 1908

the customary invitation to help ourselves to all the limes we could carry. There was a lack of legitimate pockets in the few clothes I had on. But I recalled the example of a Florida girl of my acquaintance, and when I embarked in the canoe a bushel of limes went with me and the bulge in my shirtwaist was aldermanic. An hour's sharp paddling brought us to Boca Grande, the Big Pass, and we camped on the beach outside; ate broiled pompano, roasted potatoes, baked bananas and drank iced limeade—without sugar. No mosquito bars were required that night and we lay on the beach just beyond the sweep of the surf and were soothed to sleep by the rhythmic crash of the breaking waves. The wind increased in the night to a fully fledged nor'wester. We pulled our canvases over us to keep off the rain of spray, and we pitied the folks in yachts and battleships. The crescendo roar of each incoming wave uplifted my spirits and the visions of a faraway boyhood came back to me, freed from the later disenchantments of a too material civilization. The never-ending procession of white-topped billows, the rushing wind, the salt spray beating on my face and the stars shining between the tops of towering palm trees beside me, were merely the materialized dreams of childhood. The postman, the messenger boy with the yellow envelope, and the bell of the telephone seemed less real to me than the lamp of Aladdin, and the automobile more of a myth than the enchanted horse. I was awakened at dawn by the voice of the Cameraman quoting: "Alone, alone, all, all alone," and as I realized our freedom from care with no one near to criticize our conduct, I wondered if ever again I could bear to commune with Nature with a hired guide beside me.

We had planned to paddle up the coast to Gasparilla Pass in the morning, but the waves were big and were breaking in white windrows that extended far toward the horizon. If need had been, we could have weathered them, but they were a bit too big to be tackled for fun, and the danger to camera and plates would have been considerable. The canoe was of little weight and we carried it across the point of beach at Boca Grande to the harbor inside and paddled along the lee of Gasparilla Island to Big Gasparilla Pass. For half a mile a manatee swam near us and we dipped our paddles with exceeding care, lest we alarm him, until rising beside the canoe with a friendly sniff, he nearly swamped us with a parting wave of his broad tail. At night the wind died out, but in the morning the sea was heavy and we made the day one of rest, visiting in the forenoon a fish camp that had been established between Big and Little Gasparilla Passes. More pompano were given us, but when we offered to pay the answer was: "We catch mullet to sell and pompano to eat."

We played on the beach all the afternoon, sometimes casting a fly in the quiet water inside the pass at a hurrying Spanish mackerel, cavally, ladyfish or sea trout that was coming in with the tide in search of its supper; sitting and musing on a worm-eaten, barnacle-covered, copper-bolted piece of timber that might have been washed up from the wreck of some old galleon; watching the crabs, which, scurrying along close to the beach, were often driven ashore by their active enemies in the water; then wandering slowly at the edge of the surf on the beach outside, we gathered multicolored shells of pompano with their living tiny tenants; traced home the trails of pretty panamas; chased to their holes the shadowy, almost transparent sand crabs that skittered along the beach; and lying prone on the sand in the shadow of a palm, dreamed dreams that pulsated with the roar of the surf in our ears.

At daylight the next morning we paddled out of the pass and down the coast past Boca Grande, where an east wind, meeting heavy rollers and a strong tide, gave us for a mile more excitement than we really cared for. Big loggerheads rose beside the canoe, dolphins played around us and once we turned out of our road that we might not disturb a great devilfish, which, lying on the surface where the waves were biggest, was being "rocked in the cradle of the deep."

At Captiva Pass we were tempted by a bunch of cavally, which were tossing the water into spray as they devoured a school of minnows. A big cavally would have kept my light fly rod busy for the rest of the day, so I tied a hunk of twine to the hook on a trolling line and the Cameraman paddled us into the melee. In an instant the lure was seized by a cavally so large that when, half an hour later, I landed him on the beach my hands were cut and burned and I was quite as exhausted as my captive. The jackfish is not a conventional food fish but a big one has a thick layer of red flesh which looks and tastes much like very tender beef. Tarpon were plentiful in the pass, but I only cared to catch them for the Cameraman who was too busy with his paddle and keeping the canoe trimmed to think of using the tools of his trade in the cranky craft and the rough water. We were scheduled to reach Punta Rassa that night, but dawdled over dinner too long. When I suggested getting under way the Cameraman demurred, said he didn't want to move and added that the big jackfish steak he had eaten made him feel as if he was lined with satin and he wanted to prolong the enjoyment of it. The lack of sweetness in our iced limeade reminded me of a bee man who lived a few miles north of Captiva Pass, and after camping on the beach for the night we paddled to his ranch. The bee man was walking barefoot among his fifty hives when we found him and was pawing over bunches of bees as fearlessly as a Bostonian would have handled beans. His enthusiasm overcame our shyness as we walked with him among the hives, yet he watched us closely, warned us a little and advised us more; and we heeded his warnings and attended strictly to his advice. Then we sat in his shack, talked bees and drank metheglyn, a beverage which I had trailed vainly in spirit from Shakespeare's time but had never before encountered in the flesh. When we left we carried with us a bottle of honey and a box of comb and envied the gods neither their ambrosia nor their nectar.

Three hours' paddling brought us to Sanibel Island, within six miles of Punta Rassa at a point once known as Oyster Creek. The name had disappeared, but the oysters remained and we roasted enough for our supper. The water was full of sea trout and I took in a score with the fly rod in the early morning. We breakfasted on their sounds, which were large, gelatinous and made a more delicious dish than the cod's tongues and sounds by which the old New Englander swears. A heavy rain squall, about noon, drove us ashore near Sanibel Light and we camped on the outside beach where we waded out in the warm surf to escape the chill of rain, wind-driven through garments of gauze. In the afternoon we wandered up the beach and made collections of shells that we hadn't room to carry.

On the following day we atoned for past laziness by paddling twenty-five miles and camping in the great hyacinth garden of the Caloosahatchie River, some miles above Fort Myers. Myers was avoided as being too conventional and calling for more clothes than we were wearing. It suggested newspapers and soft drinks, tempted us with candy and cakes and invited us to invest in tinned and bottled luxuries that were subversive of the spirit of our excursion. Our camp that night was in a little cove on the north bank of the river that was free from flowers, but a change of wind before morning hemmed us in with a hundred acres of the tentacled bulbs of the water hyacinth. Forcing our way through the mass was difficult work, for it was imponderable as a bubble to pressure or thrust of paddle, but clung to the canoe like the shirt of Nessus to the son of Jupiter. We ascended the Orange River a few miles, through hyacinths that often extended from bank to bank and found the residents waging a war of extermination against the plague, by forming a cordon of boats across the stream, hoping to drive and drag the whole tangled, floating mass down to its mouth.

Our canoe rested low in the water, as we descended the Caloosahatchie River, because of the grapefruit and oranges that had been contributed to our commissary. It was afternoon when we arrived at Punta Rassa, but as the breeze favored we started down the coast, arriving at dusk at Carlos Pass, the entrance to Estere Bay. The olden-time charm of the bay had departed for us and we preferred camping on the beach to entering it. It had become the home of the Koreshan Unity,* a band of fanatics and imbeciles, under the hypnotic control of an apostle of undiluted bosh.

Our itinerary was interfered with on the following day by a couple of heavy squalls, the fear of which drove us on the beach, although only one of them reached us. While ashore we roasted a few bunches of oysters which we gathered from mangrove trees and broiled some mangrove snappers which I took with the fly rod.

Marco had been our home for many months at a time, and we spent twenty-four hours there, for auld lang syne, helping ourselves to sugar apples, sapadilloes, alligator pears and cocoanuts, until our

* Cooperative community established 1894 by Cyrus Reed Teed (1839–1908), American physician who called himself Koresh (Hebrew *Koresh* Cyrus), founder of the Koreshan System of Religio-Science to reestablish church and state on a basis of divine fellowship; author of *The Cellular Cosmogony,* or *The Earth a Concave Sphere* (Guiding Star Publishing House, 1905), dedicated "to all men in all grades of progress in their liberation from the thraldom of ignorance and the hells of the competitive system"; and other volumes of Koreshan literature. The present-day Koreshan Unity, Inc., Estero, Florida, publishes *The American Eagle,* a monthly paper. W. T.

canoe looked like a fruit freighter. When the usual afternoon storm came on we watched the gathering clouds from the protection of the piazza, our only concession to convention during the cruise.

From Marco to Coon Key the usual route is inside, among the keys, but we chose to follow the beach and our next stop was at Caxambas where one and a half million pineapples were growing on a single plantation—when we arrived. These figures had been reduced when we left. The weather got troublesome and from Caxambas to Coon Key we spent half our time getting on the beach and behind trees and began to wonder what would be the effect on our health if our clothes happened to get dry. The tide was beginning to pour out of West Pass when we reached it at noon, so we camped on the pretty beach at its mouth, and roasted clams which we took from a nearby clam bar. Fortunately we unloaded the canoe before going for the clams, since we capsized the craft while getting aboard. The Cameraman utilized the afternoon by photographing some pelicans and an osprey's nest.

We went up the Pass with a rush in the morning and paddled among the pretty keys of Chokoloskee Bay to Everglade, which we had often made our cruising headquarters. One can here get ripe guavas from the trees 366 days of the year, if it happens to be leap year. A small boy resident, who knew of my weakness for guavas and sugarcane, nearly swamped the canoe with baskets full of the fruit and stalks of cane twelve feet long.

From Everglade our course lay among the Ten Thousand Islands with no convenient beaches at hand, but with the prospect good of having to hunt camping ground and evict moccasins after dark; wherefore I added a lantern and a bottle of kerosene to our equipment. For four days we paddled amid a wilderness of keys without knowing, or seeking to know, where we were. At times we were in rivers, deep and swift, where fish abounded and dolphins played about the canoe. At other times broad shallow bays spread out, from which grass-choked, currentless waterways led us, by routes that were crooked and long, back to the starting point. Yet in no hour was there lack of life and interest. At every turn in our course herons flew up from the water, while snakebirds dropped from the trees above; turtles, alligators and fish of many varieties disturbed the water; moccasins made lively the bits of soil that rose above the surface, while night herons croaked about our camps and owls hooted at us by night. It was hard to find ground solid enough for camp or campfire and the wood of the red mangrove was nearly as combustible as asbestos, but we managed to broil a brace of ducks each day and bake an occasional hoecake. For the rest, the half of a rich, creamy avocado pear as a salad and a couple of pineapples for dessert sufficed to keep us going.

One afternoon we failed to find a place to camp, although we prolonged the search by lantern light well into the night, and were finally compelled to pile enough branches in a shallow place to keep us from drowning while we tried to sleep. I slept on, or in, my canvas which proved its waterproof quality by holding the barrel of water that poured over it soon after I laid down for the night. In the morning the Cameraman rolled out of his bed into the water—to dry himself, he said—and we rustled enough fire to broil a bird which we ate while we sat on a branch in the water. We gathered cocoa plums and wild grapes; watched the ways of birds, reptiles and fish; and laughed at the deluge of the daily rain squall until the morning of our fifth day in the unknown wilderness when the Cameraman gave me a shock by producing an empty water can and quoting in tones worthy of the Ancient Mariner:

> Water, water, everywhere,
> Nor any drop to drink.

The one danger of the country in which we were picnicking had befallen us, and it was time to hustle. There was fresh water to the east of us—an ocean of it, the Everglades—but no road to it that we knew. West of us lay the Gulf of Mexico, which we could probably find in a day, after which a few hours would give us the water we wanted. We couldn't wait so long. We were thirsty already. Somewhere south of us were big rivers which ran from the Glades to the Gulf and south we headed our canoe. Always our road twisted, often it turned us back and we had to stop frequently to fight the tendency, born of imagined thirst, to paddle with a fierceness that would have run into a panic or ended in exhaustion. After some twenty miles of paddling, which scarcely advanced us half that distance, we found a stream with land on its borders and the wooded banks of a river. Its current flowed to the west, but we strove against it, keeping to the eddies and the banks until the river broke up into creeks and the water came fresh and sweet from the Everglades. We drank and we drank, we filled ourselves and our can with the beautiful water; and we camped joyfully upon a high bank which overlooked the lovely river and stretched bars that we didn't need between a palmetto and a fig tree, under a canopy of widespreading, fruit-laden wild grapevine.

The head of the river was unfamiliar to us and as we explored, the creeks subdivided and one after another ended in tangles which shut out the canoe and another day had departed when we entered the open water of the Everglades. For two days we zig-zagged among the little sloughs of clear water that spiderweb the southern Everglades, working always to the south. We dodged strands of heavy sawgrass, paddled over submerged meadows covered with white water lilies and followed the faint trail of Indian canoes until we struck the headwaters of Harney River and slept, once more, on our camping ground among the lime trees. While the Cameraman and I were enjoying the peace of the wilderness after supper, eating limes and chewing sugarcane, it occurred to us to figure up how much of our month had gone. It ended our dream of peace. Two days only of our month were left, for on the morning of the third day we must take the mail boat up the coast to connect with the train which we were to take for the North.

Half an hour after daylight in the morning we were paddling swiftly down the grass-choked river; past the almost deserted rookery, the otter slides, and the pools where the tarpon play; through the swift, crooked creek and the larger stream it leads to; across Tussock Bay, with its picturesque keys and Indian camping ground; and by way of lower Harney River to the Gulf of Mexico. Near Seminole Point, we made our final camp in a cruise of a month, without a guide, without a compass, and without a suggestion of actual peril from the beginning to the end.

Charles Phelps Cushing

If Cushing had set out—which he did not—to caricature a canoe trip, he hardly could have done better than this. The conveyance was a cross between raft and canoe, the paddle a cut-down oar, the guide a young country boy. As for canoeing—it consisted of shoving off from the shore with two or three strokes into the gentle current, letting the river do the work, and now and again poling clear of a snag. It was not a parody, however, because in those currents "float" trips were a principal means of navigation. Most of the time the author contented himself with sitting on a campstool plunk in the middle of the boat, smoking his pipe, fishing a little and, when the spirit moved him, snapping the camera shutter. An unaggressive, nonsporting sort of passage, rustic, ageless, and in accord with Ozarkian rivers and hills. Ozark is an American rendering of the name of an eighteenth-century French trading post, Aux Arcs. The French are said to have shortened long Indian names to first syllables only; thus aux Arcs *referred to going up into the country of the Arkansas tribes.*

FLOATING THROUGH THE OZARKS *

If, as a boy or as a somewhat older dreamer, you ever sat upon a bank beside some hurrying watercourse, flipping chips into the current, and watched them ride out of sight around a bend and longed to go floating with them on a journey of adventure, you can easily understand the passion that draws hundreds of sportsmen to southern Missouri and northern Arkansas every summer to take "floats" down the swift, clear rivers of the Ozark hills. . . .

In the Ozarks the idea works out in this wise: you sit on a camp stool in a flat-bottomed boat which is twenty feet or worse in length and never more than three broad at the widest point. Of necessity, your first reflection will be that the craft is a cross between a log raft and a canoe—too heavy for speed and modeled too much on the lines of a toothpick to be safe. The guide, no fancy stage hero of the north woods, but a plain country boy in faded blue overalls, sits on a roll of oilcloth-covered baggage and steers with a paddle, which is nothing more impressive than an old oar chopped off halfway down the handle. The cook box, the tent and its jointed pole, the two cots, the potatoes and onions and bread and bacon and eggs are protected from spray by the tent canvas. The whole cargo is carefully stowed in a way that preserves the balance, and you may stand up if you like and cast for bass without much fear of being upset.

To sit on the camp stool and smoke while the current whirls you through a panorama of hill country appears to be the sanest form of enjoyment on such an expedition, but, unfortunately, most of us pack with our baggage the city man's restless desire to be doing something in which there are possibilities of excitement. In consequence, nearly everyone brings a rifle or a camera or fishing

* *Outing,* August 1911.

JAMES AND WHITE RIVERS

tackle, or all. My own obsession was to be taking pictures; so, with a camera on shortened tripod legs and sighting and firing like a gunner on a battleship, I floated down the James and the White in southern Missouri, shooting pictures. . . . Yet the happiest man, no doubt, would be he who could sit smoking in contentment without even the presence of a fishhook to annoy him—just thinking that here, at last, was one of his boyhood's ambitions being realized. He is floating on a splinter toward the sea!

Nothing serious need be on his mind, not even the thought of the expense of the trip. For the services of Jim or Earnie or the Old Man's Son he is charged only $1.50 a day, and the guide is supposed to do every stroke of the work. Fifty cents a day is the rent for the boat, fifty for the tent, twenty for the cots and bedding: two travelers could make a four-day float for $16, *plus* the price of food and the cost of shipping the boat home. The pleasant feature of the latter item is that at the end of a four or five days' float on one of these wriggly Ozark streams you are likely to find yourself not over twenty miles from where you started. . . . For one example, the White River in a single county in Arkansas (Baxter) winds one hundred and twenty-five miles. . . .

This region has none of the flavor of professionalism and pose that sometimes may be detected in the Maine woods. You simply float, hunt along shore, fish for bass, shoot a few frogs and turtles, and after a camp-cooked meal enjoy your pipe. . . .

Jim's in the boat. You're in yourself. The small chain that serves for a hawser clinks musically, dramatically, on the floor. Jim dips his paddle and makes a little whirlpool of water with it. We're off! Jim quits paddling after the third stroke. In this there is evidence that already we are into the swing of the running methods, for the river, not the boatman, does the work.

The current has the splinter now for a plaything. It takes joy in the possession, gurgling, slapping the flat keel, once whirling us toward a tree that hangs so low over the water that it almost brushes off the crew. Where the boat floats so swiftly, curiosity can travel no farther in advance than the next bend; as in a speeding motor car, the tourist, until he is accustomed to the pace, takes more interest in the road just ahead than in any graceful silhouette on the skyline. The boat scoots under a bridge, the last one to be seen for five days. . . . The town of Galena whisks by. Leave it with few regrets and no description. Another wriggle or two of the current and towns are just a memory.

We glided past a few new bungalows, in one of which a phonograph was blaring through a horn large enough for a concert hall. Downstream a little way a gray-haired man who might have been a banker was fishing in a bathing suit. "Fish bitin'?" asked Jim. The boat passed so swiftly that the latter part of the short reply was considerably fainter than the first: "Not—today—think—they—must be nesting." Jim only chuckled. A few rods more and we watched in fascination while a young man with red hair dived off the end of a log like a startled turtle. But one wriggle farther in the course of the stream and we came to an end of all that faintly suggested the city.

There was a sharp turn just ahead, with a snag sticking out and bobbing a little in the middle of the narrow passage. We swept close under a willow branch. The waves of the riffle loudly slapped the keel; the boat grazed the stump, jerked, slid by. Jim worked fast with the paddle and breathed through his mouth, not as physical culture would advise. When we had left that rapid behind, I felt that this was an introduction to open country. After that, when a spot of red on the silver surface of the river marked a shoal ahead, I had no anxiety for the camera, for Jim had proved himself a real boatman. For his part, Jim put down the paddle and rolled a cigarette.

Only a portion of the land near the river—or, for that matter, on the hills—was under cultivation. That gave the fields some of the charm that belongs to any sort of rarity. Over one open space between the treetops we saw a farmer stacking hay. Just a flash and he was left behind. Another time we heard a terrific clatter, something like a runaway on cobblestones. "What's that?" I asked excitedly. Jim shouted with laughter. "I 'low somebody's plowin'," he said. The noise was of stones striking the metal of a cultivator's teeth. . . .

Jim had a penchant for spring water, and we stopped to taste at many landings. I suspected that some thirsty tourist had once told him that the mark of a good guide is a knowledge of the location of all the springs. . . .

The minutes of that afternoon fled at as fast a pace as the river. A little before sunset I began to cast for bass—promptly snagged the minnow and snapped the line. The current was taking the boat so fast that there was no time for maneuvers. After that I sat down, considerably relieved, and took more comfort in enjoying the scenery. In the deepening shadows the hills seemed to loom higher; the limestone bluffs appeared more sheer and jagged. I found no trouble then to believe Jim when he "guessed" that some of the crests were five hundred feet above the waterline of the river. In the dim light in some of the bends, the slap of little waves on the keel in the riffles sounded somehow weird. The chip on which we floated appeared to go twice as fast when it rushed by masses of strange shadows.

It was much too dark for a safe passage over shoals when we came to an opening in the solid wall of trees and heard voices at a ford. It was Cape Fair, Jim said, and a good place to spend the night. On the east was a high hill; on the other shore, where we landed on a bank of pebbles, a giant tree. The faintest sort of red glow on the skyline back of that showed where the sun had gone down. Jim drove four stakes into the pebbles, a blow to each stake, hooked the corners of the tent ropes over them, stuck a pole up under the center of the canvas, and there was our pyramid tent ready for the night. I made up cots and unloaded the boat cargo; Jim had a fire going and the dinner under way in another two minutes. . . .

There is a danger, perhaps, in dwelling too long on that first day; but the things that happen in the opening chapter are symbols far more impressive and interesting than a whole sleepy morning of the fourth day, when you merely sit in the sun and enjoy life like a turtle. On the first, everything thrills; on the fourth, the whole world takes a nap. . . . I recalled no noise through that night but the dripping of dew, like a spring rain, from the giant tree. Then I smelled the aroma of coffee, heard twigs crackling on the cookfire, and knew it was morning. We were half an hour late, Jim declared. I looked at my watch and put it back without remembering what it told. And no matter!

Jim's in the boat. You're in yourself. The chain clinks musically on the floor. Jim dips his paddle and it make a little whirlpool in the water—once, twice, three times, and rests. . . . You begin to see that there is something like a refrain in the incidents of your trip; and that in this recurrence of the familiar there is something as comforting as the voice of old friends.

We floated that day into a land of cliffs, higher than those of the day before, but simply old friends of greater stature. Back of these rose-peaked hills, now with elevation enough to be dignified by the name of "balds." Beside us in the morning floated a fisherman and his wife and a guide in a splinter boat which sat unusually low in the water. He kept close to the shore, casting with accuracy to the edge of the bank, with words of encouragement and advice to the fish all the while and occasionally praising his own skill. The wife smiled approvingly and the guide sat with a fixed grin.

We came to Virgin Bluffs. Seven hundred feet in their perpendicular of white limestone, Jim said, and whether he was telling a "stretcher" or not would have been difficult to dispute. They were the more impressive because in Virgin Shoals, at their base, the water caught the boat with a jerk and plunged it through a hundred yards of rough water in which there were intervals where the riffles could not have been much higher without deserving to be called waves.

When the river is full, they run as high as two feet, Jim averred. Now—"aw, shucks, these ain't much." I can't recall now even what time in the morning we ran these shoals, or whether Jim really had to work very hard to get through without shipping water. Stone ledges and trees whisked by; the camera snapped four times; and the next we noticed was that a flock of tame ducks was following along behind us like friendly pups.

I began to long, soon thereafter, for something to do besides sit on a camp stool and think. The shoals, no doubt, stir the blood. Jim advised stopping at a convenient wooded island to cut a pawpaw for a boat pole. "Push a little with it an' you'll feel better," he said. The prescription was excellent and comes to you now highly recommended as an appetizer. Poling is a science in the Ozarks, for the reason that it is the only way to make head in taking a boat upstream. It is indispensable also for the raftsmen. We passed one tie-raft which made me think of a partially submerged train of box cars. Here and there, like brakemen for the train, the raftsmen waved and shouted.

In deep shade near the head of an island, sitting on black loam beside a spring where imagination must have made the place seem ten degrees cooler than reality, we had luncheon without the trouble of heating coffee, and speculated about the advantages and drawbacks of various ways of making a living. Jim told of how tired a guide gets sometimes after a long day of paddling for fishermen, particularly when a heavy string of bass drags behind the boat to make work twice as hard. He related that one guide of his acquaintance trailed a string of fish over some willows in a rapids on purpose to lose it and make paddling easier. It wouldn't be fair to tell which guide this was.

I took the paddle that afternoon and ran a few of the shoals. To be at the helm of an Ozark splinter is by no means the same thing as managing a canoe. It is necessary to head the splinter sooner before you plunge into the riffle, but you may count on this homemade boat to keep from being whirled around unless there is evident cause. The blade area of Jim's paddle seemed to be small as compared with a good broad canoe paddle, but perhaps the heavy, stiff wood is necessary when the piece of oar is called upon suddenly in a rapids to serve as a pole.

Once in a while we came to a ford. When Jim talked to anyone who happened to be there, it was in a low, natural tone which carried a great distance without apparent effort. All the natives, when they are near the river, use these tones, while the stranger will shout and raise a startling rumpus with the echoes. . . .

Jim told the names of as many of the balds as he could remember; and added that they were growing as valuable nowadays for raising Angora goats as for delighting painters. Now and then he could point to a moving spot of white on the cliffs and declare it was another goat. I wondered if the owners of these animals captured their property by shooting them like mountain goats, or if they only seined for them or caught them in traps. Certainly no one could hope to give chase to a goat on one of those declivities.

Late in the afternoon Jim cast for bass and in short order caught two in succession. "They're nestin', all right," he remarked, grinning. "I 'low we dropped right into one of the nests."

We camped that night on a bar of pebbles, near where the James flows into the White. When we ran inshore and looked back up the river, Bald Joe, one of the highest of the cones in the neighborhood, was still touched with sunlight at its tip.

We had an unusually large dinner that night—the reward of a day of more than ordinary exertion—and ate two strong, raw onions for the relish course. I had become so fond of our crude old boat that I asked Jim what a new one would cost. As I recall it now he said he " 'lowed about seven or eight dollars." The wood was

"Once in a long time we met another float-trip party," from *Outing,* August 1911

cheap enough, he explained, but you have to hire a blacksmith to make some of the iron clamps.

Jim had lived in this section of the Ozarks most of his life and appeared to be fairly representative. He rather shrank from peering into the future and took all the more interest in each day's meals and smokes. . . .

How far he differed from the ordinary professional guide may be seen in the fact that at times he couldn't have been accused of being exactly taciturn. I was almost asleep that night when I heard him drawl:

"Ever et a citron?"

I was not, at that time, among those who have been so blessed. I had almost drowsed away again when I heard:

"Blame near like a watermelon—outside."

Another long pause. Then I was raised up in my cot, startled to hear:

"But when you cut into it, it ain't."

Dimly I recall that long, long after that I heard the single word "green." Is that, I wonder, the true inwardness of citron?

The next morning, to compensate for the laziness of the day before, we were up before five. When the sun struck over the treetops across the river, driving long rays here and there through the smoke-like mist, I never felt more helpless as an artist than when I adjusted the camera to attempt to record a symphony of white and gold and silver.

The cooking and packing all worked now with system and speed. And now . . . Jim's in the boat. You're in yourself. The chain clinks on the splinter's bottom. Dip. Dip. Dip. The old, sweet refrain again!

With every hour that day time went lazily. I basked in the sunlight; stopped gladly at every spring; ate and dozed with all the contentment of an aged cat. Once in a while Jim hit the water with the flat side of his paddle and made a sound like a shot. When the turtles tumbled off into the water at that alarm we always chuckled. "Right smart a bluff," Jim remarked about a towering cliff. And I answered with a sleepy nod. . . .

As a photographer, however, I continued to be active on a few occasions. The light coming from around a bend, as if the Morning Sun made his home just behind a clump of river-bank trees, the simplicity of outline of a bald and its reflection in the water—such combinations as these gave me almost as much delight as ever, though outwardly I greeted them with little enthusiasm. The endless compositions in which the triangle dominated recurred like a theme in music; and I once found myself wondering if any sort of tent but a pyramid would dare hold up its head in that land of conical balds.

There came a day when I felt identified with the chip on which we floated. Time became a joke; business a dimly remembered annoyance. . . . We came to Branson after four days of floating, a distance estimated by Jim as nearly two hundred miles, and guessed by me as at least half that much. . . .

Anna Kalland

For 150 miles, from New York to Troy, the Hudson ebbs and flows with the ocean. A canoeist catching the tide can move up the river as easily as down. But the heavy traffic—deep-water vessels and tugs with long tows—is dangerous for small craft.

When a man said they would not be able to paddle up the Hudson River by themselves—and furthermore should not—that was all the two nurses needed to hear. They felt challenged, no doubt, but there was more to it than that; the river trip offered a change, a release from daily city and hospital routines.

IT CAN'T BE DONE *

"Two lone women up the Hudson River in a canoe! Sleeping on the banks where the railroads run—cooking your own grub for the tramps to eat! Gosh! You don't know when you are well off. The steamers will swamp you—it's awfully rough, anyway—and the barge crews! Why in the name of common sense don't you ship your canoe out to a lake somewhere and sleep at a hotel—if paddle you must!

"Wouldn't see a sister of mine do it—that's all!"

When a man says that, further remarks are not in order. We made none, nor did we mention such small matters as a .38-caliber, mother-of-pearl handled and a beauty; a blackjack and a nightstick lent by a friendly cop; a hypodermic syringe to be filled with plain water, but called vitriol (this last idea, however, was given up as being too Borgian). . . .

Yes—we had "gone up the river," though not in the New York sense of the word—but in the good canoe *Ward Fifty,* hope of adventure paddling bow, hope of adventure paddling stern, a goodly supply of potatoes, bacon, Aunt Jemima, and Mocha and Java to feed it, oilskins and a tarpauline to keep it dry. And the sharp-edged, newly sandpapered and varnished paddles reached out for more, always more of the muddy, oily river; a soft pat, a firm swish—and eighteen feet of Old Town slipped by all the old week-end landmarks.

As we turned a point north of Bloomer's Landing, there was the beach sacred to canoeists. It was a mass of color that belonged: canoes of many shades along the level, sandy beach, with gray, white, green, and khaki tents blending with the thousand tints of the Indian summer woodlands. The misty afternoon light was sifting down from the rocky, leafy heights like huge shafts of blue-gray

* *Outing,* March 1923.

311

mist, taking life from the many campfires, while promontory after promontory rose ahead of us, the last fading into the river and the blue distance.

As we sat in front of our own campfire, we scarcely offered a thought to patients, night messengers with flickering tapers, blinding our eyes as we stumbled out of bed, notes from night nurses saying that someone had "ceased to breathe," telephone bells, ambulance clangings, and ether vapors—all—all of them were buried in the subcellar of our consciousness.

More like a memory did the past seem after we had rolled up in our blankets on a strip of hard ground, termed by Judy "the back fence," our heads in tufts of green grass, grasshoppers chirping and katydids saying: Katy did—Katy did—she did—she didn't—over and over again.

We unrolled early the next morning and made haste to get started before the wind came up. . . .

The mists were hanging low over Tappan Zee, that wonderful cruising place for ghosts and goblins. As it closed in about us and our paddles plied silently in an oily sea, we expected any moment to sight the "storm-ship" that comes and goes, "flying swiftly before a wind which no one can feel," or the boat of Rambout Van Dam rowing forever and ever on these haunted waters, or the headless horseman riding toward Teller's Point along the Old Post Road.

But we reached Teller's Point all alone, mists and visions alike gone before a wind that had its own way with Haverstraw Bay. So this was Haverstraw Bay! We had heard many descriptions of it. . . . But the reality outdid them all. It sluiced as much of itself as possible over our bow and sides, and all afternoon it was a game of hitting square, now tacking, now going straight before, taking advantage of lulls, always with a growing attachment to our ship that rode like a log, running away from the following sea, each tryout egging us on to press her closer and closer.

With the wind there was a blistering sun, which tormented our faces and arms and backs as all that afternoon we paddled and paddled toward the Highlands. At Stony Point we had to give up. There was no passing thereof 'til the wind had died down. Our soft muscles did not turn her to starboard one single point. . . .

So we beached *Ward Fifty* in a cove below the point and got

HUDSON RIVER

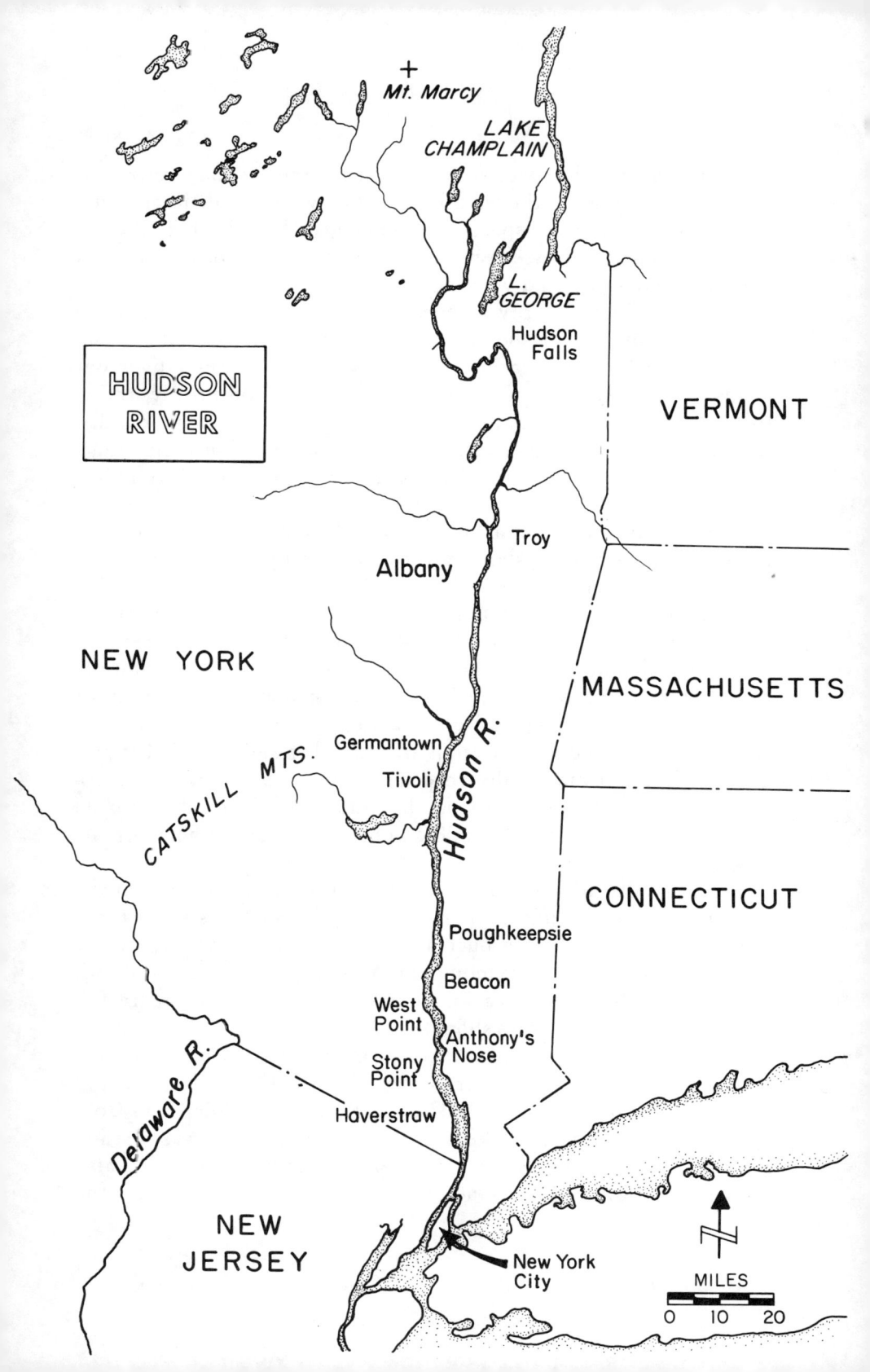

ready for chow. The place seemed too near the railroad tracks for night camp and, when the wind had died down, we pulled out, heading north, sparing as to speed and comments. We felt hurt all over, crosswise and lengthwise, each muscle fussing to find a position it had not tried and found wanting.

About an hour later we found ourselves half asleep, making camp on a small sandy beach on the West Shore. No sooner had we rolled up than the trains began to thunder by, right over our heads. But we were too tired to move and dozed off fitfully, trying to find a spot on our anatomies that didn't call for help. Finally, when the milk cans began rattling overhead, we again took refuge on the river, which flowed like a silent protest between rumbling shores.

It must have been about five or six o'clock in the morning when the watchman of Iona Island saw a blue waif of a smoke trail skyward from an outpost of the island. There was a gruel pot trying to come to a boil. Gruel? Yes. That seemed to be the dish tacitly agreed upon as most becoming to our status of mind and flesh.

The watchman probably began worrying about his ammunition, for we saw him coming toward us in rapid strides, the white tail of his little dog bobbing up and down among the gray stones, like the tail of a rabbit. We made friends with the dog and attended to our gruel and oranges in an absorbed manner that precluded interruption. He allowed us to finish our breakfast and carefully watched our intentions as we slowly paddled upstream into the heart of the Highlands.

With one day of arduous labors behind us, every neuron on the jump from the night under the railroad track, our faces so blistered from the sun that it even hurt us to laugh, we felt totally out of place in these grand surroundings. But as we slowly forged ahead, we gradually forgot our various hurts, and the paddles again fell in of themselves as paddles should.

Late in the afternoon we saw the promontory of Beacon run into the wide still waters, that were beginning to take on shadows and evening tints. Storm King, Old Crow's Nest, West Point, and Cold Springs had been duly marked off on our map, which was already aspiring to the oily appearance of a hospital deck of cards. We also marked off Pollopel's Island (Bannerman's Island), once the dwelling place of a ghost, now inhabited by an ogre of an arsenal, creeping down to the water's edge. Looking at the architecture, we felt the ghost had shown its good taste in departing, and mentioned this in our marginal notes.

We made camp at Beacon in our most finished style. There was even a neat trench dug around the tent, which consisted of a tarpaulin tied to the canoe on one side, and belayed to stakes driven into the ground on the other. With the main house built, one of us got into shore togs (a skirt and sweater worn over the bathing suit) and went foraging, while the other built the kitchen and procured wood and water.

The night was clear, and we rolled up in front of the fire, outside of the tent, watching the "funiculaire" crawling up the side of the mountain like a golden caterpillar, listening to the soft lapping of the waves on the beach, agreeing with Henry Hudson that "it is a good land to fall in with, and a pleasant land to see." We finally slept 'til the tide had come and gone and was coming again.

It looked like a promising day, but a wind came up, a wind which gathered into a storm as the day wore on. We marked our chart "Stormy Day at Beacon" and lay down on the rocks to enjoy it. The gray-green waves, topped with white, were racing toward us, breaking against the tall grasses, but where they struck the sun-built road across the waters, they played in all the colors of the shore. There was a little bit of yellow from the goldenrod, a little bit of red from the thorn apple, a touch of violet and purple from the asters, silver from the willow trees—it was like an oriental mosaic on a background of delicate green.

That night we crept under our good ship, for it looked like rain, and before long, huge drops were tambourining on our roof, trickling, we hoped, into the waiting trench. Some did; others were of an inquisitive nature and wandered into windblown places, looking for knees and backs to slide downhill. But the ropes held and, after we had wrapped our oilskins about the firewood, we returned once more to the tent, to be lulled away by the tides, the wind, and the dripping rains.

The next morning was clear and calm. We broke camp and stocked up with firewood and water. We hoped to make at least twenty miles that day, bringing us to about seventy miles from

New York. We hailed the cantilever bridge at Poughkeepsie in the late afternoon and registered ourselves and *Ward Fifty* at the Yacht Club. . . . The commodore treated us to much good advice, and a glowing description of a beautiful island a little farther upstream, an island where none but campers were allowed.

We swept under the bridge on a strong tide and pushed on, passing bend after bend. The sun had gone down on our search for the island, but the moonlight lay white over the wide reaches; the air was so filled with light that we seemed to be drinking it in with each breath. Our brains were visited by strange visions of islands created out of clouds and promontories and trees, rising in grotesque forms out of the all-pervading, illusory light.

The commodore had told us it was about five miles beyond Poughkeepsie, but we counted it nearer ten when our canoe finally took the sands of Esopus Island. It was all as he had said—and more. Near the landing place were three huge logs placed on end, with a fresh balsam bough stuck in at the top. A little farther ashore was a bed of balsam boughs, all turned down and ready. If we had found slippers and a dressing gown tossed across it, we should have been no more amazed. There was also a grate placed over bricks, which were still warm.

"Campers," we said, almost with one breath.

It was the handshake of experts in a life of give and take, connoting membership in a club as exclusive as it is delightful, although members but seldom meet.

After dinner we stretched out in front of the burning logs, oblivious to the fact that the mundane motions were still going on. Before us was a picture exquisitely framed and hung. We curled up in the corner thereof, where the signature of the artist should have been, and watched it, 'til the white light was gone and the stars were alone. . . .

The green thing beneath us moved rhythmically and smoothly all day long. The sun was gradually changing our skins from a bourgeois lobster to a dull coppery red, which would have been quite artistic had it not been for the huge flakes of skin which persisted in coming off and dropping into everything. Yet we felt that we were arriving. Our appetites were all that we ever asked of our patients—and more; we supplemented our visits to grocery stores by calls at farm kitchens, leaving the money on the doorsill and helping ourselves when the owners were away. . . .

We paddled for a long time, the sun shining, the waters glistening, the miles slipping away. . . .

We passed Cruger's Island, where, according to Indian tradition, no one ever died; we paddled through North Bay where Fulton played with his "Folly," and toward evening reached Tivoli of frivolous name and an excellent grocery store. It was twilight when we left Tivoli, and what we should have done was to look for a camping place then and there. We didn't. We felt like moving on, and move on we did, 'til the shores seemed like long, undulating black masses, we ourselves a black mite moving between them.

The east shore was unfriendly for camping purposes and, near Germantown, we crossed to the west side of the river. We paddled on, waiting for the moon to light the way. Instead of the moon came black clouds, borne on a strong north wind, and all was not so well with us. We hugged the shore to keep out of the wind, looking for a possible camping place. But every desirable spot seemed occupied by workmen's shacks; what seemed an inviting sand beach proved to be a white cliff overhanging the river.

We crawled on and on, against the wind. It was a strange and sinister thing, this moving along on dark waters under a stormy, threatening sky. At time we seemed to be standing still; at others we shot forward or downhill with headlong speed; now the waters were choppy; again we struck a snag that set us worrying about the boat. Remembering our night under the railroad track, we were determined not to make asses of ourselves this time.

On toward midnight, having doubled back on our tracks, we tied up to an old float, and fell asleep in the bottom of the canoe, too tired to take bearings, too sleepy to care. We had paddled over forty miles that day, part of the time against a strong wind and tide. When I unfolded myself in the morning, Judy greeted me from the raft, where she had squatted in the attitude of a meditating oriental:

"See that shack—and that one?"

I looked, and seeing, beheld them both, close to our canoe. They were covered with black tarpaper and invisible at night. . . .

But the Providence which is partial to women, children, and asses seemed to be with us, and so we took heart and began pushing our canoe through the mud, taking a photograph of our moorings as we went. We waded in mud to our knees, guiding her tenderly away from stones and wire and broken glass. She was a most particular, persnickety sort of a canoe; wouldn't even let us inside 'til all that mud had been washed off. Then we headed for the river, where a

"Yes, we had gone up the river—in the good canoe *Ward Fifty,* from *Outing,* March 1932

strong north wind made upstream progress impossible. We tacked across and camped out near North Germantown for the day and night.

It had not rained since the second night at Beacon; it was ideal Indian summer weather, summer heat and mosquitoes gone with the dog days. The next day we passed through the ice industry belt. There were huge icehouses where the harvest had been stacked away during the winter season. Out they came, from the dark, damp places, crystalline blocks, traveling down the incline in pairs, acting like two good pals coming home of a Saturday night, melting into the waiting barge.

In the afternoon the towers and spires of Albany rose out of the river. We did not land, but made speed to reach a landing place before dark.

As it looked like rain, we tied our canoe to the piles under a pier and slept in the bottom of it. As if by some mysterious communication, we both awoke just in time to see the *Trojan* bear down upon us in the small hours of the morning, paddles going at full speed. A few more minutes, and we would have been smashed against the piles by the breakers. We got out from under in due time, and without a scratch. We proceeded leisurely upstream, and this time we didn't even blush at our asininity. We were beginning to think that our lives were charmed.

We should soon reach Troy and the first lock, where we had been told that no canoe was ever taken through by itself. Accordingly, we kept close to the fairway and were on the lookout for a possible tow. We finally marked a barge, with her load waterline barely showing, as worthy of our attention: she was easy to board —she looked hospitable. We hailed the captain, who proved to be a French Canadian. No man ever walked a ship's plank more proud of his ship than he. To be sure, she was only a barge, but we had our weakness for our own *Ward Fifty* and understood.

Shortly before noon the whole float was locked through and we anchored near the east shore. We were given the freedom of the kitchen and set out to prepare the food, having invited our host for dinner. He, meanwhile, had mysteriously disappeared. There was no boat, no gangplank, no means of communication with the shore that we could see. Yet he was gone. But the dinner was cooking, and so we set the table in the cabin, hoping all would be well.

What a cabin! Neat! Even the crazy-quilt on the narrow cot was hanging in an exact plumb line. The walls were covered with pictures—of beautiful ladies—society ladies. None but the Vans and the Vers, Donnas and Signoras had a place. There were no personal effects—and yet the strange personality of the man was there.

As we peered through the cabin window to get a possible glimpse of him, we saw him arriving through the air, balancing himself on a pole stuck into the river bed. It was neatly done and we told him so. Clean-shaven and blue-chinned, he bowed politely. We bowed him into the cabin for dinner, where the table was steaming like an altar with steak and potatoes and corn on the cob. . . .

The last week it was a question of making good time, and yet we took no towing 'til the last Sunday. So all the week we paddled, our muscles getting harder and harder. And the passing show continued all up and down the mighty artery of the Empire State, supplying the wants of thousands, touching, it seemed, the remotest ends of the earth. . . .

SOURCES

Bishop, Nathaniel Holmes. *Four Months in a Sneak-Box: A Boat Voyage of 2600 Miles Down the Ohio and Mississippi Rivers, and Along the Gulf of Mexico.* Boston: Lee and Shepard, 1879.
―――――. *Voyage of the Paper Canoe: A Geographical Journey of 2500 miles, From Quebec to the Gulf of Mexico, During the Years 1874–5.* Boston: Lee and Shepard, 1878.
Browne, George Elmer. "Canoeing Down the Androscoggin." *Outing,* July 1898.
Chichester, Edward L. "The Cruise of the *Sybaris* and *Shaw Shaw*." *Outing,* May, June 1889.
Cushing, Charles Phelps. "Floating Through the Ozarks." *Outing,* August 1911.
Dimock, Anthony Weston. "Yachting in a Canoe." *Outing,* September 1908. Reprinted in his book *Florida Enchantments,* rev. ed. New York: Frederick A. Stokes Company, 1926.
Kalland, Anna. "It Can't Be Done." *Outing,* March 1923.
Knowles, Isobel. "Two Girls in a Canoe." *Cosmopolitan Magazine,* October 1905.
O'Reilly, John Boyle. *Athletics and Manly Sport.* Boston: Pilot Publishing Company, 1890. Earlier edition titled *Ethics of Boxing and Manly Sport,* Boston, Ticknor & Fields, 1888, included canoeing the Connecticut, Susquehanna, and Delaware Rivers. "Down the Susquehanna in a Canoe" was published in *Outing,* January 1885.
Remington, Frederic. "Black Water and Shallows." *Harper's New Monthly Magazine,* August 1893.
Stanton, Gerrit Smith. *"Where the Sportsman Loves to Linger": A Narrative of the Most Popular Canoe Trips in Maine.* New York: J. S. Ogilvie Publishing Company, c. 1905.
Thoreau, Henry David. *The Journal of Henry D. Thoreau.* Edited by Brad-

ford Torrey and Francis H. Allen. Boston: Houghton Mifflin Company, 1906, reprinted 1949, 14 vols.

Thwaites, Reuben Gold. *Historic Waterways: Six Hundred Miles of Canoeing Down the Rock, Fox, and Wisconsin Rivers.* Chicago: A. C. McClurg and Company, 1890.

Wing, Ralph K. "Canoeing on the Genesee." *Outing,* December 1885.

INDEX

"Abeham" (guide), 201–202, 207, 209, 211
Adirondack Mountains, 32
Adney, Edwin Tappan, *xiv*n
Alabama, 89, 90
Albany, New York, 318
Albemarle Sound, 194
Aldrich, Thomas Bailey, 223*n*
Allagash Falls, Maine, 268
Allagash River, Maine, *xvi*, 258, 264, 266, 268–71, 274
Allegany County, New York, 107
Allegheny Mountains, 103
Allegheny River, 60–61
Altamaha River, 49
Alton, Illinois, 77
American Eagle, The (periodical), 293*n*
Androscoggin River, 243–54
Apalachicola, Florida, 94
Appalaken, Pennsylvania, 164
Arkansas, 81, 297, 299
Assabet River, 9, 11–18, 21–25
Athens, Pennsylvania, 164, 165
Athletics and Manly Sport (O'Reilly), 149–211
Aunt Rhody's Pond, Martha's Vineyard, *xiii*
Avon, New York, 115

Baker's Farm, Concord, 21
Bald Joe Mountain, 306
Ball's Hill, on the Assabet, 15, 25
Bangor, Maine, 257, 258, 275
Bangor and Aroostook Railroad, 257, 271
Bangor House, Bangor, 257
Bannerman's Island (Pollopel's Island), 314–15

Bark Canoes and Skin Boats of North America, The (Adney and Chapelle), *xiv*n
Barnegat Bay, New Jersey, 60
Bath, Maine, 254
Baxter County, Arkansas, 301
Bayou Caden, Mississippi, 88–89
Bayou du Chien Creek, 80
Bayou La Fourche, Louisiana, 81
Bay St. Louis, 87
Beach, J. C., 34
Beacon, New York, 314, 315, 318
Bear Point, Alabama, 90
Beaver Kill, 223–26, 229
Bedford, Massachusetts, 15
Belfast, New York, 107
Belle Fontaine Point, Mississippi, 88
Belvidere, New Jersey, 171, 182–83
Bennett's Point, South Carolina, 46
Bergelund, Captain Johs., 48
Berlin Falls, New Hampshire, 246
Bethel, New Hampshire, 248
Big Eddy on the West Branch, Maine, 271
Big Foul Rift, *see* Great Foul Rift
Big Grave Creek, 65
Big Lagoon, Alabama, 90
Big Sandy River, 71
Biloxi, Mississippi, 88, 96
Binghamton, New York, 158–59
Bishop, Nathaniel Holmes, 27, 29–101
Bittern Cliff, Assabet River, 24
"Black Water and Shallows" (Remington), 233–40
Blennerhasset's Island, 60, 66, 69
Bloomer's Landing, New York, 311
Blue Creek, Florida, 99, 100
Boca Grande, Florida, 290, 291
Bombay Hook, New Jersey, 35

323

Bon Secours Bay, 89
Boone, Daniel, 72
Boston, Massachusetts, 84, 151
Boston and Maine Railroad, 151
Bower's Beach Hotel, 36
Bowlin Pitch, Maine, 274
Bradford's Island, 56
Brandenburg, Kentucky, 76
Branson, Missouri, 307
Brattleboro, Vermont, 156
Brébeuf, Jean, *ix–x, xiii–xiv*
British Army, 148
Bromidon Brook, 157, 158
Brown, Dr. John, quoted, 219
Browne, George Elmer, 241, 243–54
Brule River, *xiv*
Brunswick, Georgia, 49
Brunswick River, 49, 50
Bull River, 46–48
Bushmill Creek, 180
Butler River, 49
Butternut Grove (Cook's Falls), 223–24, 230
Buzzard's Bay, Massachusetts, *xi*

Cadosia Creek, 230
Cairo, Illinois, 61, 71, 79
Caloosahatchie River, 292–93
Camden County, North Carolina, 187
Canada, 109
Cannonsville, New York, 223
"Canoeing Down the Androscoggin" (Browne), 243–54
"Canoeing on the Connecticut" (O'Reilly), 149–58
"Canoeing in the Dismal Swamp" (O'Reilly), 187–211
"Canoeing on the Genesee" (Wing), 105–17
Canton, New York, 163*n*, 173, 231
Canyons of the Colorado (Powell), *xv*
Cape Cod, Massachusetts, *xi*
Cape Delaware, 36
Cape Fair, Missouri, 303
Cape Fear, North Carolina, 40, 44–45
Cape Hatteras, North Carolina, 40
Cape Henlopen, Delaware, 33, 40

Capens Rips, on the Androscoggin, 250–51
Cape San Blas, Florida, 92–93
Captiva Pass, Florida, 291, 292
Carbon Cliff, Illinois, 145, 146
Caribbean Sea, *xiii*
Carlisle Bridge, Concord, 15, 25
Carlos Pass, Florida, 293
Cass, Lewis, *xv*
Castle Garden, New York, 32
Catfish Bay, 128
Catfish River, 125, 127–34
Catskill Mountains, 217
Caxambas, Florida, 294
Cedar Hammock, Georgia, 49
Cedar Keys, Florida, 55, 96, 98
Cellular Cosmogony, or The Earth a Concave Sphere, The (Teed), 293*n*
Chalk Bluff, Illinois, 80
Chamberlain Lake, 265, 272
Champlain, Samuel de, *xiii*
Channing, William Ellery, 15
Chapelle, Howard I., *xivn*
Charles River, 173
Charleston, South Carolina, 45, 48
Charlotte Harbor, Florida, 283, 288
Chase's Carry, Maine, 265–66, 270
Chelsea, Massachusetts, 255
Chenango River, 215–23
Cherry River, 140
Chesuncook, Maine, 271, 272
Chesuncook Lake, 261, 263, 264, 271, 272–73
Chicago, Burlington and Quincy Railroad, 145, 146
Chichester, Edward L., 213, 215–30
Chickasaw Bluff, 80
Choctawhatchee Bay, 91
Chokoloskee Bay, 294
Church Flats, South Carolina, 45
Churchill Lake, 261, 265, 266
Cincinnati, Ohio, 66, 73, 74
Clark, William, *xv*
Clark Rapids, on the Androscoggin, 252–53
Cleveland, Illinois, 145
Coffeelos Lake, Maine, 272
Cold Spring, New York, 314

INDEX

325

Coleridge, Samuel Taylor, quoted, 295
Coloma, Illinois, 145, 146
Colonel's Island, 49, 50, 53
Columbia, Pennsylvania, 185
Columbia River, *xv*
Columbia University, 255
Columbus, Christopher, *xiii*
Columbus, Florida, 55
Combahee River, 46
Company of Jesus, *xiv*n, 123
Concord, Massachusetts, 3, 12*n*, 15, 16
Concord River, South Branch (Sudbury River), 11–14, 25
Connecticut River, 149–58, 167, 169, 175
Connors, Maine, 264, 268
Cook's Falls (Butternut Grove), New York, 223–24, 230
Coon Key, Florida, 294
Coosaw River, 46
Covington, Kentucky, 73
Crooked Island, Florida, 91, 92
Crooked Island Bay, 91
Crooked Rips, of the Androscoggin, 253
Crow's Nest Mountain, 314
Cruger's Island, 317
"Cruise of the *Sybaris* and *Shaw Shaw*, The" (Chichester), 215–30
Cumberland Sound, 48, 51
Currituck County, North Carolina, 187
Cushing, Charles Phelps, 297, 299–307

Dahoo River, 45
Darien River, 49
Dauntless (vessel), 227
Dauphine Island, 89
Deadman's Bay, Florida, 100
Death's Eddy Rift, 174, 179
Deep Creek, Virginia, 194, 195, 196, 199, 206
Deer Island Chainbridge, Newburyport, 175
Delancy, New York, 219
Delaware, 34
Delaware Bay, 35–36

Delaware River, 171–87; East Branch, *xvi*, 223–30; West Branch, 216–23, 224
Delaware Water Gap, 180–81, 182
Delhi, New York, 216–17, 218
Diamond Shoals, 40
Dimock, Anthony Weston, 283, 285–96
Dimock, Julian, 283
Dismal Swamp of Virginia and North Carolina, 187–211
Dismal Swamp Canal, 191–92, 194–202
Dorchester, Massachusetts, 119
"Down the Delaware River in a Canoe" (O'Reilly), 171–87
"Down the Susquehanna in a Canoe" (O'Reilly), 158–71
Duluth, Daniel Graysolon, sieur, *xv*
Dutton & Rixford (firm), 51–52
Dutton, Georgia, 51–52

Eagle Lake, 265, 272
East Branch, of the Delaware, *xvi*, 223–30
East Branch, of the Penobscot, 258, 271, 274–75
Easton, Pennsylvania, 174
East Pascagoula, Mississippi, 88
East Pass, Florida, 91
East River, New York, 257
Elizabeth City, North Carolina, 194
Elizabeth River, 192, 194, 206
Elsinborough, New Jersey, 34
Erie, Illinois, 143, 144
Erie Canal, 117
Esopus Island, 316
Estere Bay, 293
Everglade, Florida, 294
Everglades, The, Florida, 283, 295, 296

Fair Haven Pond, Massachusetts, 5, 14, 16, 18, 20, 25; insects of, 21; storm on, 24
Felicité (vessel), 83
Fenholloway River, 96
Fernandina, Florida, 98
First Lake, Madison, 128, 129

326   INDEX

"Floating Through the Ozarks" (Cushing), 299–307
Florida, 29, 51, 84, 90, 195; Dimock in, 283, 285–96
Fort Delaware, 34
Fort Donaldson, Tennessee, 80
Fort Gaines, 89
Fort Kent, 270, 271
Fort Morgan, 89
Fort Myers, Florida, 292–93
Fort Pickens, Florida, 91
Fourfold Creek, 71
Four Months in a Sneak-Box (Bishop), 57–101
Foxcroft, Maine, 265
Fox Hole, on the Penobscot, 261
France, *xiii*
Franklin, Benjamin, 39
Freedom, Pennsylvania, 62
French Creek, Pennsylvania, 61
French's Creek, Kentucky, 76
Fulton, Robert, 317
Fulton, Wisconsin, 134

Galena, Missouri, 302
Gasparilla Island, 290
Gasparilla Pass, Florida, 290–91
Gasparilla Sound, 283
Gates County, North Carolina, 187
Gatineau, Nicholas, 277
Gatineau River, 277, 279–82
Geary, lockman of the Dismal Swamp, 196
General's Cut, Georgia, 49
Genesee River, 103, 105–17
Geneseo, New York, 114–15
Georgia, 48, 51, 266
Germantown, New York, 317
Gilead, New Hampshire, 248
Gloucester, Massachusetts, 241
Gorham, New Hampshire, 246, 248
Grand Lake, Maine, 274
Grant's Pass, Mississippi, 89
Graveline Bayou, 88
Great Foul Rift, of the Delaware, 171, 174–75, 176, 182–87
Great Lakes, *xiii*; Ontario, 103, 105; Superior, *xiv*
Green Corner, Maine, 252

Grindstone, Maine, 272, 274, 275
Guiteras, Dr. Ramon, 149–57 *passim;* on the Delaware, 171, 173, 174, 177, 181–82, 183, 185
Gulf of Mexico, *xiv,* 29, 51, 78, 295, 296; Bishop voyage on, 83–95
Gulf of St. Lawrence, 29

Hamden, New York, 220
Hancock, New York, 229, 230
Hanover, New Hampshire, 156
Harney River, 283, 296
Harrisburg, Pennsylvania, 160
Harrison (guide), 233, 238–39, 240
Hartford, Connecticut, 156
Hartford City, Ohio, 70
Haskell Rock, Maine, 274–75
Hatteras Inlet, 40–41, 44
Haverhill, Massachusetts, 175
Haverstraw Bay, 312
Helena Sound, 46
Henry, Patrick, 194
Herrick, Robert, quoted, 187
Hickman, Kentucky, 80
Highlands, New York, 312, 314
"Historic Waterways" (Thwaites), 121–46
Hog Island, 39
Holyoke, Massachusetts, 151
Horserace, on the Allagash, 270
Hubbard, Frank, 151
Hubbard Bathing Place, Assabet River, 17
Hudson, Henry, quoted, 315
Hudson River, 29, 31–33, 141, 309, 311–20
Huntington, Ohio, 71
Hutchinson's Island, 46

Illinois, 80, 124–46
Illinois River, *xiv*
Inerarity's Point, 90
Iona Island, 314
Ireland, 148
Irish Bayou, 84
Irondequoit, New York, 103
Island No. 1, Mississippi River, 80, 81
"It Can't Be Done" (Kalland), 311–20

INDEX

J. P. & M. Railroad, 55
James River, 301, 305
Janesville, Wisconsin, 135
Jehossee Island, 45
Jekyl Creek, 49
Jekyl Sound, 49
Jericho Canal, of the Dismal Swamp, 204–205
Jersey City, New Jersey, 32
Jesuit Relations and Allied Documents, The (Thwaites, ed.), xivn
Joe Eckel's Bar, Mississippi River, 81
Jointer Creek, 49, 50–51
Jolliet, Louis, *xiv*
Journal (Thoreau), 3, 5–25
Jug Island, Florida, 99

Kalland, Anna, 309, 311–20
Kentucky, 71, 72–73, 74, 75, 76, 80
Kentucky River, 77
Kill Van Kull Strait, 32, 33
Kineo, Maine, 257, 258, 272–73
King, Rudolph A., 201
King's Creek, 63
Knight & Brother, C. P. (firm), 33
Knowles, Isobel, 277, 279–82
Koresan Unity (Koreshan System of Religio-Science), 293n
Krider, John, 33

Laépède, Bernard Delaville, comte de, 55
Lake Borgne, 85
Lake Champlain, 31, 151
Lake Drummond, in the Dismal Swamp, 195, 201, 205; drainage of, 188, 190–91, 199; extent of, 187, 202–203; fishing, 196, 204
Lake George, 31
Lake Koshkonong, 134
Lake Ontario, 103, 105
Lake Pontchartrain, 83, 84–95
Lakeside, Wisconsin, 124
Lake Superior, *xiv*
LaSalle, Robert Cavelier, sieur de, *xiv*
Latham Station, Illinois, 138–39
Lavey, Jacob, 35
League Island, New York, 34

Ledge Island Rips, on the Androscoggin, 252
Lee's Cliff, Assabet River, 17
le Jeune, Father Paul, *xiv*n
Letart's Landing, Ohio, 70
Lewes, Delaware, 36
Lewis, Meriwether, *xv*
Lewis's, New York, 110–11
Lewiston, Maine, 253, 254
Light of St. Joseph, Louisiana, 86–87
Little Egg Harbor, New Jersey, 60
Little Foul Rift, Delaware River, 171, 174–75, 183–84
Little River, Virginia, 206
Live Oak, Florida, 54
Long Island, New York, 255
Louisiana, 81, 91, 96
Louisville, Kentucky, 74, 77
Love Creek, 36
Lyndon, Illinois, 142–43

McGregor, John "Rob Roy," 122n
McPhee, John, cited, xvin
Madison, Wisconsin, 121, 124–25
Maine, 243, 257–75, 301
Maine Steamship Company, 257
Maine Woods, The (Thoreau), *xvi*
Mallory's Grove, New York, 222
Manley, Atwood, cited, 163n
Marco, Florida, 294
Marcus Hook, Pennsylvania, 34
Maria Theresa (canoe), 27, 29–101
Marjorie Daw (Aldrich), 223n
Marquette, Jacques, *xiv*
Martha's Vineyard, Massachusetts, *ix–xiii*
Martial Miles Meadow, Concord, 14
Massachusetts, *xi*, 84, 283
Maysville, Kentucky, 72–73
Medford, Massachusetts, 27
Megalloway River, 244
Meredith, Morris, 151
Merrimack River, 175
Merrymeeting Bay, 254
Miakka River, 285, 287–88
Michigan Territory, *xv*
Middletown, Connecticut, 151, 156
Milan, Illinois, 146
Milford, Pennsylvania, 176, 177, 178

Miller's Falls, Haverhill, 175
Mispillion Creek, 36
Mississippi, 85
Mississippi River, *xiv*, 61, 67, 74; Bishop on, 79–82; Rock River junction, 144–46
Mississippi Sound, 89
Missouri, 80, 81, 299, 301
Missouri River, *xv*
Mobile, Alabama, 89
Mobile Bay, 89
Mondongo Key, Florida, 288
Monongahela River, 60–61
Moosehead Lake, 257–58, 260, 273
Moosehorn River, 261
Moseley, Edward A., 171, 173, 185, 186; quoted, 177, 178, 187; in the Dismal Swamp, 191, 193, 195, 196, 200–201, 206–207, 208, 210–11
Moundsville, Ohio, 65
Mount Hazen, 246
Mount Hope Cemetery, Rochester, 117
Mount Katahdin, 264, 270
Mount Maria, 246, 248
Mount Morris, New York, 109, 110, 113–14
Mud Pond Carry, Maine, 264–65, 272, 273
Murderkill Creek, 35, 36

Narrative Journal of Travels . . . through the Great Chain of American Lakes to the Sources of the Mississippi, *xv*
Nansemond County, Virginia, 187
Nansemond River, 205, 206
Natchez, Mississippi, 80
Necoochee (canoe), 233–40
New Basin Canal, 83
Newburg, Indiana, 78
Newburyport, Massachusetts, 175
New Castle, Delaware, 34
New Hampshire, 152, 157
New Hope, Pennsylvania, *xvi*
New Jersey, 32, 34, 57, 176
New Madrid, Missouri, 80, 81
New Orleans, Louisiana, 69, 82, 83, 84, 96, 98

Newry, New Hampshire, 248
New York City, New York, 32, 84, 216, 257, 283, 309, 316
New York State, 103, 105–17, 309–20
Niagara Falls, 187
Norcross, Maine, 271
Norfolk, Virginia, 34, 40; Dismal Swamp and, 192, 193, 194
Northampton, Massachusetts, 169
North Bay, New York, 31
North Carolina, 40–45, 187, 194
Northeast Carry, on the Penobscot, 258, 260, 261, 273
North Edisto River, 45
North Germantown, New York, 318
North River (Assabet River), Massachusetts, 9, 11–18, 21–25
North River, Virginia, 206
North Star (vessel), 257
Northwest River, Virginia, 199, 206
Norwich, New York, 215, 216
Nut Meadow Brook, Massachusetts, 14

Oak Point, Mississippi, 88
Ocean County, New Jersey, 27
Ocilla River, 95
Ocracoke Inlet, 41
Ogdensburg, New York, 231
Ohio River, 60–79
Oil Creek, 61
Okefenokee Swamp, 51, 52–54
Old Town Hammock, Florida, 56
Ontario, Canada, 231
Orange River, 293
Oregon, Illinois, 141
O'Reilly, John Boyle, 148–211
Ottawa, Ontario, 277
Ottawa River, *xiii*, 277
Ott's Farm, Madison, 124
Oyster Creek, 292
Ozark Mountains, 297, 299–307

Pamlico River, 40
Pan-Handle Railroad, 64
Pantry Brook, 12*n*
Partelow (canoe builder), 163, 173
Pascagoula, Mississippi, 88

INDEX

Pasquotank County, North Carolina, 187
Pasquotank River, 194
Patch, Sam, 105
Peace River, 283, 285
Pea Patch Island, 34
Peedee River, 55
Pennsylvania, 34, 107, 183, 185, 186; floods of, 160–61
Penobscot River, 257, 271, 274–75; West Branch, 258, 260–61, 264, 270, 273
Pensacola Bay, 91
Perdido River, 89–90
Perquimans River, 206
Peterson's Rips, on the Androscoggin, 251–52
Philadelphia, Pennsylvania, 31, 32, 33, 34, 39; Delaware River trip to, 171, 175, 176, 180
Piffard, New York, 115
Pine Stream Falls, Maine, 261
Pittsburgh, Pennsylvania, 60–61, 64, 79; riots of, 160–61
Plunkett, H. G., 86, 87
Point aux Herbes Lighthouse, Louisiana, 84, 85
Polis, Joe, *xvi*
Pollopel's Island (Bannerman's Island), 314–315
Pope's Springs, Wisconsin, 135
Portsmouth, Ohio, 72
Portage, New York, 109, 110, 111, 112, 113
Port Jervis, New York: Delaware River trip from, 171, 173, 175, 176, 178, 180, 181
Poughkeepsie, New York, 316
Powell, John Wesley, *xv*
Presidential Range, of the White Mountains, 246, 248
Princess Anne County, Virginia, 187
Prophetstown, Illinois, 143
Punta Gorda, Florida, 285
Punta Rassa, Florida, 292, 293

Quebec City, Quebec, *xiii*, 29, 31
Quebec Province, Canada, 277

Racine Boat Company, 122*n*, 173
Raritan Bay, 32
Read's Creek, New York, 227
Reedy Island, New Jersey, 35
Reelfoot Bayou, 80
Rehoboth Sound, 36
Reigelsville, Pennsylvania, 181
Remington, Frederic, 231, 233–40
Rice Lake, Ontario, 231, 233
Richardson's Landing, Kentucky, 76–77
Richmond, Virginia, 192–93
Riddle, Captain M. H., 84
Riddle (vessel), 84, 85, 90, 98
Ripogenus Gorge, Maine, 271
Ripogenus Lake, 271
Riverside, Massachusetts, 163
Rixford, Georgia, 51
Robbin's Reef, New York, 32–33
Rob Roy (vessel), 122*n*
Rochester, New York, 103, 105, 110, 113, 116–17
Rochester, University of, 103
Rockford, Illinois, 140
Rock Island, Florida, 96
Rock Island, Illinois, 146
Rock Rift, New York, 225
Rock River, 124–27, 133, 134–46
Rockton, Illinois, 137, 138
Rocky Mountains, 187
Rocky Rips, on the Penobscot, 261
Rome, Ohio, 72
Roper, John L., 195
Roscoe, Illinois, 137–38
Round Pond, Maine, 268
Rumford, Maine, 249
Rumford Falls, 249
Rurik (vessel), 48
Rush, New York, 116
Rushton, John Henry, 163*n*, 173
Rushton and His Times in American Canoeing (Manley), 163*n*
Russia, 48

Sacajawea, *xv*
"Saddles," 84–85, 86–87, 90–91, 92, 93; illness of, 95–99
St. Andrew's Bay, 91
St. Andrew's Sound, 49, 92

Saint Croix River, *xiv, xv*
St. Helena, New York, 113
St. John River, 258, 264, 268
St. Joseph's Bay, 92
St. Joseph's Sound, 94
St. Lawrence River, *xiii, xiv,* 31, 231
St. Mark's River, 93, 95, 96
St. Mary's, Georgia, 51
St. Mary's River, 48, 51, 52–54
St. Vincent's Sound, 95
Salem Cove, New Jersey, 34
Salt River, 77
Sanibel Island, Florida, 292
Santa Rosa Island, Florida, 91
Savannah, Georgia, 54
Savannah River, 48
Sawmill Rift, on the Delaware, 174
Schoolcraft, Henry Rowe, *xv*
Seaman, Captain Hazelton, 58, 60
Second Lake, Madison, 125, 127, 128
Seminole Point, Florida, 283, 296
Shakespeare, William, 292
Shaw Shaw (canoe), 215–30
Shelborn, New Hampshire, 248
Sherman, William Tecumseh, 265–66
Sherwood House, Delhi, New York, 218
Shieldsboro, Louisiana, 83, 86, 87
Simpson (Chichester companion), 213, 215–23 *passim*
Slaughter Beach, 36–37
Smith, J., 158, 161–62, 170; singing beach of, 165–66
Smith, John, *xiii*
Snake River, *xv*
Sourdnahunk Dead Water, Maine, 270, 272
South Carolina, 45, 55
Spring Creek, Florida, 97, 98, 99
Springfield, Massachusetts, 156
Stair Falls, Maine, 274
Stanton, Elizabeth Cady, 255
Stanton, Gerrit Smith, 255, 257–75
Stanton, Henry Brewster, 255
Staten Island, New York, 32
Stebbinsville, Wisconsin, 132–33
Steubenville, Ohio, 64
Stewart's Ferry, Florida, 53
Stono River, 45
Stony Point, New York, 312

Storm King Mountain, 314
Stoughton, Wisconsin, 130, 131
Styron's, North Carolina, 41
Sudbury River (Concord River South Branch), 11–14, 25
Suffolk, Virginia, 193, 201
Survival of the Bark Canoe, The (McPhee), *xvi*n
Susquehanna River, 158–71, 175, 185
Suwanee River, 51, 54–56, 100
Sybaris (canoe), 215–30

Tappan Zee, 312
Tashmoo Lake, Martha's Vineyard, *ix–xiii*
Teed, Cyrus Reed, 293*n*
Teller, Walter, *ix–xvii*
Teller's Point, New York, 312
Telos Lake, 272, 273, 274
Tennessee, 80
Ten Thousand Islands, Florida, 294
"Theme and Variations" (Teller), *ix–xvii*
Third Lake, Madison, 124–25
Thoreau, Henry David, *xvi*, 3, 5–25
Thoreau, the Poet-Naturalist (Channing), 15*n*
Thousand Miles in the Rob Roy Canoe, A (McGregor), 122*n*
Three Mile Cut, Georgia, 49
Three Mile Island, Indiana, 78
Thwaites, Jessie (Mrs. Reuben Gold Thwaites), 119
Thwaites, Reuben Gold, *xiv*n, 119, 121–46
Tiger River, 72
Tinkers' Rips, on the Androscoggin, 246
Tioga Center, Pennsylvania, 169
Tivoli, New York, 317
Towanda, Pennsylvania, 160, 163, 167, 168–69
Traubel, Horace, cited, 148*n*
Trenton, New Jersey, 171, 175
Trenton Falls, 174, 175
Trojan (vessel), 319
Troy, New York, 29, 31, 33, 309, 319
Turner's Falls, Massachusetts, 156
Turvill's Bay, Wisconsin, 124
Tussock Bay, 296

INDEX

331

Twin Brook Rapids, of the Allagash, 269–70
"Two Girls in a Canoe" (Knowles), 279–82

Umbazooksus Lake, 264, 273
Umbazooksus River, 264, 265, 272, 273
Umsaskis Lake, 264, 266–68
United States Army Corps of Engineers, 81
United States Coast Survey, 29; in Florida, 92, 93, 97
United States Congress, 194

Van Dam, Rambout, 312
Vikings, *xiii*
Virgin Bluffs, Missouri, 304
Virginia, 60, 71, 187, 194, 206
Virgin Shoals, Missouri, 304
Voyage of the Paper Canoe (Bishop), 29–56, 57

Waccamaw Swamp, 52
Wadmelaw River, 45
Wadmelaw Sound, 45
Wallace, Captain, in the Dismal Swamp, 193, 196, 198, 199
Wallaceton, Virginia, 198, 199
Wall Street and the Wilds (Dimock), 283
Walpack Bend, Pennsylvania, 178, 179, 180
Walton, Izaak, 127
Walton, New York, 221, 222
Wappoo Creek, 45
Ward Fifty (canoe), 311–20
Warrior Creek, Florida, 99
Washington, George, 194; quoted, 190
Washington, D.C., 201
"Washington's Ditch," in the Dismal Swamp, 194, 205
Watchapreague Inlet, 41

Waters & Sons, E., 29
Watteau, Antoine, 186
Week on the Concord and Merrimack Rivers, A (Thoreau), *xvi*
Welles's Falls, 174
West Branch River, of the Delaware, 215, 216–23, 224
West Branch River, of the Penobscot, 258, 260–61, 264, 270, 273
West Creek, New Jersey, 57
West New Brighton, New York, 33
West Pascagoula, Mississippi, 88
West Pass, Florida, 294
West Point, New York, 314
Wheeling, West Virginia, 64
"Where the Sportsman Loves to Linger" (Stanton), 257–75
Whetstone, Maine, 275
White (Browne's companion), 243–54
White Mountains, Presidential range of, 246, 248
White River, Arkansas, 301, 305
White River, Massachusetts, 151
White River Junction, Massachusetts, 151, 157
Whitman, Walt, quoted, 148
Wilkes-Barre, Pennsylvania, 163
Williams, R. F., 50
Wing, Ralph K., 103, 105–17
Wisconsin, *xiii*, 119, 128, 131
Wisconsin River, *xiv*
Wisconsin State Historical Society, 119
With Walt Whitman in Camden (Traubel), 148*n*
Wolf Island, Illinois, 80
Wood's Bridge, Assabet River, 22

"Yachting in a Canoe" (Dimock), 285–96
Yale University, 231